BPMN 2.0
Handbook

BPMN 2.0 Handbook

Methods, Concepts, Case Studies and Standards in Business Process Management Notation

Foreword by

Dr. Bruce Silver

Published in association with the
Workflow Management Coalition

17 Years of Thought-Process Leadership

Edited by

Layna Fischer

Future Strategies Inc., Book Division
Lighthouse Point, Florida

BPMN 2.0 Handbook

Copyright © 2011 by Future Strategies Inc.

ISBN-13: 978-0-9819870-3-3

Published by Future Strategies Inc., Book Division

3640-B3 North Federal Highway #421
Lighthouse Point FL 33064 USA
954.782.3376 fax 954.719.3746
www.FutStrat.com; books@FutStrat.com

Publisher's Cataloging-in-Publication Data

Library of Congress Catalog Card LCCN No. 2010940580

BPMN 2.0 Handbook:
/Layna Fischer (editor)

p. cm.

Includes bibliographical references, appendices and index.

ISBN 9780981987033

1. Business Process Management Notation. 2. BPMN 2.0 Standard 3. Technological Innovation. 4. Business Process Management. 5. Business Process Technology. 6. Organizational Change 7. Management Information Systems. 8. Office Practice Automation. 9. Business Process Technology. 10. Electronic Commerce. 11. Process Analysis

Fischer, Layna (editor)

Table of Contents

SECTION 3—Reference and Appendices

Foreword

Finalization of the BPMN 2.0 standard in OMG marks a major milestone in the evolution of business process modeling. We now have a tool-independent graphical process definition language that is widely adopted by both business and IT for purposes ranging from basic process documentation to detailed performance analysis, requirements specification, and executable design. While the notation on the diagram surface seems little changed from BPMN 1.2, under the covers there is much that is new: a formal UML metamodel, more precisely defined operational semantics, and an XML Schema and conformance classes supporting model interchange. As such it represents "something new" for a broad spectrum of process modelers, from business process analysts and architects to BPM academics to process automation engine designers.

The *BPMN 2.0 Handbook* illustrates this diversity of interest in the new standard. In addition to discussion of BPMN 2.0's technical features, we have examples of its application in business and government, its relation to SOA and process execution, and its suitability as a business-readable communication tool. We also have many suggestions for how BPMN could be extended, improved, or enhanced to meet the broader goals of business process management.

One thing you won't read much about in the Handbook is the arduous path and hard work it took to complete the BPMN 2.0 specification. I was a "fringe" member of the BPMN 2.0 team from the fall of 2008 until publication of the beta spec and launch of the Finalization Task Force (FTF) in the summer of 2009. As such I got to see for myself how this sausage was made, and as you might suspect, it was not a pretty sight. I tried to represent the interests of the majority of existing BPMN users, typically business process analysts and architects modeling non-executable processes, and I often felt overwhelmed by the focus on process execution. But however frustrating the process seemed at times, it was ultimately "fair" and achieved a remarkable result. For that we owe a debt of gratitude to the managers of the BPMN 2.0 spec development effort in OMG. We owe an equally large debt to two Handbook authors, Robert Shapiro and Denis Gagné, who succeeded where I could not in two critical parts of the spec—process modeling conformance classes and a proper XML schema for diagram graphics information—developing and driving them from near-oblivion at the start of FTF to inclusion in the final standard. When model interchange among BPMN tools eventually becomes commonplace, we will all have Robert and Denis to thank.

What most people fail to realize is that a specification as wide-ranging as BPMN 2.0 is of necessity a "political" document as much as a technical one. It is a negotiated settlement of competing interests and aims. In this case, OMG initially tried to take its abstract, language-independent Business Process Definition Metamodel and simply rebrand it BPMN 2.0, even though its graphical notation, almost an afterthought, had only passing resemblance to BPMN 1.2 and its terminology no similarity at all. While that may have served the purposes of OMG's broader Model Driven Architecture effort, it was a bit too abstract for BPM tool vendors looking to bridge the gap between business-oriented process modeling and executable process design. Led by IBM, Oracle, and SAP, a competing BPMN 2.0 proposal was put forward. In the end the two efforts were merged, although the IBM-Oracle-SAP ideas, which took the existing BPMN notation and armed each shape with execution-oriented semantics, mostly carried the day.

So, in the end, BPMN 2.0 had to accommodate and harmonize the needs and interests of three constituencies: one group thinking about executable BPMN, another thinking about a way to link BPMN to other OMG standards under the MDA banner, and a small but insistent minority pleading with the team not to forget about the vast majority of existing BPMN users, who cared little about either of those things. That might explain the seemingly odd choice of what to put in and what to leave out of the standard. There is no doubt some "pork" in there, included to win the support of some particular interest group, while something like simulation—a mainstay of most process modeling tools today and a topic covered in the Handbook—was left out entirely. But BPMN 2.0 never aspired to cover all the modeling needs of BPM. If it had tried to include the wishlists of some authors in the Handbook, I doubt we would have gotten any spec at all through the committee. BPMN 2.0 exists because it doesn't try to do too much. Like all negotiations, it achieved as much as it possibly could get agreement on.

An unfortunate consequence of the focus on execution semantics in the spec is a bit of a backlash against BPMN 2.0 from business-oriented practitioners. We sometimes hear that BPMN is too complicated for business users, and that it mainly serves the needs of BPMS vendors. That's too bad, because in my experience most BPMN users today are not trying to automate anything, but simply document and analyze their existing processes. The BPMN spec could have addressed that issue, but did not consider that its mission. For example, there are no rules, best practices, and diagram examples intended to promote "good" BPMN —clear, business-readable, and well-structured—anywhere in the spec. For that reason I am particularly interested in the Handbook articles by Allweyer, Silingas and Miliviciene, Kuehn et al., and Navarro-Suarez et al., all of which touch on the topic of making BPMN more consumable by business.

The good news is that we don't have to change BPMN 2.0 in order to create "good" process models. The spec provides room to create good models just as easily as bad ones, and offers plenty of "value-add" opportunity for both tool vendors and service providers to promote (and even enforce) best modeling practices for business and technical users within the confines of the spec as it is. As BPMN 2.0 tools are only beginning to enter the marketplace, this Handbook is not the last word on BPMN 2.0, but the start of a long and lively discussion.

Bruce Silver, Principal, Bruce Silver Associates

Introduction

Layna Fischer, Future Strategies Inc. USA

Authored by members of WfMC, OMG and other key participants in the development of BPMN 2.0, the **BPMN 2.0 Handbook** brings together industry thought-leaders and international experts in this space.

Exclusive and unique contributions examine a variety of aspects that start with an introduction of what's new in BPMN 2.0, and look closely at interchange, analytics, conformance, optimization, simulation and more from a technical perspective. The authors also address the business imperative for adoption of the standard by examining best practice guidelines, BPMN business strategy, the human interface and real-life case studies. Other critical chapters tackle the practical aspects of making a BPMN 2.0 model executable and the basic timeline analysis of a BPMN 2.0 model.

FOREWORD
Bruce Silver, Principal, Bruce Silver Associates

The *BPMN 2.0 Handbook* illustrates this diversity of interest in the new standard. In addition to discussion of BPMN 2.0's technical features, we have examples of its application in business and government, its relation to SOA and process execution, and its suitability as a business-readable communication tool. We also have many suggestions for how BPMN could be extended, improved, or enhanced to meet the broader goals of business process management.

SECTION 1—Guide to BPMN 2.0 Technical Aspects

NEW CAPABILITIES FOR PROCESS AND INTERACTION MODELING IN BPMN 2.0
Stephen A. White PhD, International Business Machines, and Conrad Bock, National Institute of Standards and Technology, USA

This paper provides a high-level introduction to new features in processes and interaction diagrams in the Business Process Model and Notation (BPMN) Version 2.0. BPMN 2.0 expands the capabilities of BPMN 1.x Process diagrams, and adds Choreography diagrams and Conversations to BPMN 1.x Collaborations for business interaction modeling. Half of the paper covers new elements in Process diagrams, including non-interrupting Events and Event Sub-Processes. The other half will cover new capabilities for modeling interactions, including the use of interactive Processes with Collaborations.

BPMN 2.0 INTERCHANGE
Denis Gagne, CEO & CTO, Trisotech, Canada

Interchange (via some form of serialization was one of the most cited shortcomings of the first version of BPMN. With the advent of BPMN 2.0 it is now possible to interchange BPMN process models and diagrams. In this chapter, we abstract away from the technical details of BPMN 2.0 interchange serialization to explore BPMN 2.0 interchange from a business perspective. We start by providing some insight as to WHY BPMN 2.0 interchange is desirable. We then postulate as to WHO benefits from such interchange and what kind of benefits each stakeholder obtains from the open interchange of BPMN 2.0. We then present in simple terms WHAT can be interchanged using the various types of BPMN 2.0 models and diagrams cautioning the reader of the pitfalls from what we call the BPMN 2.0 devil's quadrants. We then argue that while BPMN 2.0 interchange standardization is required, it is not sufficient, and explain HOW interchange conformance verification and validation can act as a catalyst to universal BPMN interchange. We conclude by postulating that the answer to "WHEN will BPMN 2.0 interchange be feasible?" is *now*.

Simulation for Business Process Management
John Januszczak, Vice President, Meta Software Corporation, USA

Simulation is a traditional analysis technique in operations management. In the context of Business Process Management (BPM), simulation models can be used to perform "what-if" analysis of process designs before they are implemented, or test changes to processing parameters before they occur, such as an increase in the volume of work to be processed. Simulation in some form is supported by many Business Process Management Suites (BPMS), as well as other process oriented analysis tools. Besides process definitions, simulation models require additional data to define a scenario such as volumes of work and arrival patterns, task processing times, resource levels and availability, and descriptions of other external events that impact the work flow. Currently there are no specific standards for business process simulation. This paper provides an overview of business process simulation, the types of information required to define a business process scenario for the purpose of simulation, and a proposed standard for defining simulation scenarios that is compatible with the Business Process Modeling Notation (BPMN and XML Process Definition Language (XPDL). The article also describes how a RESTful web services API can be developed to support the standard. By providing a standard interchange format and/or a standard API, various artifacts currently available in the event logs of BPM systems could be used to generate baseline simulation scenarios useful in operational decision making and addressing near term processing issues, as well as long term process design.

Collaborative Activities inside Pools
Michele Chinosi, Grantholder, European Commission, Joint Research Centre (JRC), Italy

Choreographies and Conversations, introduced with BPMN 2.0, will make modelers able to describe interactions among different Participants as well as messages exchange. Often enough different Participants have to accomplish the same task. This can be now easily and clearly represented using BPMN 2.0. BPMN 2.0 does not specify the usage of Lanes neither their meaning. However, Lanes are sometimes used to specify internal roles or departments. In this context it could happen that modelers want to represent an Activity performed by different roles or offices together (e.g., attending the same meeting, collaborative writing of a document). Such situation has been modeled so far by using merging Gateways placed before the activities, but this patch does not solve a related problem. BPMN forces to draw elements within Lanes boundaries. This means that, at least conceptually, one Activity is lead by the subject which the containing Lane is linked to, which is not necessarily true. Some experiments revealed how much the means to model such inner collaboration is a desirable feature.

Multi-faceted BPM
Marco Brambilla, Researcher, Politecnico di Milano, Italy and Stefano Butti, CEO, Web Models S.r.l. - WebRatio, Italy

We propose an integrated design approach to BPM that comprises modeling of business processes, application structure, master data, and user interaction, together with automatic model transformations among them. In this way, it is possible to work at different levels of abstraction and get quick prototypes to be discussed with the customers, but also generate production applications to be delivered as finalized systems. Indeed, the models allow the designers and analysts to work on orthogonal aspects of the design, and to fine tune the final application in several ways, e.g., by integrating the visual identity of the organization, plugging in new components, or connecting the business process to legacy applications via Web Services. The paper presents the different models that we deem essential for complete enterprise application design together with the model transformations among them and the benefits obtained by adopting the approach.

We describe which peculiar aspects of BPMN 2.0 have proven useful in our approach and we explain their role. We also mention which ones we decided not to support and why. To demonstrate the feasibility and advantages, we show the approach at work on a set of real industrial applications.

Refactoring BPMN Models
Darius Silingas, Principal Consultant and Edita Mileviciene, Cameo Business Modeler Product Manager, No Magic Europe, Lithuania

BPMN is already acknowledged as a de facto standard for business process modeling. However, it still takes a long journey to raise the maturity of business process modeling practice. The notation, examples, fundamental process patterns, and basic style guidelines are already covered in BPMN books and articles. However, in practice most business process modelers do a lot of mistakes that make their BPMN models over complex, difficult to understand and maintain. There is a lack of discussion on "bad smells" in BPMN models, and how to apply business process patterns in order to make the BPMN models compliant with the best practices. This paper is filling in this gap by identifying and analyzing the most typical BPMN "bad smells", explaining what best practices are violated, and demonstrating how to refactor BPMN models to get rid of the "bad smells". Each of the presented BPMN "bad smells" is illustrated by two BPMN 2.0 diagrams – the original version and the refactored version. The paper is based on extensive authors' BPMN consultancy in banking, telecommunication, defence, and software domains.

Admission Process Optimization with BPMN (case study)
Jack Xue, Butler University and Manager of IT Architecture, Conseco Service LLC, USA

The Business Process Modeling Notation (BPMN) is an increasingly important standard for business process design and optimization and has enjoyed high levels of attention in academic research and business practice. In this paper, experiences are shared from a project using BPMN to design and optimize an online admission process. This process is optimized by choosing a subset of incoming requests such that the revenue of the service provider is maximized. The admission decision is based on an estimation of requests' service times, and the rewards associated with serving these requests within their Quality of Service (QoS) bounds with respect to a limited resource. Experiments demonstrated the effectiveness of the admission process in a middleware service.

Workflow Patterns using BPMN 2.0
Vishal Saxena, Founder and CEO, Roubroo, USA

Over the past few years, workflow patterns have become a touchstone of workflow standards and products. The Workflow Patterns initiative is a joint effort of Eindhoven University of Technology (led by Professor Wil van der Aalst) and Queensland University of Technology (led by Professor Arthur ter Hofstede) which started in 1999. The aim of this initiative is to provide a conceptual basis for process technology. In particular, the research provides a thorough examination of the various perspectives (control flow, data, resource, and exception handling) that need to be supported by a workflow language or a business process modelling language. In this paper we would present how these workflow patterns can be modeled using BPMN 2.0. We will identify what are the advantages of using BPMN 2.0 when modeling these patterns. Further, we will focus on specific constructs in BPMN 2.0 that let the users extend the workflow patterns if required. Our initial intent is to target the various control flow patterns. We would cover data flow patterns as well.

Analytics for Performance Optimization of BPMN2.0 Business Processes
Robert Shapiro, SVP Research, Global 360, USA and Hartmann Genrich, Consultant, Germany

We describe a new approach to process improvement based on the combined use of statistics and simulation to study the structural aspects of process models. Past efforts to use simulation focused on resource optimization have led to some significant successes when coupled with Workforce Management scheduling technology, but that approach has not been particularly successful in making structural improvements in the actual processes. The difficulty of preparing satisfactorily detailed schedules, combined with the structural complexities introduced in particular by the event and looping structures in BPMN, requires a fresh look at the problem.

MAKING A BPMN 2.0 MODEL EXECUTABLE

Lloyd Dugan, Senior Project Director/CTO, Information Engineering Services, Inc., and Nathaniel Palmer, Executive Director, WfMC, USA

The advent of BPMN 2.0 provides a breakthrough in bridging the communication divide through two notable advances. One is an expanded iconic set offering more procedural and message-level behavior than before. The other, and most controversial, is a new serialization format containing implementation details for an executing platform. This chapter proposes a set of minimum characteristics for an executable BPMN 2.0 model as well as modeling guidelines that ensure modeled elements map to executing components. This approach applies to all areas of BPMN modeling, but is also necessary for leveraging the emerging class of BPMS environment where processes orchestrate services within a Service Component Architecture (SCA) composite. The result is a design pattern for implementing BPMN processes that is particularly applicable to applications that run as services and leverage SOA components.

Yet the advent of a serialization format does not alone resolve the issues otherwise surrounding executable models. Well-designed models require the first principles of modeling to ensure that design-time BPMN constructs follow the necessary characteristics of an executable model. This is particularly important for environments that purge the BPMS layer of most (if not all) core business logic, instead orchestrating invoked services that components of capabilities. In the examples that follow, this approach is illustrated by using specific task types and swimlanes to map to SCA components. Also presented is the recommended approach for mapping an XML expression of BPMN, either the serialized version of BPMN or XPDL, to and from an XML expression of an SCA composite.

BESPOKE ENTERPRISE ARCHITECTURE: TAILORING BPMN 2.0 USING CONFORMANCE CLASSES

Dennis E. Wisnosky, Office of the Deputy Chief Management Officer, Department of Defense, and Michael zur Muehlen Ph.D., Center for Business Process Innovation, Stevens Institute of Technology, USA

Government agencies have to fulfill their mission while being fiscally responsible and maintaining customer focus. Understanding the agencies' end-to-end processes and mission threads is essential to ensure that both performance and compliance objectives are met. Increasingly, Enterprise Architectures are used to document end-to-end business operations and to prove compliance to rules and regulations. Enterprise Architecture covers the creation of analytical or prescriptive models of organizations to understand, manage, or change the enterprise. The models that describe different architecture facets are typically organized according to the views they describe, such as process, data, rules and organization models, among others. For organizations that engage in multiple architecture projects, a systematic organization of these views is essential; only if the views and their representations are consistent across different projects can an organization efficiently identify organizational and technical interfaces, streamline cross-functional operations, and assert compliance to rules and regulations.

A number of obstacles to consistent architecture efforts exist to date: Divergent viewpoints, different frameworks, multiple modeling methods, and inconsistent interpretations of individual methods. This paper reports on the development of a methodology for the creation of architecture models that is centered around BPMN and is based on the notion of a common vocabulary.

SECTION 2—Guide to the Business Imperative for BPMN

BEST PRACTICE GUIDELINES FOR BPMN 2.0

Gerardo Navarro-Suarez, Jakob Freund and Matthias Schrepfer, camunda services GmbH, Germany

In practice modeling projects often tend to be quite large. Adopting BPMN 2.0 eases the creation of process models for business and technical projects. However, the creation of models in large modeling projects is still not a trivial task. The introduction of modeling guidelines guides and supports modeling projects. This article introduces an approach to establish such modeling guidelines for individual modeling projects using BPMN 2.0 as modeling notation. The article discusses the concept of modeling guidelines and shows why their application can help to apply BPMN 2.0 in practice. A framework for the creation of guidelines is described in detail. Real-world examples illustrate the use of modeling guidelines and constitute the effectiveness of best practice guidelines.

BPMN FOR BUSINESS PROFESSIONALS: MAKING BPMN 2.0 FIT FOR FULL BUSINESS USE

Tobias Rausch, Harald Kuehn, BOC AG, Marion Murzek, BOC GmbH, Austria and Thomas Brennan, BOC Ltd, Ireland

Addressing users throughout the business is one of the key goals of BPMN 2.0. At the same time "BPMN is constrained to support only the concepts of modeling that are applicable to business processes. This means that other types of modeling done by organizations for business purpose is out of scope for BPMN." While this is understandable when defining a standard, it is essential for organizations to have support for BPM scenarios such as work instructions, organizational analysis, process costing, ICS/ERM etc.

This paper shows how BPMN 2.0 could be extended with business relevant concepts to support business-analysis (e.g. creating risk reports by assigning risks/controls to tasks). This will be demonstrated by looking at different real-life scenarios and how BPMN processes are linked with organizational data, resources, information, risks and controls and thereby allowing rich business analysis, reporting and simulation. There has been much discussion about BPMN's first letter and this paper illustrates how users are offered both a standard for describing process models and support of their key business application scenarios.

BPMN AND BUSINESS STRATEGY: ONE SIZE DOES NOT FIT ALL

Lionel Loiseau, Head of BPM Competency Center, BNP Paribas and Michael Ferrari, Independent BPM Consultant and Business Analyst, France.

In BPM, we would like to conciliate the management-oriented abstraction necessary to fully grasp the essence of a process with the exhaustiveness and realism that are essential to an automated solution. But one size does not fit all!

This led us to develop a classification of the various business process modeling plans and a gradual approach aimed at defining how to move smoothly from one plan to another. Our classification takes into account the required levels of abstraction, the legacy notations, the significant number of existing process models as well as the contribution of the BPMN notation.

While traditional BPMN approaches present three levels of process modeling, respectively descriptive, analytic and exhaustive, our classification connects BPMN to strategy, indicators, business rules and risks, and breaks down further the separation between general process models and organized process models. In this paper, we detail and justify our approach and our classification, as well as explain how they are used in our company. We also shed a new light on the role of the BPM analyst, an emerging position blending several skills, notations, and collaborative tools.

HUMAN-READABLE BPMN DIAGRAMS

Thomas Allweyer, Professor, University of Applied Sciences Kaiserslautern, Germany

The Object Management Group has published a useful non-normative document for BPMN modelers: "BPMN 2.0 by Example". While the specification of the BPMN standard describes the BPMN diagrams, elements, and their meanings, the examples document provides suggestions of how to use BPMN for modeling real processes. The reader can get valuable insights and hints for his own modeling practice. This paper discusses one of the models, the E-Mail Voting Example. The E-Mail Voting Example describes how a distributed working group discusses issues and votes on them by e-mail. This process was used during the development of BPMN. The authors claim that "This process is small, but fairly complex [...], and it will help illustrate that BPMN can handle simple and unusual business processes and still be easily understandable for readers of the Diagram".

BUSINESS PROCESS INTEGRATION IN A DEFENSE PRODUCT-FOCUSED COMPANY (CASE STUDY)
Kerry M. Finn, Enterprise SOA Lead and J. Bryan Lail, Chief Architect, Raytheon Company, USA

A common language for integrating processes across silos is a significant enabler in ways both obvious and subtle. Once the business organizations that touch a product or execution life cycle can agree on the first priorities where tighter integration is very clearly going to yield measurable benefits, then the common process language immediately leads to communicating one shared model across leadership and stakeholders. From there, modern methods and tools lead to validated processes, key performance indicators that can be tracked during execution, behavior and cultural changes, and executable processes that automate and parallelize legacy practices. This paper describes how BPMN 2.0 can promote a balance of business agility and enterprise efficiency. The approach takes two tiers to execute for a product-focused company, which the authors call horizontal and vertical integration. The methods and common language around BPMN apply to internal business operations for any sizeable company; however, the approach for applying the methods to the actual products of a defense company is different. The dual benefits come from focusing on the information management for those products in either the battle-space or the business space; this paper will study both areas and deliver a common theme for BPI.

SECTION 3—Reference and Appendices

REFERENCE GUIDE—XPDL 2.2: INCORPORATING BPMN 2.0 PROCESS MODELING EXTENSIONS
Robert M. Shapiro, WfMC Chair XPDL Technical Committee, USA

XPDL2.2 is intended as a preliminary release which supports the graphical extensions to process modeling contained in BPMN2.0. In fact, the BPMN specification addresses four different areas of modeling, referred to as Process Modeling, Process Execution, BPEL Process Execution, and Choreography Modeling. In this reference guide, we focus only on Process Modeling. Within that we define several sub-classes to support process interchange between tools. This is discussed in a later section of this paper. Here we discuss significant additions in XPDL 2.2.

Appendices

- Authors' appendix
- BPMN 20 Supporting organizations
- XPDL Implementations
- BPMN 2.0 Glossary
- Index
- Further Reading in BPM and BPMN

BPMN 2.0 HANDBOOK COMPANION CD
Additional Material

A Companion CD is planned for release in early 2011 which will contain, in addition to the full *Digital Edition of the BPMN 2.0 Handbook*, substantial material on BPMN 2.0 helpful to readers. This includes free BPMN and XPDL Verification/Validation files, webinars, videos, product specs, tools, free/trial modelers etc.

Several Handbook authors have contributed additional files and explanatory diagrams to the CD. This additional material gives readers exposure to a larger resource on BPMN 2.0 and XPDL than a book alone can offer.

An early mock-up of the CD has been posted to http://bpmnhandbook.com/

Section 1

Guide to BPMN 2.0 Technical Aspects

New Capabilities for Process and Interaction Modeling in BPMN 2.0

Stephen A. White PhD, International Business Machines, and Conrad Bock, National Institute of Standards and Technology, USA

1   INTRODUCTION

This paper provides a high-level introduction to new features in processes and interaction diagrams in the Business Process Model and Notation (BPMN) Version 2.0 [1]. BPMN 2 expands the capabilities of BPMN 1.x Process and Collaboration diagrams, and adds Choreography diagrams for business interaction modeling. Half of the paper covers new elements in Process diagrams, including non-interrupting Events and Event Sub-Processes. The other half covers new capabilities for modeling interactions, including Conversations, and interactive Processes in Collaborations. The paper assumes familiarity with earlier versions of BPMN.

BPMN provides a view of processes (how things get done) with flow charts tailored for business processes and interactions. In addition, BPMN 2 has two ways to model business interactions: Collaborations and Choreographies, the first emphasizing participants, and the second the sequence of interactions. Choreographies are new to BPMN 2.

The primary purposes of BPMN 2 are threefold:
- First, to provide a notation that is readily understandable by all business users, from business analysts creating initial drafts of the processes, to those performing processes or implementing technology to automate them, and finally, to business people who will manage and monitor those processes.
- Second, to support the notation with an internal model that has formal execution semantics enabling process model execution, as well as declarative semantics to relate processes and interactions.
- Third, to provide a standard interchange format for transfer of process and interaction models, and detailed visual information, between modeling tools.

These features of BPMN 2 create a standardized bridge between the business process design and process implementation.

1.1   The Origins of BPMN

The BPMN 1.0 specification was developed by the Business Process Management Institute (BPMI), now merged with the Object Management Group (OMG), and released to the public in May, 2004. BPMN was adopted as an OMG standard in February, 2006. Work on BPMN continued within the OMG and BPMN 1.1 was completed in June, 2007, BPMN 1.2 was completed in June, 2008, and BPMN 2.0 was completed in June, 2010. The term "BPMN 1.x" is used in this paper to represent the 1.0, 1.1 and 1.2 versions of BPMN.

1.2 *New BPMN Modeling Capabilities*

The basic look-and-feel of BPMN has not significantly changed in BPMN 2, especially for process modeling. The updates to process and interaction modeling are described in the following sections.

In addition to process and interaction enhancements, BPMN 2 defines four new Conformance Levels to support different modeling requirements:

- Process: includes Collaboration, but not Choreography and Execution.
- Process Execution: for execution engines.
- Business Process Execution Language (BPEL) Execution: for BPEL execution engines [2].
- Choreography: for Choreography tools. Process and Execution are not required.

Furthermore, the Process Conformance level is divided into three sub-levels:

- Descriptive: elements for high-level modeling.
- Analytic: elements consistent with the Department of Defense Architecture Framework [3] .
- Common executable; elements for models that can be executed.

2 PROCESS MODELS

A common use of BPMN is for modeling business processes, sometimes in the context of collaborations. BPMN 1.x diagrams are basically the same in BPMN 2, but BPMN 2 adds significant support for more advanced process modeling patterns. The major areas updated include: Activities, Events, Gateways, and Data.

2.1 *Updated Activities*

BPMN 2 Activities are updated in the following ways:

- Markers for Task types
- A new Business Rule Task
- Changes in Multi-Instance markers
- New Global Tasks
- New Call Activities
- New Event Sub-Processes

The sections below will describe these changes.

Markers for Tasks

BPMN 1.x was developed with various types of Tasks (atomic Activities). These provide a set of predefined Tasks, such as sending or receiving a message. BPMN has a User Task, Service Task, Receive Task, Send Task, Manual Task, and Script Task, as well as an undefined Task. In BPMN 2, a Business Rule Task is added (see next section).

In BPMN 1.x the Task types were a part of the BPMN model, but there was no visualization to distinguish the Task types. In BPMN 2, distinguishing markers are added to the Task types (see Figure 1) in the upper left corner of the shape, except for the undefined Task (now called an Abstract Task).

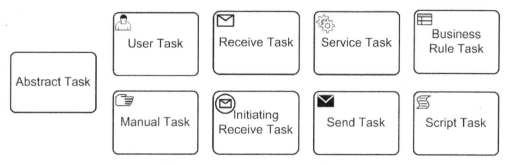

Figure 1: Task types and their markers

Note that the Receive Task has two variations. A standard Receive Task has a marker in the shape of an envelope. A Receive Task that is used to start (initiate) a Process has a marker that looks like the Message Start Event.

Business Rule Task

A new Task type is added in BPMN 2—the Business Rule Task (see Figure 2). This Task represents an Activity in the Process where a business rule engine evaluates Process data and returns the results. Process data can be updated based on the results, which can then affect the flow of the Process through a Gateway, for example.

Figure 2: A Business Rule Task

Multi-Instance Markers

BPMN 2 adds notation to distinguish between the two types of Multi-Instance Activities: sequential and parallel. The parallel Multi-Instance Activity maintains the BPMN 1.x notation of three vertical lines (see the Activity on the left in Figure 3). The sequential Multi-Instance Activity now uses three horizontal lines (see the Activity on the right in Figure 3).

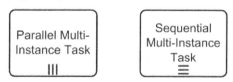

Figure 3: Parallel and sequential multi-instance Task markers

Global Tasks

Global Tasks are new elements in BPMN 2 that enable modelers to create libraries of reusable atomic Tasks that can be called into a Process through a Call Activity (see the next section). Global Tasks are not graphical elements themselves, but are reused by graphical elements. Of the types of Process (embedded) Tasks (see Figure 1, above), only Business Rule, Manual, Script, and User types can be Global Tasks.

Call Activities

BPMN 1.x provided the capability of reusing one Process in the flow of another. BPMN 2 modifies and expands this capability. The Sub-Process types *reusable* and *reference* in BPMN 1.x are replaced with a Call Activity in BPMN 2. The remaining BPMN 1.x Sub-Process type *embedded* becomes the BPMN 2 Sub-Process element.

The Call Activity is an Activity that reuses either a previously defined Global Task (see previous section) or a Process. Call Activities are distinguished from other "local" Activities by their thick border (see Figure 4). When a Call Activity reuses a Global Task, the marker for that type of Task will be visible in the upper left corner. When a Call Activity reuses a Process, the plus sign marker of a Sub-Process will be visible in the bottom center.

Figure 4: Call Activities

A notation pattern introduced in BPMN 2.0 is that thin boundaries represent elements local to the diagram and thick boundaries represent elements that reuse global elements. The pattern is used in Collaboration and Choreography diagrams (see section 3.1.3).

Event Sub-Processes

Event Sub-Processes are a new element in BPMN 2 that combine the characteristics of boundary Events and Sub-Processes. They are similar to boundary Events, except are placed inside the Activity (a Process or Sub-Process—they cannot be used for a Task). They are Sub-Processes in that they are a compound Activity—an Activity that has lower-level Activities as part of its definition.

The Event Sub-Process is distinguished from a normal Sub-Process by its dotted line border and the specific Event type that triggers it shown in the upper left corner of the shape (see Figure 5). If the Event Sub-Process is expanded, then the marker is not shown (because the Start Event is visible), but the dotted border remains (see Figure 6).

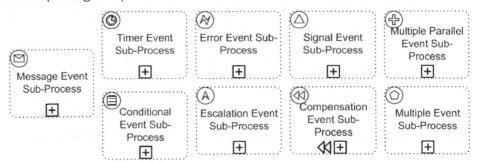

Figure 5: Event Sub-Process types and their markers

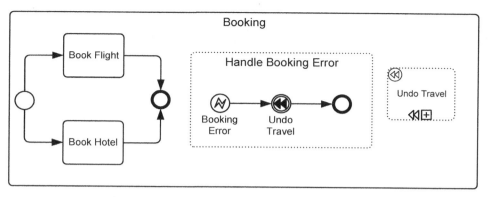

Figure 6: An expanded Event Sub-Process

An Event Sub-Process is a Sub-Process that is initiated only when its Start Event occurs. An Event Sub-Process is contained within a Process, but it is outside the main flow of that Process. That is, as the Process flows from its normal Start Event to End Event, the Event Sub-Process will not be initiated. The Event Sub-Process can only be initiated if its Start Event is triggered. Unlike a normal Sub-Process, an Event Sub-Process can only have one Start Event and that Start Event must have a trigger. As with boundary Events, Event Sub-Process can be set to either interrupt its parent Process or not.

Event Sub-Processes set to interrupt will stop its parent Process, when the triggering event occurs, and begin performing the internal Activities of the Event Sub-Process. While the main flow of the Process has been stopped, the Process as a whole will not have completed until all the active Event Sub-Processes have been completed. Event Sub-Processes that do not interrupt will run in parallel with the main Process flow and can be triggered multiple times during the lifetime of the main Process.

Visually, interrupting and non-interrupting Event Sub-Processes are distinguished by the border of the marker for collapsed Event Sub-Processes or the border of the Start Event for expanded Event Sub-Processes. Non-interrupting Event Sub-Process markers have a dashed border (see Figure 7).

Figure 7: Interrupting and non-interrupting Event Sub-Processes

As with boundary Events, not all kinds of Event Sub-Processes can be non-interrupting. The Event Sub-Processes that do not have non-interrupting options are Compensation and Error. The remaining Event Sub-Processes that do have non-interrupting options are Conditional, Escalation, Message, Multiple, Multiple Parallel, Signal, and Timer.

2.2 *Updated Events*

A major enhancement to the behavior of Events in BPMN 2 is boundary Events that trigger without interrupting the Activity. In addition, two new types of Events are introduced: Escalation and Multiple Parallel.

Non-Interrupting Events

One of the unique characteristics of BPMN 1.x was the innovation of placing Events on the boundaries of Activities (boundary Events) to show that those Activities might be interrupted during their performance (see Figure 8).

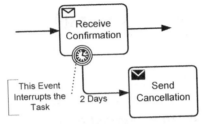

Figure 8: Use of interrupting boundary Events

However, some business process patterns require the boundary Event to be triggered without interrupting the original Activity. Thus, the Activity would continue being performed while a parallel path is triggered. With BPMN 1.x there are alternative ways of modeling this behavior, but they are complex and require many additional modeling elements. In BPMN 2, the capabilities of boundary Events are upgraded to enable triggering without interrupting the source Activity. An interrupting boundary Event maintains the BPMN 1.x double lined border (see Figure 8, above). A non-interrupting boundary Event has dashed lines for its border (see Figure 9).

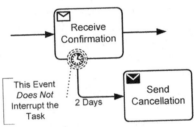

Figure 9: Use of non-interrupting boundary Events

Some boundary Events do not have a non-interrupting option. These Events are the Cancel, Compensation, and Error Events. The boundary Events that do have a non-interrupting option are Conditional, Escalation, Message, Multiple, Multiple Parallel, Signal, and Timer.

Escalation Events

Escalation Events are added in BPMN 2. In concept, they are similar to Errors, but are generally less critical. They usually represent a situation requiring human intervention. Unlike Error Events, they do not need to interrupt when attached to Activity boundaries. Escalation Events can be used for Start Events (for Event Sub-Processes), catch and throw Intermediate Events in the main Process flow, boundary Intermediate Events, and End Events (see Figure 10).

Escalation Events

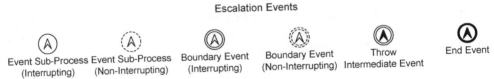

Figure 10: Escalation Events

Multiple Parallel Events

Multiple Events can respond to more than one Event type for a single Event on the diagram. For example, there might be multiple ways to start a Process. Instead of creating a separate Start Event for each of these ways (which is also possible), the modeler might want to have less clutter and combine them into a single Start Event on the diagram. The Multiple Event can respond to any combination of valid Event types, including multiple definitions of the same type (for example, multiple unique Messages).

The Multiple Events behave exclusively. That is, if any one of the defined Event types for the Event is triggered, then it is the only one responded to, and the Process flow will continue from the Event. Any triggering of any other of the Event types would be independent. In the case of Start Events, any new trigger would create a separate Process instance.

In BPMN 2, the Multiple Event capability is expanded to support parallel dependency between the types of Events defined for a single Multiple Event. In this case, *all* of the Event types defined for the Event must be triggered before the Process flow can continue. This variation of the Multiple Event is called the Multiple Parallel Event.

The Multiple Parallel Event marker is distinguished from the Multiple Event and looks like the Parallel Gateway marker (a plus sign—see Figure 11). The plus sign is unfilled to indicate that it is used in "catch" situations.

Multiple Event   Multiple Parallel
(Exclusive)   Event

Figure 11: Multiple Event types

Multiple Parallel Events can be used for Start Events, catch Intermediate Events in the main Process flow, and boundary Intermediate Events. They are not used for throw Intermediate Events or End Events, since these types of Events already throw all of the defined Event types in parallel.

2.3 Updated Gateways

Most of the changes to Gateways in BPMN 2 are for the Event Gateways. In BPMN 1.x Event Gateways could be set to initiate a Process or not. In BPMN 2 there is a visual differentiation between Event Gateways that initiate a Process and those that do not. The normal Event Gateway, one that does not initiate a Process, maintains the original internal marker that looks like a Multiple Intermediate Event (see left Gateway in Figure 12). The Event Gateway that does initiate a Process now has an internal marker that looks like a Multiple Start Event (see middle Gateway in Figure 12).

Non-   Initiating   Multiple Parallel
Initiating   (Initiating)

Figure 12: Event Gateway variations

Both the initiating and non-initiating versions of the Event Gateway are exclusive. This means that of the multiple Events that follow the Gateway, only one of them can be triggered each time the Gateway is used. However, to fill the requirements of some business process patterns, a new variation of the Event Gateway is added in BPMN 2—the Multiple Parallel Event Gateway. This Gateway requires that *all* of the Events that follow the Gateway must be triggered before the Process can be initiated (this Gateway is only used for initiating a Process). The internal marker for this variation looks like the new Multiple Parallel Start Event (see right Gateway in Figure 12, above).

2.4 Updated Data Elements

In BPMN 1.x data was considered an Artifact and not a main part of the Process flow. While the flow of data is still separated from Sequence Flow, data becomes first class elements in BPMN 2. Many technical and graphical changes are made to how data can be modeled. The technical changes are mainly of interest to the tool implementers and advanced modelers, but there are new graphical data elements, including: Data Input, Data Output, and Data Store (see Figure 13).

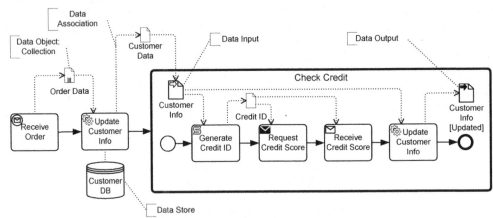

Figure 13: A Process with changes to BPMN data elements highlighted

Data Associations

In BPMN 1.x a connector between a Data Object and an Activity was an Association (a dotted line). BPMN 2 transforms these lines into new elements called Data Associations. Associations are still used for connecting Artifacts to elements, such as a Text Annotation to an Activity, but Data Associations are used exclusively between data elements and Activities or Events. They also add mechanisms for the transfer and transformation of data as it passes through the Process. Both Associations and Data Associations use the same dotted line—thus, BPMN 1.x and BPMN 2 diagrams will look the same in this regard (see Figure 13, above).

Data Inputs and Outputs

Data Inputs and Data Outputs were a part of BPMN 1.x for Activities and Processes. These elements were hidden attributes of the model. In BPMN 2 the Data Inputs and Data Outputs for Processes can be visualized (there is no place to visualize the Data Inputs or Outputs of Tasks). Data Inputs and Data Outputs share the same basic shape as a Data Object, but there are markers in the upper left corner of the shape to distinguish them. A Data Input has an unfilled arrow marker (see the "Customer Info" element in the middle of Figure 13, above). A Data Output has an filled arrow marker (see the "Customer Info [Updated]" element at the right side of Figure 13, above).

Data Stores

Data Stores are a new element for BPMN 2. They represent basic organizational data stores, repositories, or databases. They are represented in a diagram with the traditional database cylinder shape (see the "Customer DB" element at the left side of Figure 13, above).

Collections

It is often the case that data elements come grouped together using the same basic structure. For example a set of orders for the same product may be sent at the same time. This is known as a collection, and BPMN 2 adds an attribute to data elements to enable modelers to define them. If a Data Object, Input, or Output is defined as a collection, then the shape will include the same marker that is used for Multi-Instance Activities (see the Data Object "Order Data" at the left side of Figure 13, above).

3   INTERACTION MODELS

Modern businesses typically provide services along with products ("solutions"), and partner with other businesses in delivering solutions.[1] For example, producers of cell phones provide mobile services, many products are paired with maintenance contracts, and shipping is usually provided by separate businesses. Services can increase potential markets by providing multiple services on a single product. New services can help differentiate businesses from competitors. They also enable businesses to focus on core value, while partnering for non-core services.

Business services are characterized by interactions between businesses and their customers and partners that are usually agreed or assumed ahead of time, and do not detail the internal activities of the participants. The interactions might be very short from start to end, or take place over a long period. Agreements determine what information, goods, or personnel are needed by whom and at what time, how complaints and unusual situations are handled, and so on. Interactions might be completed in advance, or have details worked out during the interaction, as in case management. Capturing service interactions in diagrams gathers requirements and solution expertise in one place, and facilitates coordination between the parties when the interaction is carried out. This helps lower costs for providers and consumers, reduce unnecessary or unsatisfactory interactions, and identify new areas for service development, including combining and adapting existing services.

This section describes interaction diagrams in BPMN 2, including the new Choreography diagram, improvements to the Collaboration diagram from BPMN 1.x, and enhancements to interactive process modeling. Section 3.1 covers interaction models in BPMN 2. Section 3.2 describes added capabilities for interactive processes needed to deploy interactions.

3.1   *Interaction Diagrams*

BPMN 2 has two diagrams for interactions: Collaboration and Choreography. The first is available in BPMN 1.x, and enhanced in BPMN 2, while the second is in BPMN 2 only. The diagrams show different aspects of interactions, sometimes

---

[1] The term "service" in the section is used in the business sense, rather than a web service or other software operation. Business services can be complicated to deliver, and require more information to specify than simpler software services such as getting stock quotes. Antoine Lonjon provided some of the points in this paragraph.

using different notations for the same concepts, or highlighting some concepts over others. Section 3.1.1 covers the concepts in common to both diagrams, while Sections 3.1.2 and 3.1.3 describe concepts available in only one of the diagrams.

3.1.1   Interaction Basics

Interaction diagrams in BPMN 2 have these elements in common:

- Participants are the interacting agents. These might be businesses, departments, or people, for example, or automated agents in software or hardware.
- Messages are sent between Participants. These can be informational or physical, including physical things that do not carry information, such as cars or furniture.
- Messages Flows occur at certain points during the interaction, between particular Participants. The same Message can be carried by more than one Message Flow.

Figure 14 shows the notations for these three basic concepts. Participants in Collaboration diagrams on the left are shown with rectangles (called "pools"), while the Choreography diagram on the right shows them as bands inside a rounded rectangle, called a Choreography Activity. Collaboration diagrams show participants much more prominently than Choreography, so are useful when relationships between Participants are the primary concern.

Messages are shown as envelopes on both interaction diagrams, with a label naming them. Message Flows show which Participants exchange the messages. In Collaboration diagrams Message Flows appear as dashed arrows with Messages optionally overlaid on them. In Choreography, Message Flows are shown as Choreography Activities, with Messages linked to them by dotted lines called Associations. The unshaded bands of Choreography Activities are Participants sending the Message, and shaded bands are the ones receiving them.

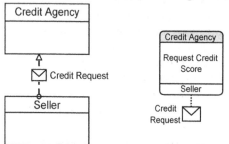

Figure 14: Basic Interaction Elements

3.1.2   Message Flow Sequence

Messages usually flow between Participants in a particular order. For example, in many retail purchasing interactions, payment is made before the product is delivered. Choreographies capture this most directly, as Sequence Flows between Choreography Activities (see Figure 15). Sequence Flow arrows indicate that the Message in the Choreography Activity at the tail of the arrow flows before the Message in Choreography Activity at the head. In this example, the Message requesting a credit score is sent before the one providing the credit score. The sending Participant in the first Message Flow is the receiver in the second, capturing a simple request-response interaction. The response may be a very long time after the request, or a very short time, depending on how much processing occurs within the receiver of the first Message.

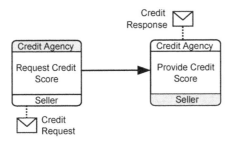

Figure 15: Message Flow Sequence in Choreography

Choreography diagrams can use Gateways to split and merge Sequence Flows in similar ways as BPMN Process diagrams, but with some restrictions due to limited Participant visibility. The rule above about Participants in sequences of Choreography Activities applies even when Gateways are present. The sender in a Choreography Activity must also be a Participant in the immediately previous Activity, either as sender or receiver, even if Gateways are interposed between the Activities. For split Gateways, which have a single Sequence Flow coming in and multiple going out, all senders in Activities after the Gateway must participate in the Activity before the Gateway. For merge Gateways, which have multiple Sequence Flows going in and a single one going out, the sender in the Activity after the Gateway must participate in all the Activities before the Gateway. The notation for Gateways in Choreography diagrams is the same as in Process diagrams.

3.1.3   Grouping Message Flow

Grouping Message Flows helps manage complicated interactions by gathering multiple flows together under a single element. Choreography diagrams support this with Activities representing multiple Message Flows (see examples on the left in Figure 16). These have two Message Flows, as indicated by the Message icons linked to the Participants sending them on the upper right. In this example the Seller sends a Credit Request Message, and the Credit Agency sends back a Credit Response. The thickness of Choreography Activity borders indicates whether the grouped Message Flows can be nested by multiple Choreography Activities, either in the same Choreography diagram or different ones. A thick border indicates they can be used in multiple Activities, while a thin border indicates they cannot. Thick-bordered Activities are Call Choreography Activities. The one on the lower left in Figure 16 is "calling" a Global Choreography Task that groups Message Flows for nesting by multiple Activities and diagrams. The thin-bordered Activity on the upper left is a Choreography Task, which groups Message Flows without a making them available for multiple Activities or diagrams (they are local to the diagram). Message icons can only be linked to Choreography Tasks. Message icons for receiving Participants are shaded to match the bands to which they are linked.

The two Choreography Activities on the left in Figure 16 do not explicitly capture sequencing of the Message Flows they group, because they do not expand to another Choreography diagram, as indicated by the absence of small plus-sign markers. However, they can represent two Message Flows at most, and the first Message to be sent is identified by linking its icon to the unshaded Participant for Choreography Tasks. These two Activities combine request and response flows between the two Participants, with the request happening first because it is the initiating Participant, and the response happening next, because it is the only one left.

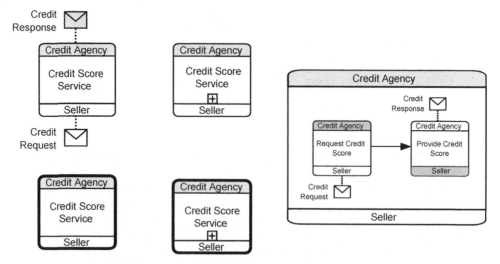

Figure 16: Grouping Message Flow

To capture sequencing of grouped Message Flows, Choreography Activities can expand to entire Choreography diagrams, as illustrated in the middle and right in Figure 16. The middle shows the collapsed forms, as indicated by the small plus-sign markers. In the expanded form shown on the right, they contain a full Choreography diagram, including Sequence Flows between nested Choreography Activities. The Activity in the lower middle is calling the Choreography diagram on the right, which is available to be reused in multiple Activities and diagrams. The Activity in the upper middle is a Sub-Choreography, which nests the diagram on the right without making it available for multiple Activities or diagrams.

Collaboration diagrams also support grouping Message Flows to manage complicated interactions, using Conversations to stand in for multiple Message Flows (see examples on the left in Figure 17). Conversations appear as hexagons with solid double lines ("pipelines") connecting Participants. The examples expand to two Message Flows shown in the middle left, the Seller sending a Credit Request message to the Credit Agency, which sends back a Credit Response. The thickness of Conversation borders indicates whether the grouped Message Flows can be reused in multiple Conversations, either in the same outer Collaboration diagram or different ones. A thick border indicates they can, while a thin border indicates they cannot. Thick-bordered Conversations are Call Conversations. The one on the lower left in Figure 17 is "calling" a Global Conversation that groups Message Flows for reuse by multiple Conversations and diagrams. The thin-bordered Conversation on the upper left groups Message Flows without making them available for multiple Conversations or diagrams. These Conversations do not have a special name, but are analogous to Tasks in Processes and Choreography in the way they group elements.[2] The Conversations on the left in Figure 17 can only group Message Flows, not other Conversations, as indicated by the absence of a small plus-sign adornment.

---

[2] The hexagon notation in general is technically called a Conversation Node.

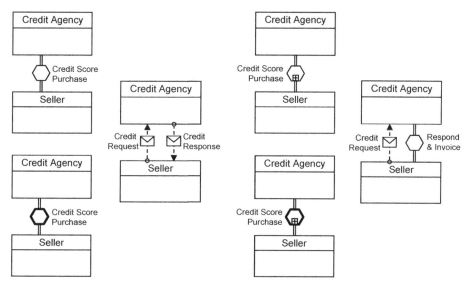

Figure 17: Conversations

To help manage complex interactions, the expansion of Conversations can include other Conversations as well as Message Flows (see examples on the right side of Figure 17). In collapsed form, these Conversations have a small plus-sign adornment. In expanded form, they appear as Message Flows and Conversations, shown on the far right. The Conversations in the lower middle right is calling the Collaboration diagram on the right, which is available to be nested in multiple Activities and diagrams. The Conversation in the upper middle right is a Sub-Conversation, which nests the diagram on the right without making it available for multiple Activities or diagrams.

3.2 Interactive Processes

Interactive Processes send and receive Messages to and from outside Participants. They are needed to deploy the interaction diagrams discussed in the previous section. Section 3.2.1 describes how Collaboration diagrams include interactive Processes within Participants. Section 3.2.2 covers interactive Processes as they appear to other Participants and to the Participants carrying them out.

3.2.1   Processes in Collaboration Diagrams

Collaboration diagrams can show how Activities in a Process interact with other Participants, by sending and receiving Messages. Processes usually interact with multiple Participants, serving or producing a product for at least one of them, with assistance from the others. Figure 18 is an example Process where a service is provided to a Customer, with assistance from a Credit Agency. Message Flows show which Tasks interact with which Participants.

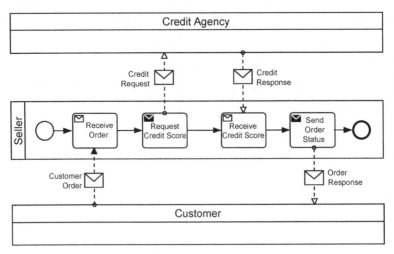

Figure 18: Process in a Collaboration

Conversations can link Process Activities and Participants by grouping many Message Flows at lower levels of Process nesting. For example, the Invoicing Conversation in Figure 19 links the Process Invoice Activity to the Invoicer Participant. The Activity calls another Process that exchanges potentially many Messages with the Invoicer (not shown for brevity). Similarly the Scheduling and Shipping Conversations might group many Message Flows to many Activities, but in this case they simplify the diagram by linking directly to the Process Participant, rather than identifying the Messages and Activities involved.

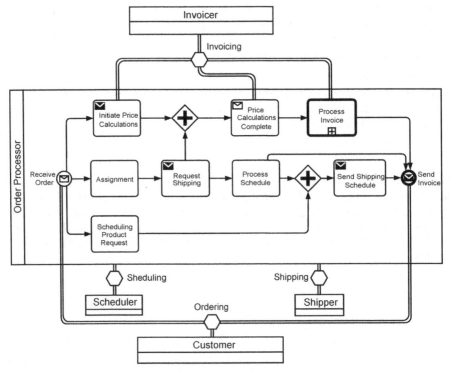

Figure 19: Process with Conversations

3.2.2 Public and Private Processes

Businesses usually do not show each other their Process models, even interactive ones, unless the models only describe interactions with other businesses. In BPMN 2, these are called public Processes, while those internal to a business are private.[3] For example, Figure 18 could be a public Process, because it only sends and receives Messages, which are Activities other Participants can detect. Figure 20 shows a possible private Process for Figure 18 containing Activities that are not interactive and usually not shown to other Participants. It uses Event notation for receiving and sending Messages, which has the same effect as the Receive and Send Tasks in Figure 18. While the private Process waits for the Credit Response Message, it searches internal records for credit information. A Parallel Gateway is used to receive the Credit Response Message even if it arrives while the internal search is underway. When the Credit Response Message arrives and the internal search is completed, the Process can continue. When the private Process is carried out it will appear to external Participants as if it were the public one in Figure 18, because the same Messages are sent in the same order to the same Participants.

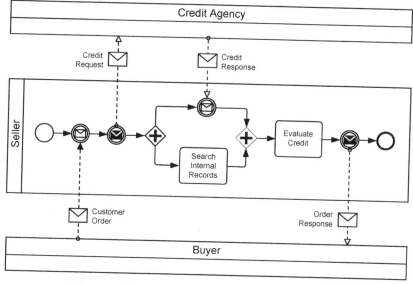

Figure 20: *Private Process for Figure 18*

A private Process supports a public one by interacting the same way as a public one, as described above. The *supports* relationship does not have a notation, but is accessible in other ways with tools supporting Process diagrams. Modelers can specify which private Processes support which public ones, for example, to declare a private Process they developed will cover the public Processes agreed to with partners. Tools might check these declarations, but it is not required for BPMN 2 compliance. The same private Process can support multiple public ones, each showing different aspects of the Private process. For example, two other public Processes can be defined from Figure 18 by removing either Customer or

---

[3] Public Processes are called "abstract" in BPMN 1.x. The name is changed in BPMN 2 to avoid confusion with Processes that act as templates for further development. Public Processes might be used as templates for private Processes, but the private Processes cannot be changed arbitrarily as those based on templates can. Private Processes must support interactions specified in public Processes (see rest of this section).

Credit Agency. These would only have Message Flows and Tasks for interacting with the remaining Participant, Credit Agency or Customer respectively. The two additional diagrams would be suitable for showing to those particular Participants. The private process in Figure 20 would support both of these public processes.

4 CONCLUSION

The new features for processes and interactions in BPMN 2 significantly broaden the range of applications of the language. Process Tasks and Events are more refined, including the use of business rules, and Event Sub-Processes enabling triggers of separate portions of a Process. Events themselves are more expressive, supporting Activity boundary Events without interruption if needed, and Multiple Events that combine events either exclusively or in conjunction with each other. Data becomes a first-class part of Process modeling in BPMN 2. Inputs and outputs are visually specified for Processes and Activities. Collections of Data Objects and Data Stores are also supported.

Interactions and interactive processes undergo a major upgrade in BPMN 2, with Collaborations grouping Message Flows into Conversations, a new Choreography diagram for specifying sequences and conditions for Message Flow, and explicit relationships between public and private interactive Processes. Collaborations show Participants more prominently, while Choreography shows sequencing of Message Flows directly. Message flow to Activities in interactive Processes can be grouped into Conversations, aligning with grouping of Activities in Processes. Public and private interactive processes can be linked to indicate which private processes support which public ones.

5 ACKNOWLEDGEMENTS

The authors thank Antoine Lonjon, Peter Denno, and J.D. Baker for their input to this paper.

Commercial equipment and materials might be identified to adequately specify certain procedures. In no case does such identification imply recommendation or endorsement by the U.S. National Institute of Standards and Technology, nor does it imply that the materials or equipment identified are necessarily the best available for the purpose.

6 REFERENCES

[1] Object Management Group, "Business Process Model and Notation (BPMN), Version 2.0, Beta 2," http://doc.omg.org/dtc/10-06-04, June 2010.

[2] Organization for the Advancement of Structured Information Standards, "Web Services Business Process Execution Language Version 2.0," April, 2007.

[3] U.S Department of Defense, "DoD Architecture Framework Version 2.0," May 2009.

BPMN 2.0 Interchange: A W5 Executive Summary

Denis Gagné, Trisotech, Canada

ABSTRACT

Interchange (via some form of serialization) was one of the most cited shortcomings of the first version of BPMN. With the advent of BPMN 2.0 it is now possible to interchange BPMN process models and diagrams. In this chapter, we abstract away from the technical details of BPMN 2.0 interchange serialization to explore BPMN 2.0 interchange from a business perspective. We start by providing some insight as to WHY BPMN 2.0 interchange is desirable. We then postulate as to WHO benefits from such interchange and what kind of benefits each stakeholder obtains from the open interchange of BPMN 2.0. We then present in simple terms WHAT can be interchanged using the various types of BPMN 2.0 models and diagrams cautioning the reader of the pitfalls from what we call the BPMN 2.0 devil's quadrants. We then argue that while BPMN 2.0 interchange standardization is required, it is not sufficient, and explain HOW interchange conformance verification and validation can act as a catalyst to universal BPMN interchange. We conclude by postulating that the answer to "WHEN will BPMN 2.0 interchange be feasible?" is *now*.

INTRODUCTION

Business Process Management (BPM) standards have the potential of delivering tremendous value to both practitioners of the BPM discipline and vendors of BPM tools and technology. In fact, the adoption of BPM as a discipline can be said to be stimulated by the existence of BPM relevant standards and facilitated by the existence of BPM enabling technology conformant to these standards [1].

As one such BPM relevant standard, BPMN's primary goal is to provide a notation that is readily understandable by all business stakeholders [2]. In the context of BPMN 2.0, the term *"Business Stakeholders"* broadly refers to the *Business Analysts* that create the initial drafts of the processes, the *Technical Developers* responsible for implementing the technology that will enable the performance of those processes, the *Business People* (employees) who will participate in, enact, manage and monitor those processes, and even extends to the *Business Partners* with whom the organization will communicate and interact during the performance of those same processes. From a process lifecycle point of view, BPMN aims to create a standardized bridge for the gap between the business process design/analysis and the process implementation/execution. In other words, BPMN aims to ease the communication amongst the various business stakeholders throughout the various lifecycle phases of a business process by offering a universally understood notation.

Along with the *"Universal Understandability"* goal of BPMN, a reasonable expectation from BPMN users is that one should be able to create a BPMN process model once and then be able to open it anywhere. This seemingly simple *"model-once-open-anywhere"* expectation actually implies two further requirements upon BPMN: 1) the existence of a file interchange capability between various tools implementing BPMN, and, 2) a unique interpretation by the tools of what has been interchanged. Put simply, not only do BPMN process models need to mean the same thing to all business stakeholders, they also need to "*mean*" the same thing for all conformant tools.

One often referred weakness of previous versions of BPMN (BPMN 1.X) was the inexistence of such *model-once-open-anywhere* capability [3]. In other words, BPMN was missing a unique standardized way for tools to electronically persist and exchange process models and diagrams. Version 2.0 of BPMN has remedied this situation, and with it, came a subtle change in the spelled out name of BPMN. With version 2.0, BPMN now stands for "Business Process **Model and Notation**" rather than the previous "Business Process Modeling Notation". The change in the spelled out name reflects the fact that BPMN is now more than just a notation.

In this chapter, we abstract away from the technical details of BPMN 2.0 interchange and present BPMN 2.0 interchange from a business perspective. The remainder of this chapter will provide a W5 executive summary of BPMN 2.0 interchange covering: **w**HY is BPMN 2.0 interchange desirable, **w**HO will benefit from BPMN 2.0 interchange, **w**HAT can be interchanged using BPMN 2.0, HO**w** is that interchange to be enabled and **w**HEN will that BPMN 2.0 interchange be possible.

WHY IS INTERCHANGE DESIRABLE?

BPMN 2.0 interchange is highly desirable to stimulate wide adoption of BPMN 2.0 and is a necessity of end user organizations for cost reduction and barrier-free repurposing and migration of BPM assets.

A benefit of BPMN 2.0 is that it promotes the use of a standard notation, terminology and unified definition of behavior. This accelerates the universal understanding and promotes wider adoption of BPMN 2.0 by reducing confusion and promoting uniqueness of skill requirements for the organization. Various stakeholder groups within the organization can now be trained to become proficient at a common visual modeling language. BPMN 2.0 training and certification can be elaborated once and widely disseminated across the organization. Not everyone in the organization needs to be proficient using the full expressiveness of BPMN 2.0, but the basic four elements, namely, *Event, Activity, Gateway* and *Sequence flow* and the simple notion of flowcharting are certainly within the grasp of anybody in an organization. Universal understanding and widespread adoption also has the effect of making it easier for organizations to compare competitive products.

Many large organizations already use different BPM systems for different types of processes and for different purposes. For example, a specific tool or suite of tools may be dedicated to *Human Centric* type of processes, while another may be used for *Integration Centric* type of processes. Alternatively, a tool may be used for modeling purposes while another is used for simulation purposes. It is imperative for the process models hosted by these disparate tools to be freely interchangeable. Having all these tools using BPMN 2.0 as their underlying language for defining the processes enables repurposing of these process model assets and may also facilitate interoperability. For example, a BPMN 2.0 process model used in one system may now be interchanged to be repurposed for simulation on another system.

Another major benefit of standardized interchange for BPMN 2.0 process models is that it will allow organizations to more easily migrate from one BPM platform to another. With BPMN 2.0 interchange, customers are no longer locked-in with one vendor. If they are dissatisfied with the services or performance of a system from a particular vendor, they can migrate their platform independent process models to another vendor whose BPM system is also based on BPMN 2.0 using interchange.

By: 1) increasing universal understanding, 2) stimulating wider adoption, 3) facilitating interoperability, 4) enabling the repurposing and migration of BPM assets from one vendor tool to another, the standardization of BPMN 2.0 interchange creates an open market of enabling technology removing some of the previous barriers. In such an open market, both "suites" and "best of breed" BPMN 2.0 product offerings can truly flourish. This stimulates faster innovation and the elaboration of point solutions addressing specific or niche business needs. The result for end user organizations is an increased return on investment (ROI) and a reduced total cost of ownership (TOC).

Simply put, BPMN 2.0 interchange is what the market wants and it is what the market needs.

WHO BENEFITS FROM INTERCHANGE?

The protagonists of BPMN 2.0 interchange can be captured into two very broad communities: End Users and Vendors. The end user community is primarily composed of the business stakeholders enumerated earlier, namely: Business Analysts, Technical Developers, Business People, and Business Partners. These business stakeholders use BPMN 2.0 in the course of completing their responsibilities within or across organizations. The vendor community is composed of any provider of BPMN 2.0 tools enabling the practice of BPM. These BPMN 2.0 enabling tools are not limited to Business Process Management Suites (BPMS). They also include function specific tools that fall in categories such as: modeling tools, analysis tools, simulation tools, reporting tools, execution engines, etc. These function specific tools are required to enable end users to efficiently and proficiently use BPMN 2.0. Each community is motivated by, and rewarded with, specific benefits from the interchange of BPMN 2.0.

Broadly speaking, BPMN 2.0 interchange allows vendors to: attract and retain customers, demonstrate market leadership, create competitive advantages, develop and maintain best practices (figure 1). For these vendors, the ability to demonstrate compliance with a widely recognized and respected standard such as BPMN 2.0 is an effective means of differentiation in a competitive marketplace. As consumers become increasingly informed about their choices, conformity to this recognized standard becomes pivotal.

To the end user community, benefits from BPMN 2.0 interchange include: choice in tools, speed of deployment, readily available skill force, flexibility and agility [4]. Standardized BPMN 2.0 means that choices made in tools today leaves open a wide range of options for later. New solutions that involve multiple hardware and software platforms can be quickly elaborated providing desired speed and flexibility of deployment. Resources that understand BPMN 2.0 and have the appropriate skills can readily be found in the market. Process model interchange between internal departments, or to external partners, that made different technology choices is possible providing flexibility. Adjustments to dispersed process models can be made quickly in response to changing business parameters and environment (e.g. new opportunities, new partners, new employees, etc.) allowing business agility (Figure 1).

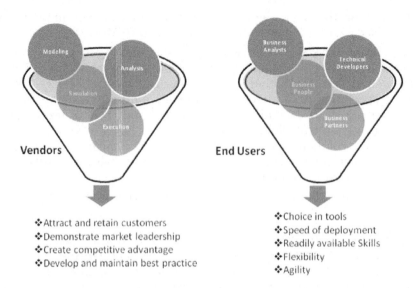

Vendors

❖ Attract and retain customers
❖ Demonstrate market leadership
❖ Create competitive advantage
❖ Develop and maintain best practice

End Users

❖ Choice in tools
❖ Speed of deployment
❖ Readily available Skills
❖ Flexibility
❖ Agility

Figure 1: Communities and their Benefits

WHAT CAN BE INTERCHANGED?

BPMN 2.0 is more than just a notation. It is a visual modeling language for business processes. Visual modeling languages have the potential of being more intuitive and faster to comprehend than their textual modeling language counterparts. However, to effectively and efficiently use these visual modeling languages it is necessary to clearly define their syntax and meaning (or semantics). This is because the diagrams of a visual modeling language are what is often used to communicate between different stakeholders. Ambiguous definition of the language can lead to misunderstandings and require extra effort to explain the intended meaning diagram by diagram.

To be clearly and unambiguously defined, the syntax of a visual language must be distinguished into a "*concrete syntax*" and an "*abstract syntax*". The concrete syntax describes the notational symbols and graphical representation of the language. The abstract syntax defines the underlying computer-interpretable representation of the language.

The concrete syntax of BPMN 2.0 is what is commonly known as the BPMN 2.0 notation. The specification provides the depictions of all the various BPMN 2.0 elements and their graphical variants. The specification also provides the rules that govern the visual appearance of the BPMN 2.0 elements.

The BPMN 2.0 abstract syntax is captured via a "*meta-model*". Meta-modeling is a popular method to define abstract syntax of languages. The BPMN 2.0 meta-model is an abstraction that describes and defines the constructs that can be used in creating a process model along with the rules and constraints that apply to these constructs. It is the means by which the proper unique structure of BPMN 2.0 process models is ensured from tool to tool.

Also included in BPMN 2.0 is a Diagram Interchange (BPMN DI) meta-model. BPMN DI is the means by which the layout of a BPMN diagram is maintained from tool to tool. Process diagrams can be considered like pictures of the process model. Many diagrams (or pictures) of the same process model are possible, each showing or hiding various aspects of the process model details. Each process diagram references the process model to uncover the details and attributes of the model behind the process diagram (or picture) (figure 2).

When modeling, the BPMN 2.0 process models created are in fact "*instances*" of the abstract syntax meta-model while the BPMN 2.0 process diagrams are "*instances*" of the BPMN DI meta-model. By *instances* we mean that a particular process model or process diagram is properly structured in accordance with the description provided by its respective meta-model (figure 2).

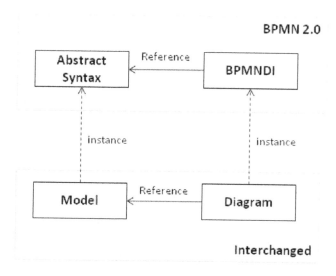

BPMN 2.0

Figure 2: What is Interchanged

For interchange, the process models and diagrams created need to be "*serialized*". Serializing is the process of converting the internal computer interpretable representation to a format that can be stored in a file. That is the electronic file format that eases the safeguard and transfer of this data between different tools.

Two interchange file formats are supported for both the abstract syntax meta-model and the BPMN DI meta-model. An XMI based file format which is an Object Management Group (OMG) interchange file format [5] and an extended marked up language (XML) schema definition (XSD) based file format.

In simple terms, interchange in BPMN 2.0 is about Models and Diagrams. That is the interchange of both the process model details and the graphical details (e.g. layout) of the many different process diagrams depicting all or portions of the model. The simplest interchange approach to ensure the unambiguous rendering of a BPMN diagram was chosen to ensure that the picture you see in all tools is as similar as possible, if not identical.

BPMN 2.0 does not aim to preserve or interchange any "tool smarts" between the source and target tools (e.g. layout smarts, efficient styling, etc.). Furthermore, BPMN 2.0 does not address, nor define, the interchange of color information within a diagram. The use of alternative colors in BPMN 2.0 is non normative as the meaning of colors might vary from tool to tool or, from user to user, potentially leading to miss-interpretations (e.g. red may mean "important" for someone and "trouble" for someone else). Finally, successful interchange of BPMN 2.0 does not ascertain that the BPMN 2.0 process model and diagrams are syntactically or semantically correct.

BPMN 2.0 is a visual modeling language; it does not guarantee that people will write useful models. As a language, BPMN 2.0 attempts to be as expressive as possible. Expressiveness is a measure of the concepts expressible in a given language. For process modeling, BPMN 2.0 is expressive enough to capture different perspective and fulfill different modeling initiatives' objectives.

BPMN 2.0 provides the ability for models and diagrams to capture both the *"orchestration"* and the *"choreography"* perspectives. The orchestration perspective defines the sequence of activities within a process, including conditions and exceptions while the choreography perspective formalizes the way business participants coordinate their interactions. In the choreography perspective, the focus is not on orchestrations of the work performed within the participants, but rather on the exchange of information or messages between these participants.

The objective of a process modeling initiative greatly influences what is included in a process model and what is excluded from it. If the objective is to create a process model to visualize or simply document the actual process, then the model should aim to be informative. These models are normally used as call to actions, for discussions between stakeholders and may provide customized views adapted to the audience. This type of model is aimed to inform and communicate. It can also be an important element of organizational training material for current or future employees. If the objective pursued by the modeling effort is to better structure or analyze the process being modeled, the process model should then aim to be more descriptive. At this level, the model must provide enough information on its detailed structure, the resources used and measures to enable its analysis. On the other hand, if the objective is to use the model to enact or automate the process, the model must then be prescriptive. It will have to prescribe clearly the instructions and parameters governing the automation of the process.

In BPMN 2.0, it is possible to draw or model the same process in many different ways, each with the intent to fulfill a specific objective or to serve a specific purpose. Combining these purposes with the breadth of the modeling expressiveness of BPMN 2.0 leads to a depiction that we call the *"BPMN 2.0 Devil's Quadrants"* (figure 3). On the one axis are opposed the purposes of succinctly communicating a common understanding of a process using simple diagrams versus modeling in complete details the process behaviors for uniform execution (unique behavior) on different platforms. On the other axis, are opposed the internal orchestration perspective focusing on sequencing of the processes activities versus the choreography perspective of the external partner interactions. Each of the four quadrants generated, captures a tradeoff combination of purpose and breadth (e.g. communicating an orchestration's perspective versus executing a choreography's perspective).

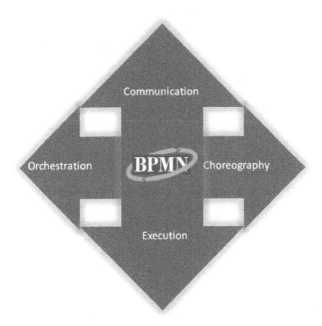

Figure 3: BPMN 2.0 Devil's Quadrants

Each BPMN 2.0 model or diagram may be quite adequate for the intended purpose but simply incorrect for other purposes. It has been postulated that "All models are wrong some are useful" [6]. Usefulness in this context is the sum of many properties and the degree to which they combine to promote understanding and effective results. It is important to note that the most accurate, or the most elegant, or even the most complete model is not necessarily the most useful. All models are incomplete. All models are a compromise. The modeler's efficiency lies in making those shrewd trade-offs that will render the model most useful to the purpose or objective at hand.

HOW INTERCHANGED CAN BE ENABLED?

BPMN 2.0 interchange standardization is not only desired but it is required. Users of BPMN 2.0 based tools rely on the assurance provided by the existence of the standardized interchange to reap its benefits. As organizations continue to make investments in BPM assets by modeling more and more of their processes using BPMN 2.0 they come to not only expect, but actually demand, the flexibility and agility provided by standardize interchange.

Standards specified using hundreds of pages like BPMN 2.0 are likely to have sections interpreted out of context or simply misinterpreted. These misconceptions and misinterpretations can generate variants in product implementations that can potentially inhibit proper interchange and deny end users the expected benefits.

Furthermore, while the BPMN 2.0 specification provides for the model-once-open-anywhere desired capability, it is also permissive enough to allow the interchange of work in progress, namely incomplete models or diagrams that may be incorrect with respect to the complete set of rules of the BPMN 2.0 syntax.

BPMN 2.0 interchange standardization is thus necessary, but it is not in itself sufficient. To truly ripe the benefits of BPMN 2.0 interchange, some form of conformance assurance needs to be in place. Independent conformance verification and validation can act as a catalyst to universal BPMN 2.0 interchange.

Verification and validation is the means by which one ensures that a product, service, or system meets specifications and that it fulfills its intended purpose. Verification is Quality Control (QC). Verification involves structural testing, also referred to as white box testing and checks that the specifications are correctly implemented by the system. Verification aims to answer the *"Are we building things right?"* question. Verification can be objective, if the specifications are sufficiently precise. Validation is Quality Assurance (QA). Validation involves functional testing, also referred to as black box testing and checks that the user's needs are met by the system. Validation aims to answer the *"Are we building the right thing?"* question. Complete validation is generally difficult to determine as it involves subjective judgments.

In the context of BPMN 2.0 interchange, we are interested in the verification and validation of the file being interchanged. For this purpose, verification can be defined as the insurance that the file being interchanged meets the specified schema (XSD), and that the structure and constraints of the abstract syntax and BPMN DI meta-models are respected. BPMN 2.0 verification can be performed for the various conformance classes and sub-classes.

Validation would normally insure intent. While we cannot validate the ultimate intent of the modeler, we redefine Validation as the insurance that no syntax rule of the language has been violated[1]. BPMN 2.0 file validation can be done at two levels: visual and complete. At the visual level, only rules that affect the depiction of the process model are validated. At the complete level all syntax rules, including those that pertain to the hidden attributes, are validated.

Simply put, in the context of BPMN 2.0 file interchange, we verify the "container" and validate the "content". For example, a BPMN 2.0 file containing incorrect references would raise verification issues, whereas a BPMN 2.0 file containing a collaboration including only one participant may be verified to be "structurally' correct but would raise validation issues as collaboration is usually between two participants.

But even with conformance assurance in place there are some potential inhibitors to the business value realization promised by BPMN 2.0 interchange. Adopters of BPMN 2.0 technology are well advised to be mindful of potential indirect lock-in and sink-holes created in the early market. Some tools, or suite, may claim to be BPMN 2.0 tools but not offer any support for interchange creating indirect vendor lock-in. The end users of such tools are able to model using BPMN 2.0 within the tool or suite, but unable to reap the benefits of BPMN 2.0 interchange creating a vendor lock-in. Some other tools may claim BPMN 2.0 support, but only import the interchange format without export capability creating a vendor sink-hole. These marketing rhetoric and unfounded claims of conformance are ill advised to vendors as they will soon antagonize their customers.

When will Interchange be Possible?

As a BPM standard, it is hard to call BPMN anything but a success. The adoption rate of the previous version of BPMN by both end user and vendor communities has been phenomenal. With BPMN 2.0, complete interchange of both process models and process diagrams is now possible correcting one of the most cited shortcomings of the previous version. Based on the broad intended adoption of

---

[1] Some will take issue with this definition of validation saying that is just another level of verification, but we want to differentiate between the notions of container and content.

BPMN 2.0 from the tool vendors' community, we can only foresee further adoption success.

To further accelerate the achievement of the full potential and all benefits of BPMN 2.0 interchange, we postulate that a self-service conformance assurance platform for BPMN 2.0 interchange files is required. A platform providing conformance verification and validation of BPMN 2.0 files. A resource that is vendor-independent but supported by them. The hope is of having as many BPMN technology vendors showcase their commitment to the open interchange of BPMN 2.0.

There is such a resource [7] that offers BPM practitioners a catalogue of cloud apps or web services accepting not only BPMN 2.0 files but various file formats relevant to BPM. These cloud apps manipulate all versions of the BPMN standard. Within this resource platform, atomic web services can be piped into one another to obtain composite services (cloud apps). Over 200 atomic web services are available at this point. The resulting cloud apps have been organized into various categories, not only addressing the desired verification and validation, but also allowing visualization, transformation, and conversion of various file formats.

The web services can be accessed via a graphical user interface (GUI) web site for ease of consumption by the general public, and are also available via a public application programming interface (API) for consumption by third party applications.

It is the goal of this platform to enable universal exchange and interchange of various process assets using various BPM standards. It aims to increase the reliability of BPM standards, and streamline their adoption as a result.

With the existence of the BPMN 2.0 interchange standard, the broad intended adoption from the tool vendors' community, and the availability of interchange conformance verification and validation, we believe that all elements are in place to assure the feasibility BPMN 2.0 interchange. The open interchange of standardized BPMN 2.0 file is possible right now.

Conclusion

In this chapter, we presented BPMN 2.0 interchange from a business perspective. A W5 executive summary of BPMN interchange was presented covering: WHY is BPMN 2.0 interchange desirable, WHO will benefit from BPMN 2.0 interchange, WHAT can be interchanged using BPMN 2.0, HOW is that interchange to be enabled and WHEN will BPMN 2.0 interchange be possible.

While BPMN 2.0 interchange delivers value to both practitioners of the BPM discipline and vendors of BPM tools and technology, it is not in itself sufficient. Independent conformance verification and validation is required to act as a catalyst to universal BPMN 2.0 interchange allowing all stakeholders to truly reap the desired benefits.

A self-service conformance verification and validation platform was promoted as an efficient independent solution to assure such conformance. These services are readily available for the process modeling conformance class and sub-classes of BPMN 2.0 at [7].

Organizations can invest in BPMN 2.0 process assets benefiting from cost reductions and barrier-free repurposing and migration of their platform independent BPM assets.

Acknowledgements

Many people have written about BPMN interchange in the past, namely Robert Shapiro, Keith Swenson, Bruce Silver and many others. Although this chapter may not reflect their particular views regarding BPMN interchange, it was certainly influenced by their insightful writings.

REFERENCES

1. Ryan K.L. Ko, Stephen S.G. Lee, Eng Wah Lee, (2009) "Business process management (BPM) standards: a survey", Business Process Management Journal, Vol. 15 Iss: 5, pp.744 – 791.
2. Object Management Group (OMG): Business Process Model and Notation (BPMN) Version 2.0, OMG report: dtc/2010-06-05, OMG, (2010).
3. Antoine Lonjon, *"The BPMN Wish List Revisited."* Object Management Group (OMG) Whitepaper: http://www.omg.org/news/whitepapers/, Retrieved November 1, 2010.
4. Stephen White, "Introduction to BPM Standards." BPMBlueworks: https://apps.lotuslive.com/bpmblueworks/blog/?author=108#, Retrieved November 1, 2010.
5. Object Management Group (OMG): MOF 2.0/XMI Mapping, Version 2.1.1, OMG Document Number: Formal/2007-12-01, OMG, (2007).
6. George E. P. Box, Norman R. Draper (1987). *Empirical Model-Building and Response Surfaces*. Wiley. p. 424.
7. www.BusinessProcessIncubator.com, Retrieved November 1, 2010.

Simulation for Business Process Management

John Januszczak, Meta Software Corp., USA

ABSTRACT

Simulation is a traditional analysis technique in operations management. In the context of Business Process Management (BPM), simulation models can be used to perform "what-if" analysis of process designs before they are implemented, or test changes to processing parameters before they occur, such as an increase in the volume of work to be processed. Simulation in some form is supported by many Business Process Management Suites (BPMS), as well as other process oriented analysis tools. Besides process definitions, simulation models require additional data to define a scenario such as volumes of work and arrival patterns, task processing times, resource levels and availability, and descriptions of other external events that impact the work flow. Currently there are no specific standards for business process simulation.

This paper provides an overview of business process simulation, the types of information required to define a business process scenario for the purpose of simulation, and a proposed standard for defining simulation scenarios that is compatible with the Business Process Modeling Notation (BPMN) and XML Process Definition Language (XPDL). The article also describes how a RESTful web services API can be developed to support the standard. By providing a standard interchange format and/or a standard API, various artifacts currently available in the event logs of BPM systems could be used to generate baseline simulation scenarios useful in operational decision making and addressing near term processing issues, as well as long term process design.

OVERVIEW OF BUSINESS PROCESS SIMULATION

Computer simulation is a useful tool for exploring the operation of a system. A model that represents certain key attributes of a system is analyzed to demonstrate the effects of alternative conditions or courses of action. Unlike optimization methods that seek to identify a better or best configuration, simulation solely attempts to measure how changes in some of the system's parameters affect the behavior of the system over time. It is exactly this *what-if* capability that makes simulation compelling as an analysis tool. The desire to look into the future in this way is not just extremely useful, but perhaps even profoundly human[1].

Simulation has been used to analyze business processes since the 1970s [2] and is now considered a standard analysis technique for operations management. Business process simulation has evolved from creating models via programming languages extended with simulation capabilities to graphical modeling tools that help generate simulation code without programming by hand. The evolution continues today with the automatic extraction of process models (*process discovery*)

---

[1] The frontal lobe of the brain in humans is disproportionately enlarged compared to lesser primates and other animals. Scientists believe that the executive functions of the frontal lobe involve the ability to recognize future consequences resulting from current actions, and to choose between good and bad actions [1].

and simulation parameters from work flow system event logs that are in turn used to generate simulation models [3]. It is therefore quite natural that simulation is a well established analysis technique in the world of Business Process Management (BPM), where process models, executable work flows and process event tracking converge [4].

Within and outside of the context of BPM, business process simulation is often used in the initial design of business processes where experimentation with the real system under study would be disruptive, cost prohibitive, or where a real process does not yet exist [5]. Business process modeling and simulation used for process or organizational (re)design provides a safe and controlled environment for testing how different processing configurations will potentially perform in the real world [9]. Therefore, simulation can also be used to enhance operational performance (for example, by reducing response times or lowering processing costs) by identifying and testing process improvements. The process models and parameters that these simulations are based on are often compiled by hand. Furthermore, the initial state of the simulation often reflects an empty process and therefore the simulation model is often *warmed up* until a steady state is achieved. Given this, simulation analysis is most often used for strategic planning purposes where the effort to compile a simulation model is practical and the results of such a steady state model are more than adequate for the desired analysis.

BUSINESS PROCESS SIMULATION DEFICIENCIES

It has been argued that even though business process simulation is compelling and easy to understand conceptually, few organizations are using it effectively or in a structured manner [4]. This can be attributed to four factors:

1. The inadequate training or skill sets of people tasked with performing simulation analysis.
2. Limitations of existing tools.
3. Oversimplified models.
4. Not using available artifacts.

It is helpful to look at each of these issues to understand how a standard for defining business process simulation models might help organizations use simulation more effectively.

Simulation Practitioner Capabilities

The concept of business process simulation is easy to understand. However, a certain amount of mathematical or industrial engineering expertise is typically required to create meaningful simulation models [8]. Lack of proper training or capabilities often lead to the processes being modeled incorrectly or not enough data being collected to properly parameterize the model [4].

While a standard format for defining business process simulation scenarios would not directly address this problem, it may offer an indirect benefit addressing the consequences of this need for specialized training. Currently, the design of simulation models, the acquisition of data to properly parameterize the model, and the analysis of simulation results typically occur in an integrated environment (for example, the design, running, and analysis of the model are performed in the same software application). In this configuration, the running of simulations and analysis of the results is usually restricted to those with simulation expertise. With a standard format for the definition of simulation model scenarios the initial design of simulation models would still require the skills of a qualified analyst, however, the running of scenarios and analysis of the output could be made more accessible to other users. For example, the simulation model designer could create a template or baseline scenario definition and specify automated queries and aggregations from various data sources (for example, BPMS event logs) *at design time*. Updated simulation parameters could be published into the baseline scenario via an application programming interface (API) based on the standard. Likewise, user interfaces that update baseline scenarios via such an API could provide a wider range of users the ability to run ad-hoc what-if scenarios by manually adjusting a subset of parameters in the simulation model. Most importantly, the design of simulation models, user interfaces for (simulation) analysis, tools that automate the population of simulation model parameters, and simulation engines can be developed independently, by separate solution providers, since they can rely on a common data specification for business process simulation.

Tool Limitations

Many Business Process Management Systems (BPMS) provide add on simulation capabilities to their process model editors or simulation via process discovery based on the system event logs. The result is often a simulation capability of limited value, to the point where at least one BPM commentator describes simulation provided by BPM solution providers as a *fake feature* [10]. Limitations mentioned include items such as the following[2]:

- Activity duration does not include the time an item of work waits at an activity before being processed. This extra wait time could be due to the queuing of work, limited processing capacity at an activity (for example due to a physical constraint) or the required processing resources being unavailable.
- Probabilities or parameters used at various activities or gateways are uncorrelated. These probabilities (or parameters) are usually highly correlated in real world business processes. Specifically, the duration of a particular activity, the probability of a particular gateway output, and/or the probability of some event occurring are often related to each other. For example, the longer an activity takes (e.g. scanning documents), the more likely an exceptional event might occur (e.g. a jam). One needs to be able to specify simulation parameters as an expression of one or more instance attributes, such as "size" or "claim value", rather than simple numbers like an absolute value or a mean and standard deviation.
- In business processes an activity will only be executed when work and resources are available for the activity in question. The availability of specific resources, whether human, machine or otherwise, is driven by their schedules and contention for equivalent resources by other activities. Simulation software should accurately model resource contention and allow detailed schedules to be defined for all resources which show when they are available to work in specific roles, or specific sets of activities.
- Most simulation tools let you assign roles to activities. However, business processes are often characterized by contingent resource assignment. For example, an activity may assign Role *A* as the primary resource, but if no

---

[2] This sample has been compiled based on various posts in Bruce Silver's BPMS Watch. For example, see http://www.brsilver.com/wordpress/2007/03/08/is-simulation-fake/ and http://www.brsilver.com/wordpress/2009/02/15/making-simulation-useful/

member of Role *A* is available, the activity may use a resource that can perform Role *B*.

- Simulation models generally start empty, reflecting no work initially present in the system. This causes inaccurate simulation results at the beginning of the simulation period. Continuous processes are always in a state where resources are already constrained by the work in progress.

A standard for defining business process simulation scenarios cannot ensure that simulation solutions include the features described above. However, a standard can ensure that the data required to make this functionality possible can be adequately defined in the definition of a simulation scenario, and interchanged between data sources and capable tools. For example, a standard can allow resource availability to be defined in such a way that a simulation model *could* show the effect of constraining resource availability on end to end activity duration (processing time plus wait time) *if* the simulation tool is capable of capturing this effect. Likewise, a standard would provide a way of defining work in progress at the start of the simulation period. Tools that support the modeling of such an initial state could initialize a simulation model to reflect such a process state captured in the simulation scenario definition.

A standard would also allow BPMS solution providers to more easily integrate robust third party simulation tools into their systems. Solution providers can exploit all the simulation relevant data in their systems without the burden of developing sophisticated simulation software from scratch, or settling for a limited feature set. BPMS providers can turn to the developers of state of the art simulation solutions and integrate these products into their systems.

Oversimplified Models & Limited Use of Available Artifacts

Lastly, there is a fundamental problem when simulation models are focused on process (re)design. Using these, it is often difficult or impossible to use simulation analysis for the purposes of operational decision making where it could be used to help solve a current concrete problem rather than a future concern [7]. The reason for this difficulty is typically due to:

- **Oversimplified or naive resource models**: Simulation models often do not reflect that fact that people work in multiple processes, that they have different efficiencies depending on the activity or type of work being performed, or that resources are not continuously available.
- **Available artifacts not being used to update simulation model parameters**: Event logs are typically used to estimate simulation parameters, often represented by some kind of distribution, instead of being used directly. This estimation is often performed at model design time and not subsequently updated by using more current data.
- **Not initializing the simulation to the current state of the business process**: In many simulation models the initial state is assumed to be empty. Sometimes this reflects reality where one can assume there is no carry over work from the periods preceding the scenario start time. Usually this is not accurate and a warm up period is used where results from the initial periods in the simulation results are disregarded. In this way, simulation cannot be used for any kind of transient analysis except for the special case where the actual operation under study starts from an empty state.

A standard for defining business process simulation scenarios helps address all of these concerns. A standard would define a rich resource model, providing not just a simple resource level by role or function, but model specific resources and their availability and efficiencies across the various roles and activities to which they may by assigned. A standard would also support a multitude of resource usage patterns such as direct, role based and contingent allocation, amongst other patterns [11]. With such a standard, tools that might naturally capture the attributes of a rich resource model, for example, scheduling systems, time and attendance systems or Human Resources Information Systems (HRIS), could interchange this data with simulation tools and update the simulation scenarios to accurately reflect the resourcing of the business processes under study.

An event detection and correlation system [6] can be used to automatically assemble and aggregate process artifacts and update the parameters used in simulation scenarios. A standard would allow such a system to easily update simulation scenario definitions. Likewise, the current state captured in production and/or work flow systems could be used to initialize the simulation model by specifying the process state using the standard.

DEFINING BUSINESS PROCESS SIMULATION SCENARIOS

Clearly, a standard for defining business process simulation scenarios would help address some of the current deficiencies with simulation in BPM. We need to understand what kind of information is required to adequately describe a business process simulation scenario in order to compile a specification for such a standard. An empirical approach would look at how existing business process simulation software defines these scenarios. A more academic approach would look at the current literature covering BPM and business process simulation. Both approaches converge on a similar set of requirements and the specification of a standard should depend on both.

One classification suggests at least three sets of information (or *perspectives*) are required in order to simulate a business process [4]:

- Control Flow
- Data/Rules
- Resource/Organization

The control flow perspective describes the ordering of activities. Activity order may be sequential, or depend on splits, joins and/or loops in the flow of work. This perspective may also be described as the *process definitions*. Since resources may participate in more than one business process, it might be useful to include multiple processes in a simulation scenario. The data/rules perspective describes decisions made within a process and the data upon which these decisions are made. The resource organization perspective describes the allocation of activities to resources, the availability and other properties of the resources and organization.

It is possible to provide structure to the resource/organization perspective [6] described above. Roles can be used to describe functions performed and the skill required to carry out these functions. In this way, resources can be described as performing work in these roles, where resources could be human, equipment or systems. The availability of resources (and therefore roles) can be modeled by specifying shifts, as well as efficiencies for each resource. Availability has also been refined to include not just when a resource can work, but also how resources divide up their work and sub periods over which a particular set of constraints may be in place [7]. It can be shown that these refinements, used to reflect the batching of work and nuanced relationships between performance and workload, can also be described in the process definition.

The data/rules perspective can be broken down into the following components [6]:

- Incoming Work
- Activity Details
- Routing Information

Incoming work, or *arrivals*, describes when work to be processed arrives into a business process and any attributes of the work that will impact how the work is processed or routed through the process. Activity details describe additional properties of the activities not captured in the process definition, but pertinent to simulation such as the duration of an activity, which may be a simple value, a complex expression based on the attributes of the work (originally defined in the incoming work and perhaps modified during the work flow), or based on some kind of distribution function. Routing information refers to information not included in the process definition that may further describe under which conditions certain paths in the work flow are taken. While routing information is usually based on rules specified in the process definition or control flow, these may instead be represented by percentages that reflect the likelihood of a certain result in a simulation model.

Lastly, the simulation model must be initialized to reflect the state of the process at the beginning of the period being simulated. While this may not be required, or may be impossible to do when using simulation for process design, or longer term strategic planning, the initial state of the simulation model becomes important when the starting point for simulation is based on a point in time in the past, the present, or the very near future. The components of such an initialization are as follows:

- progress state of work items currently being processed ("work in progress")
- attributes of work items currently in process
- busy resources

For example, when starting a simulation scenario at 9:00 AM on such and such a day, the scenario definition would identify the work items in progress and their attributes, which activity they are being processed at, and if being worked on, which specific resource is performing the work at that point in time.

PROPOSED STANDARD

The current state of simulation in BPM is characterized by a lack of specific standards for business process model simulation [8]. XPDL provides for the interchange of a limited, but incomplete, set of simulation attributes. However, XPDL is an interchange format for *business process definitions*. It is designed to exchange the graphical layout and semantics of a business process definition between different BPM products, not simulation parameters. An interchange format for business process simulation scenario data as described in the previous section would allow for the exchange of this kind of data between BPM products, business process analytics tools, other process aware information systems[3] and simulation solutions.

Ideally, a proposed standard would be simple, yet complete in that it can adequately describe most business process simulation scenarios. It should be vendor

---

[3] Examples of process aware information systems include BPMS, other workflow management systems, enterprise resource planning (ERP) systems, process centric middleware and line of business applications, and call center systems [7].

neutral, but extensible so that particular solutions can use the standard for inter-change, yet derive from, and extend it where convenient to capture elements or structures particular to a given solution or specialized use case.

A standard for defining business process simulation scenarios would specify the following categories of information:
- Process Definitions
- Scenario Meta Data
- Scenario Context
- Simulation Options
- Event Parameters
- Resourcing Parameters
- Activity Parameters

The definition of business processes is already covered by existing standards and schemas such as BPMN and XPDL. These standards are relatively mature, so it would be wise to leverage the existing standards work in the area of process defi-nition. As such, the scenario definitions defined using a standard for business process simulation models would be loosely coupled to a process definition represented in BPMN or XPDL (or even another process definition mechanism for that matter). For example, activity parameters (like activity duration) defined us-ing the business process simulation standard could refer to activities in a corres-ponding BPMN diagram or XPDL document.

By using an existing standard for process definitions we can focus on describing in greater detail the rest of the components that are required in a proposed stan-dard for business process simulation scenarios[4].

Scenario Meta Data

Scenario Meta Data describes the scenario itself, including a name or unique identifier for the scenario, the author, the tool that generated the scenario defini-tion, as well as scenario creation and modification timestamps.

Scenario Context

The context describes some general conditions and global configurations under which the business process scenario will be simulated. Table 1 describes the ele-ments of the scenario context.

Element	Description
Is Calendar Based	When the beginning and end of a scenario are specified by calendar date/time this is set to TRUE. If the run length is defined by an end time specified in clock units this is set to FALSE.
Begin Date/Time	If the scenario is calendar based, this specifies the sce-nario starting date/time. For example, 9/21/2009 12:00:00 AM. If the scenario is not calendar based, this element is not required, and if present should be ig-nored.

---

[4] The complete draft specification of the standard being proposed can be found at http://sim4bpm.com/specification/. The resulting xml schema can be found at http://sim4bpm.com/schemas/scenario.xsd. Those interested in providing simulation (or other scenario based modeling) support for BPM applications, are encouraged to get involved with the specification effort.

End Date/Time	If the scenario is calendar based, this specifies the scenario ending date/time. For example, 9/28/2009 12:00:00 PM. If the scenario is not calendar based, this represents the scenario length defined in terms of the specified clock units. For example, if the clock units are MINUTE, then an end date/time of 2880 represents a scenario that runs for 2 days.
Clock Units	DAY, HOUR, MINUTE, or SECOND. The default unit of measure for time expressions.
Scheduling Method	CONCURRENT or EXCLUSIVE. Concurrent scheduling represents a global state where all resources can play any role to which they are assigned when they are available for productive work. Exclusive scheduling indicates that the roles which a resource can play at any given time are specified explicitly in the resource's schedule.
Resource Selection	LIST, RANDOM, PERFORMANCE. List means that an attempt to acquire a resource is done in the order by which they are specified (for a given role). Alternatively, the resources can be acquired randomly for a given role or in order of performance where the resources that have the highest performance in a given role are acquired first depending on availability.

Table 1: Scenario Context

Simulation Options

The simulation engine may have useful options which can be set by the client. Table 2 describes these options.

Element	**Description**
Seed Type	The seed is used to control the simulator's (pseudo) random number generator. SYSTEM or SPECIFIED. If specified, the simulator uses the seed value below.
Seed Value	An integer seed value. This can be used to force two simulation runs to use the same random numbers.
Animation	Some simulation packages support animation. If animation is supported and can be toggled on or off, this option allows one to specify whether to animate the running simulation. Animation may be turned off in situations where only the results of a simulation are of primary concern. Valid values for this option are ON or OFF.
Initialization	A simulation may require the initialization of various simulation resources. This field could be used to specify any logic, script, application, etc. used to perform this initialization. The specific format of the contents of this parameter is left unspecified on purpose as this may vary greatly from application to application.
Termination	A simulation may require the termination of various simulation resources. This field could be used to specify any logic, script, application, etc. used to perform this

| | termination. The specific format of the contents of this parameter is left unspecified on purpose as this may vary greatly from application to application. |

Table 2: Simulation Options

There are various elements in this proposed standard that might be used to store logic, a script, or some blob of data. The simulation options initialization and termination elements are examples of where this occurs. The application consuming the scenario definition may provide support for its own programming language, logic, scripting, etc. A given tool may support the definition of variables, procedures, and/or various data types amongst other possible structures. Elements such as the simulation options initialization and termination specify no particular format for their values. What is populated in these elements could depend on the application(s) being used. For example, a simulation application might read in the value of the initialization element and use that to initialize the simulation model. This value might include logic to open files, or set the initial values for variables used by the simulator.

Event Parameters

Within a business process scenario, events occur that affect the flow of the process. An event can initiate a process, or occur during a process flow, or perhaps even terminate a process flow. From a simulation scenario perspective, an event represents the instantiation or injection of a process instance or "token" of work in the work flow. The process instance can be instantiated at any point in the process, and therefore could be associated with a process start event or an intermediate event. To initialize the state of the process at the beginning of a scenario's period, we can also instantiate tokens of work at process activities.

From a BPMN perspective you can make a direct mapping between scenario events and business process model events. Unlike BPMN, simulation scenario events also include the instantiation of work in progress at process activities. Simulation scenario events are not differentiated by trigger types. Event parameters are described in Table 3.

Element	Description
Event ID	A unique identifier for the event.
Process Name	The process name or id (e.g. as defined in the process model).
Data Source	Specifies the source system or scenario of the event data.
Destination	The location in the process where the event takes place. Events may occur at places other than the start of a process to represent the work in progress at the start date/time of the scenario. In general, this is a reference to an event or activity in the process model.
Event Time	The date and time at which the event into the process takes place.
Occurrences	How many times the event occurs. This could be a statistical distribution.
Frequency	The time between occurrences. This could be a statistical distribution.
Quantity	Allows multiple events with the same attributes to occur at the given event time. This could be a statistical distribution.

Field Values	Data field values for the event. Since events instantiate tokens in the simulation, the field values can be used to describe the attributes of the injected token. To initialize the state of the process at the beginning of the simulation period, these values may include the resource currently working on the token.

Table 3: Event Parameters

Each unit of work injected into a simulated business process has a set of attributes which are quantified by the values of a set of data fields. Practically speaking, field values are attributes that correspond to either numeric facts about an instance of work, and therefore behave like *measures* in the online analytics processing (OLAP) sense of the word, or are used to identify different types of instances of work, and behave like *dimensions* in the OLAP sense. Field values that correspond to this later case have certain characteristics. We would expect the possible values of such field values to be bounded. As a bounded list, field values that identify an instance of work in such a way are in fact enumerations. This is an important distinction because an enumeration will allow us to associate a name as well as other attributes with each possible value. You can think of this like how attributes and/or hierarchies describe primary keys for an OLAP dimension. For example, arrival event parameters may have a field value that specifies a geographic location. There may be other attributes for a specific location such as address, city, country, etc. It is left to the specific application as to how this might be implemented.

Resourcing Parameters

Resourcing parameters describe the roles and resources used to process the work in a business process. Roles typically represent skill sets where a skill set represents the expertise required to perform a given set of activities. A resource may have multiple skill sets, and therefore resources may be assigned to multiple roles. Roles may be loosely coupled to the roles or performer types described in the process definitions. Resources represent the actual instances of the performers of work in the process. Resources may be assigned to a role, a specific set of work according to specific characteristics of the work, to specific activities or some combination of the preceding. Resources are also characterized by their availability to perform work in a given scenario. Table 4 describes how resources would be defined in the proposed standard.

Element	Description
Name	A unique identifier for the resource.
Department	Associates the resource with an organizational unit. This could be used for reporting purposes.
Quantity	A resource could represent multiple instances of a resource with identical attributes.
Cost	Resources often have costs associated with them (e.g. salary, hourly rate, etc.). This field can be used to calculate costs by resource usage or availability.
Assignments	Specifies that type of work the resource is assigned to work on. This is how a resource is assigned to a specific role, a specific class of work, and perhaps a specific set of activities. An assignment represents a role and list of data field values that must be true in order for the resource instance to work

	on those items. For example, a resource performing role X might only work at location Y and on work associated with customer Z. Proficiency may vary by role, customer, or any field value combination.
Shift Segments	Shift segments are used to describe the availability of resources during the scenario. Furthermore, a shift segment can optionally be dedicated to a particular assignment (see above).

Table 4: Resourcing Parameters

Activity Parameters

Activity parameters describe how work is processed at a given activity (see Table 5). There may optionally be multiple sets of parameters for a given activity to represent how these parameters may vary from one kind of work item to another when processed at the same activity.

Element	Description
Activity Name	A unique identifier for the activity (e.g. references an activity in the process model).
Field Values	Describes the type of work for which the activity parameters apply. For the same activity, different parameters may apply depending on the attributes of the work item being processed at the activity.
Priority	The relative ranking of activities. The performing of one activity could take precedence over the performing of another.
Resource Acquisition	Specifies how, and which, resources are acquired to perform the activity. This could be the specification of a role or set of roles, a specific resource or set of resources, or some kind of logic or expression that dynamically specifies the acquisition of resources according to the work being processed or state of the scenario.
Duration	Specifies the duration of performing the activity once any resources specified are acquired. This could be an absolute value, some kind of statistical distribution, or some logic or expression that specifies the duration based on the work being processed, the resources being used or the state of the scenario.
Additional Operations	Used to specify any custom logic or processing that must be executed prior to any acquired resources being released.
Resource Release	Specifies how, and which, resources are released when the activity is completed.
Weights/Conditions/Routing Information	The type of output produced by an activity may depend on relative percentages or weights, or on some other condition or set of conditions.

Table 5: Activity Parameters

A RESTFUL API

The standard described above specifies an xml schema[5] for defining the components of a business process simulation scenario in an xml document. This suggests a simple way to define business process simulation scenarios via a RESTful[6] web service. Since the proposed standard describes a way of defining data, the methods of the hypertext transport protocol (HTTP) are more than sufficient for the purposes of defining a web services based API for such a schema. For example, consider the following URL where a web service for defining simulation scenarios is being hosted on "myhost":

> http://myhost/scenarios/

A **GET** request to this URL could return a list of scenario definitions in the format specified by the standard's schema. A **POST** request to this URL could include a payload of xml data that describes a new scenario defined using the standard's xml schema. Such a request would add a new scenario definition based on the xml payload included with the request.

Other data formats based on the standard could easily be supported. Providing support for other formats could make it easier for some clients to consume the data provided by the service. Table 6 illustrates how other formats could be supported by such an API.

URL	Data Format Returned
http://myhost/scenarios/	html
http://myhost/scenarios.xml	xml
http://myhost/scenarios.json	JavaScript object notation
http://myhost/scenarios.atom	Atom syndication format

Table 6: Web Service Data Formats

The point to be made is that a standard for business process simulation scenarios might provide different levels of abstraction. An xml schema provides a very formalized and detailed standard for the specification of the scenario data format. A standards based API as described above provides more freedom. Tools could use the standard's schema for the data passed to and from the API, and their own schema and data formats internally.

We leave the complete specification of such a web service API for another paper. However, it is useful to consider some examples of retrieving and updating subcomponents of a scenario via such an API. Table 7 demonstrates this for select components of a simulation scenario definition.

URL	HTTP Method	Action
http://myhost/scenarios/AsIs/Context/	GET	Retrieves the context of the "AsIs" scenario.
http://myhost/scenarios/AsIs/Context/	PUT	Updates the context of the "AsIs" scenario. The data payload of the request contains an appropriate representation of the sce-

---

[5] This xml schema can be found at http://sim4bpm.com/schemas/scenario.xsd.

[6] Representational State Transfer (REST) is a style of software architecture for the web [12].

		nario context as described in the standard (for example an xml representation of the context conforming to the standard's xml schema).
http://myhost/scenarios/AsIs/ Resourcing/Resources/ JohnDoe/ShiftSegments/	GET	Retrieves the shift segments for the "JohnDoe" resource in the "AsIs" scenario.
http://myhost/scenarios/AsIs/ Resourcing/Resources/ JohnDoe/ShiftSegments/	POST	Adds a new shift segment for the "JohnDoe" resource in the "AsIs" scenario. The data payload of the request contains an appropriate representation of a shift segment as described in the standard.
http://myhost/scenarios/AsIs/ Resourcing/Resources/ JohnDoe/	PUT	Updates the "JohnDoe" resource in the "AsIs" scenario. The data payload of the request contains an appropriate representation of a resource as described in the standard.
http://myhost/scenarios/AsIs/ Resourcing/Resources/ JohnDoe/	DELETE	Deletes the "JohnDoe" resource in the "AsIs" scenario.

Table 7: Web Service Samples

This kind of web service API is also relatively straightforward to implement. Figure 1 shows an HTTP **GET** request for a scenario (named "Baseline") returning an html response from a web application implementing the suggested API.

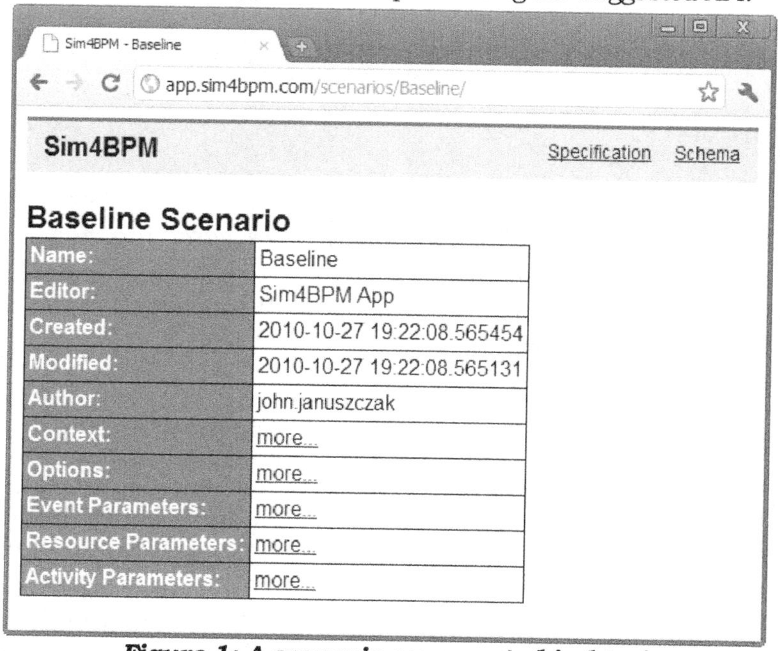

Figure 1: A scenario represented in html

Figure 2 shows the response of a **GET** request for an html representation of the scenario's context while Figure 3 shows the response of the same request for an xml representation.

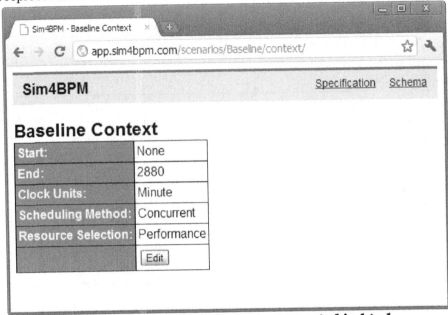

Figure 2: A scenario's context represented in html

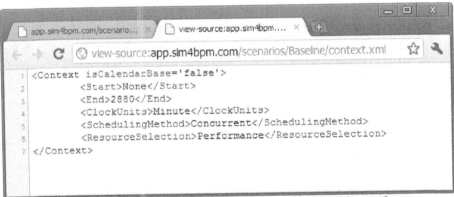

Figure 3: A scenario's context represented in xml

Other web, mobile and desktop based applications could programmatically interact with the web service via such an xml format. We merely show the xml in the browser to illustrate the contents of an xml response.

CONCLUSION

Simulation can be a powerful technique for analyzing business processes. Due to several deficiencies, creating and maintaining simulation models is often time consuming and expensive. Besides this, the nature of how simulation models are created and maintained (if at all) makes it difficult to use them for operational decision support even though conceptually simulation could provide tremendous value for such an application.

The kinds of information required to define a business process simulation scenario for the purposes of simulation is well known, and mostly consistent across existing business process simulation solutions and the literature that addresses this topic. By developing a standard schema for the specification of business process simulation scenarios, business process management systems, process aware information systems, and even specialized line of business applications could exchange data with simulation solutions. This would allow for the automatic update and initialization of simulation models which would enable the use of simulation analysis for the purposes of operational decision making.

Lastly, a web based API could easily be developed from such a standard, allowing the interchange of data over HTTP, and a further layer of abstraction for solution providers. This allows for simulation as a service and supporting simulation analysis in cloud based BPM solutions.

REFERENCES

1. Burgess, Paul W. Theory and Methodology in Executive Function Research. Methodology of frontal and executive function. East Sussex, U.K.: Psychology P, 1997. 83-84.
2. Shannon, Robert E. Systems simulation: the art and science. Englewood Cliffs, NJ: Prentice-Hall, 1975.
3. Rozinat, R.S. Mans, M. Song, and W.M.P. van der Aalst. Discovering Simulation Models. BETA Working Paper Series, WP 223, Eindhoven University of Technology, Eindhoven, 2007.
4. Van der Aalst, Wil M. P. Business Process Simulation Revisited. Enterprise and Organizational Modeling and Simulation 6th International Workshop, Eomas 2010, Held at Caise 2010, Hammamet, Tunisia, June 7-8, 2010, Revised Selected Papers. Springer Verlag, 2010.
5. Klafehn, Keith, Jay Weinroth, and Jess Boronico. Computer simulation in operations management. Westport, CT: Quorum, 1996.
6. Zur Muehlen, Michael, and Robert Shapiro. Business Process Analytics. Handbook on Business Process Management. Berlin: Springer-Verlag GmbH, 2009.
7. Van der Aalst, Wil M. P., J. Nakatumba, A. Rozinat, and N. Russell. Business Process Simulation: How to get it right? In J. vom Brocke and M. Rosemann, editors, International Handbook on Business Process Management, Springer-Verlag, Berlin, 2009
8. Gagné, Denis. Modeling and Simulation in Business Process Management. http://www.slideshare.net/dgagne/modeling-and-simulation-in-business-process-management
9. Barjis, Joseph, and Alexander Verbraeck. The Relevance of Modeling and Simulation in Enterprise and Organizational Study. Enterprise and Organizational Modeling and Simulation 6th International Workshop, Eomas 2010, Held at Caise 2010, Hammamet, Tunisia, June 7-8, 2010, Revised Selected Papers. Springer Verlag, 2010.
10. Silver, Bruce. Is Simulation Fake? in BPMS Watch. http://www.brsilver.com/wordpress/2007/03/08/is-simulation-fake/
11. N. Russell, A.H.M. ter Hofstede, D. Edmond, and W.M.P. van der Aalst. Workflow Resource Patterns. BETA Working Paper Series, WP 127, Eindhoven University of Technology, Eindhoven, 2004.
12. Fielding, Roy T., Taylor, Richard N. Principled Design of the Modern Web Architecture. ACM Transactions on Internet Technology, Association for Computing Machinery, New York, 2002

Collaborative Activities Inside Pools

Michele Chinosi, European Commission Joint Research Centre, Italy

INTRODUCTION

Choreographies and Conversations, introduced with BPMN 2.0, will make modelers able to describe interactions among different Participants as well as messages exchange. Often enough different Participants have to accomplish the same task. This can be now easily and clearly represented using BPMN 2.0. BPMN 2.0 does not specify the usage of Lanes neither their meaning. However, Lanes are sometimes used to specify internal roles or departments.

In this context it could happen that modelers want to represent an Activity performed by different roles or offices together (e.g., attending the same meeting, collaborative writing of a document). Such situation has been modeled so far by using merging Gateways placed before the activities, but this patch does not solve a related problem. BPMN forces to draw elements within Lanes boundaries. This means that, at least conceptually, one Activity is lead by the subject which the containing Lane is linked to, which is not necessarily true. Some experiments revealed how much the means to model such inner collaboration is a desirable feature.

ANALYSIS OF THE PROBLEM

BPMN allows people to model many different scenarios involving one or more participants, simple or complex activities, splitting and merging paths, messages exchange, different points of view, and so forth. With the advent of BPMN 2.0 a very big interest has been put on how to better represent the relationships among different participants (also known as Collaborations), in particular through the introduction of Conversation diagrams and Choreographies. Now it is possible to model a complex message exchange among multiple participants focusing on messages and relationships among the involved actors/roles. However, one of the most common scenarios both in private and in public sectors is represented by shared activities, or, to put it better, the need to model one single Activity involving more than one participant at the same time. Common examples of such shared or collaborative activities are meetings, conferences, working groups with same goals to achieve, as well as new scenarios faced out in the last years, like cloud computing, collaborative real-time document writing, collaborative modeling. Probably one of the most well-known example which excited many users in 2009/2010 was the launch of the Google Wave collaborative platform[1].

BPMN offers different ways to model a business process. It is possible to model a private process, a public process, a collaborative process as well as the already mentioned Choreographies and Conversation diagrams. The usual way (actually, it is a common practice inherited from BPMN 1.2) to model an activities flow performed by different actors/roles is describing the business process from the point

---

[1] http://wave.google.com/about.html

of view of public or collaborative diagrams (i.e., highlighting the messages exchange among the participants). An explicative example on how to model a collaborative Activity by using BPMN 2.0 is shown hereinafter.

A meeting with regional partners

Figure 1 shows an example diagram in which there are two participants (the Project Manager and Regional Partners). The depicted scenario focuses on a general project management procedure for a company with many regional partners worldwide. This Business Process Diagram (BPD) also takes advantage of the possibility introduced in BPMN 2.0 to mark a Pool as Multi-Instance if the Participant defined for the Pool is a Multi-Instance Participant, as it is in this example.

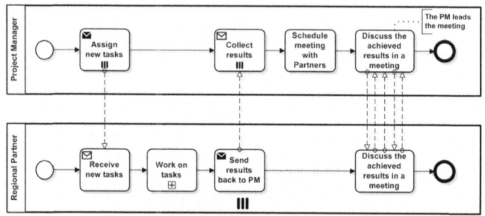

Figure 1: The Project Management example

The last Task in both Pools represents a meeting between the two Participants leaded by the Project Manager. It is possible to have the same Task in different Pools because each Task belongs to a different Participant even if Participants are physically in the same place at the same time doing the same things.

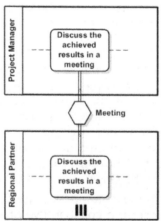

Figure 2: Using a Conversation instead of multiple Message Flows

Message Flows can represent in this case the speeches given by attendees. It is not mandatory to show them, unless there is the need to specify the subject of the speeches. Nevertheless modelers have to keep in mind that they are asked to model an abstract process, not a particular instance of a process. To use Message Flows with no labels or messages just to represent a discussion happening at a certain point should be avoided. Instead, the same process can be modeled more concisely and neat using a Conversation, as shown in Figure 2. By using a Conversation it is possible to model a meeting avoiding the risk to model only one particular instance of a process rather than a general process. Furthermore, the same BPD can be also represented from a different point of view using a Choreography, as in Figure 3. The biggest advantage of using a Choreography in this case is that all the private details can be left hidden focusing only on relationships among Participants.

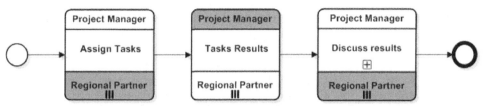

Figure 3: The Choreography associated to the example process

Finally, there is another way to deal with collaborative activities in a Collaborative Process context, especially if it is not important to show the messages exchange. BPMN 2.0 introduces the concept of Global Tasks and Call Activities. It is possible to define a Task or a Sub-Process as Global Task referencing it from any other Process using a Call Activity (even if under certain constraints). Thus, once the main Participant of a shared Activity has been identified, modelers can put the Global Task element in its Process while putting relating Call Activities in all the other involved Processes.

But so far nothing new has been shown, apart from giving few hints on using new BPMN 2.0 characteristics to model collaborative scenarios including shared activities. However, we dealt with multiple Participants represented with different Pools, where most common troubles regard representation or synchronization issues. To model shared activities in an internal context is a more complex problem, somehow concerning meaning (*semantic* is probably a too strong term in this context) often imposed to Lanes.

DO LANES HAVE A MEANING?

The definition of Lanes as it is written in BPMN specifications is somehow misleading. "BPMN does not specify the usage of Lanes" neither their implicit or explicit meaning. In fact, "the meaning of the Lanes is up to the modeler". Lanes have to be treated just as "sub-partitions within a Process (often within a Pool)", and used "to organize and categorize Activities within a Pool". In practice, "Lanes are often used for such things as internal roles, systems, an internal department, etc"[2].

It is clear that Lanes do not have a *semantic* and that *meaning* refers just to the name modelers give to Lanes, even if the difference between "semantic" and "meaning" is not always clear. In computer science, the term *semantic* is applied to certain types of data structures specifically designed and used for representing information content[3], and this definition is coherent with the definition of Lanes provided by BPMN specifications. In semantics, the term *meaning* refers to the ob-

---

[2] Business Process Model and Notation (BPMN), Version 2.0, OMG Document Number dtc/2010-06-05

[3] http://en.wikipedia.org/wiki/Semantics

jects or concept that a word or phrase denotes, or that which a sentence says. In other words, the meaning is inferred from objects or concepts expressed by words, phrases or sentences[4]. Furthermore, Lanes do not have a Participant associated to them, but instead they inherit the Participant from the owning Pool. However, the statement "the meaning of the Lanes is up to the modeler" leads modelers to believe that giving Lanes a meaning is permitted, thus pretending to use Lanes as they were nested Pools.

It is difficult in general to see a Lane only as a graphical container intended to categorize and organize Activities in a Process. By giving names to Lanes, modelers tend to implicitly associate also a meaning (or at least a behavior) to the associated roles. This practice becomes more marked considering the goals most modelers have in mind when they start modeling a process in BPMN. Many conducted experiments, along with a web sentiment analysis on this topic, revealed how the 90% of modelers loves BPMN as a graphical mean to document processes, while only the remaining 10% is also really interested in simulating, deploying, executing, exporting business processes using BPMN. By considering BPMN only from a graphical point of view, modelers cannot be aware of the big differences in terms of properties, attributes and relationships that lie behind the definitions of Pools and Lanes, especially if they choose to use BPMN editors with only graphical shapes support. Moreover, common practices misguide modelers to give Lanes a name representing roles or functions implicitly applying to them also a semantic, thus modeling business processes having in mind a separation of duties more than a mere graphical arrangement of the Activities.

In this context, it could happen that at a certain point in the middle of a process diagram modelers want to represent an Activity performed by different roles or offices together (e.g., attending the same meeting, collaborative writing of a document), thus changing the granularity level and the point of view on the process. Unfortunately, it is not always possible to change from a private to a collaborative level in the middle of a process (at least, not in an intuitive way).

Summing up, it is possible to outline the problem using a general question: when in the midst of a Swimlane diagram you need to model a shared Task, how do you model it if a Task can only belong to one Swimlane? Before BPMN, many would just extend a Task across Swimlanes. How do we handle this in BPMN?

Such situation has been tackled so far by using different techniques like Gateways placed before and/or after the activities. In such cases, where it becomes important to model interactions among different Participants, Pools should be used instead. A big debate is still ongoing, and during the last two years many attempts have been proposed through printed books[5] and web communities. One of the longest discussions on this topic took place in the *BPMN-Community*'s forum[6]. Some valuable proposals are reported in the following.

---

[4] http://en.wikipedia.org/wiki/Meaning

[5] See for instance: Silver B., "BPMN Method & Style", Cody-Cassidy Press, 2009; Debevoise T and Geneva R., "The Microguide to Process Modeling in BPMN", Booksurge Publishing, 2008; Sharp A. and McDermott P., "Workflow Modeling", Artech House Pub., 2001.

[6] See for example http://en.bpmn-community.org/forum/78/ and http://en.bpmn-community.org/forum/17/, last accessed 25th of October, 2010.

COLLABORATIVE ACTIVITIES INSIDE THE SAME POOL

The example scenario is the one depicted in Figure 4, where a single report for a project is prepared by multiple actors/roles working together in real time (e.g., in meetings) or near-real-time (communicating continuously). To fill the report is an internal process for a company, involving different roles performed by colleagues.

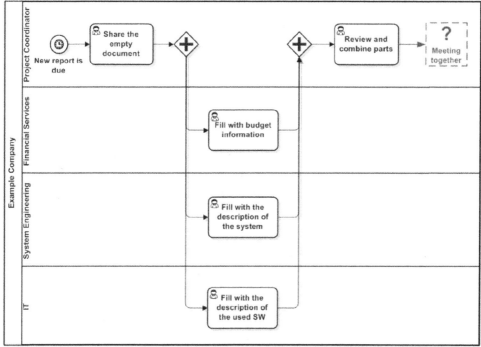

Figure 4: Example scenario for collaborative activities inside a Pool

From this point of view it is fair to model the process using one single Pool with multiple Lanes, one for each actor/role, because there is no messages exchange among different Participants but just an internal documental workflow. Quite at the end of the process a final meeting is foreseen, attended by all of the contributing authors. But how to model (or, better, graphically represent) at that point an Activity performed together by all the roles? As a matter of facts, most users would prefer seeing in an intuitive way this kind of collaborative activity on a model (considering that BPMN aims to be an easily readable notation understandable by all users from business users to technicians) rather than sifting through textual properties and attributes values, like instead technicians or computer scientists love to do.

Solution #1: Duplicate Tasks in each Lane

The first solution consists in duplicating the Task for each involved Lane, like in Figure 5, maybe also grouping all the Tasks together within a Group to improve the readability of the diagram (Figure 6).

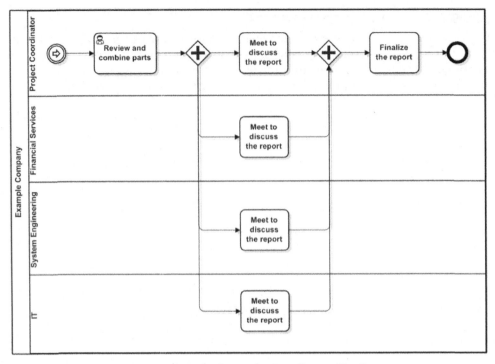

Figure 5: Solution #1 - Duplicate Tasks

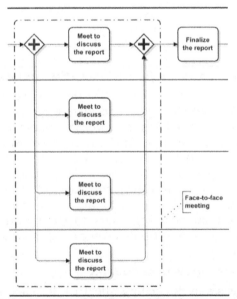

Figure 6: Solution #1 - Duplicated Tasks grouped together

But this solution introduces many problems. Duplicated Tasks are not multiple copies of the same original Task, otherwise the diagram will not be valid with respect to the BPMN specifications, even if, at least conceptually, it could seem so (and probably this is the meaning the author intended to pass to the reader). Instead, all the Tasks have different IDs, even if they share the same label, thus resulting in a diagram with multiple separate Tasks performing the same action in parallel (they are put in between two Parallel Gateways). Moreover, there may occur coherence problems, because modelers have to guarantee that all the properties values match among the Tasks, as well as refactoring problems due to the necessity to reflect each modification affecting one Task to all the others. Even from a graphical point of view this solution should be avoided. In the shown example there are only four Lanes, and they are contiguous. If the number of the Lanes is higher, or if Lanes are not contiguous but separated by other Lanes, the diagram will become complex and messy. In fact, each involved role/actor should have the same Activity in its Lane while BPMN does not allow to have multi-instance Lanes to represent multiple subjects sharing the same Activities set as it does for multi-instance Pools. Besides, obviously, it is always necessary to synchronize all the Activities with a Parallel Gateway.

Solution #2: Assign different Tasks to actors/roles

To solve some of the problems of the first solution, supposing it is feasible to slightly change the description of the modeled scenario, it would be possible to assign different Tasks to each actor/role, by decomposing the original Task in smaller actions, like in Figure 7. All the roles/actors keep on collaborating to the same shared Task, even if in this diagram all the single parts have been explicitly represented.

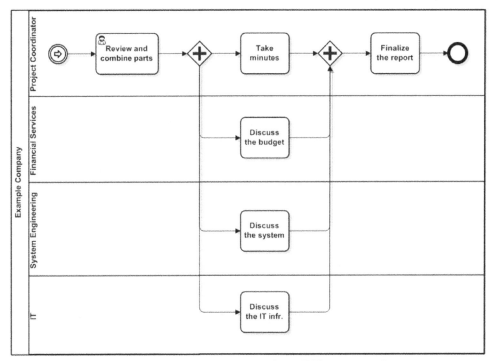

Figure 7: Solution #2 - Assign different Tasks

The depicted solution has fewer problems than the first one, but nevertheless other difficulties face out, especially affecting the modeler more than they were only syntactical or validation issues. In fact, there could be too many actions to invent: each actor/role should have its own action to perform but it is not necessarily true that for each actor/role there exists a particular action to perform. In case of a meeting, many actors/roles have just to attend the meeting, doing nothing special other than listening to the speeches. Another issue concerns the semantic aspect of the diagram whose meaning became weaker by adopting this solution: looking at the diagram, the first impression is not of a meeting, but of different activities taking place at the same time.

Solution #3: Create a separate Lane to represents actors/roles as group

Another approach introduces a new Lane within the Pool to represent the group of actors/roles involved in a common Task. This would permit avoiding Tasks repetition and reducing the activities number. The solution is presented in Figure 8.

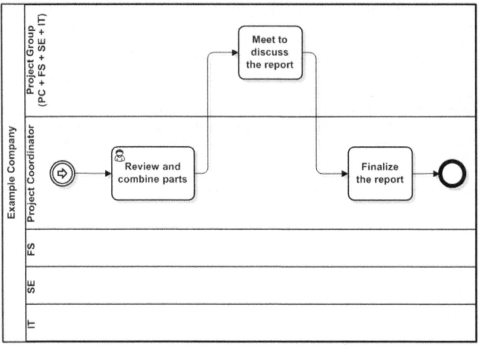

Figure 8: Solution #3 - Create a separate Lane

But also in this case there could be problems. First of all, the complexity of the model increases because a new Lane has been added, perhaps for just one Task. Another difficulty for modelers will come out if in the process there are different groups of actors/roles, for example if after the plenary meeting in the example another meeting between the Project Coordinator and Financial Services takes place. By adopting this solution, each time a shared Activity has to be modeled for a new group of actors/roles, a new Lane will be added to the process.

A slight variation of this solution, presented in Figure 9, uses the nested Lanes mechanism. Although the diagram may looks better, this variation prevents modelers from adding now other groups if needed. Moreover, multiple nesting, although "legal", often confuses the business users.

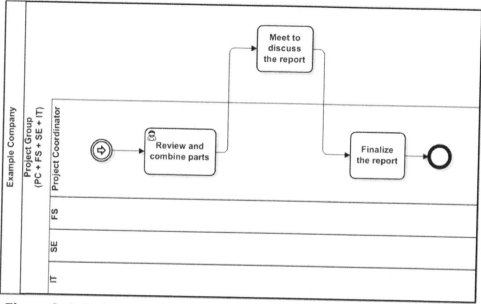

Figure 9: Solution #3 - Create a separate Lane for groups nesting all the other involved Lanes

Solution #4: Shared activities are modeled in a separate Process

The last considered approach, completely different from the others mentioned so far, uses Call Activities calling a different Process where the shared activity has been modeled in a Pool holding a single Lane representing the group of actors/roles performing the action. An example is shown in Figure 10.

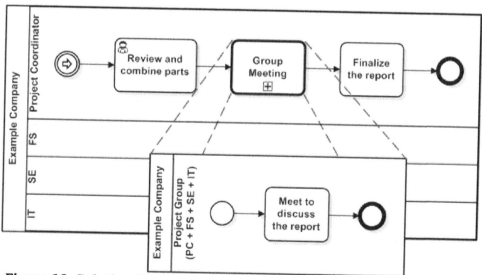

Figure 10: Solution #4 - Shared activities modeled as a separate Process

It is worth noting that the Call Activity is contained in the Lane pertaining to the actor/role responsible for leading the meeting. In other words, modelers could model the shared activities involving multiple actors/roles in a separate Process (one for each Activity and for each group of actors/roles) placing the Call Activity inside the Lane of the actor/role which is supposed to be the main performer of that activity. The biggest disadvantage is that each simple Task representing a shared or collaborative activity will have a related Process, compelling modelers to define every property and attribute to be BPMN compliant. Thus, the complexity of the whole BPD will increase quite exponentially.

Representing shared Artifacts

The depicted problem of representing shared tasks or collaborative activities becomes even more complex at the time that Data Objects should be added to the diagram, especially if the process describes a collaborative editing of the same document. Among the solutions presented so far, only the third and the fourth solutions can be used to represent a single Data Object edited by different actors/roles at the same time. The second solution can be used only in the context of a common document whose different sections are edited independently by different actors/roles (see Figure 11 on the left), while the first solution would require to add a single Data Object with multiple Data Associations, one for each Task. A trivial solution in this case would be to link through a Data Association one Data Object to a common incoming Sequence Flow of each Task, doing the same for the output of the editing Task (like in Figure 11 on the right), but thus skipping the representation of the editing process of the document.

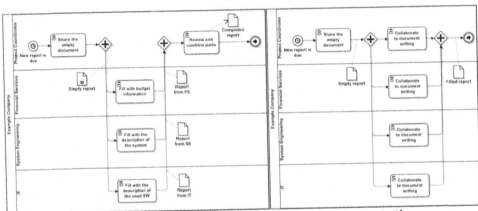

Figure 11: Possible shared Data Objects representations

PROPOSED SOLUTIONS

In this section some other solutions will be delineated. Unlike solutions discussed so far, arisen from common practices, the following originate from BPMN 2.0 specifications, in order to provide alternatives on one hand to fulfill as much as possible users' requirements, while on the other hand being compliant with BPMN specifications as well. While the first two proposals presented here will follow as much as possible the BPMN specs, the last one will suggest an extension to BPMN to meet both the requirements of representing collaborative activities and keeping the diagram easily readable.

Use the Performer class

BPMN 2.0 introduces the Performer class, which defines the resource that will perform or will be responsible for an Activity. The performer can be specified in the form of a specific individual, a group, an organization role or position, or an organization. The Performer element does not have attributes or model associations other than ones inherited from the BaseElement.

This solution is fully BPMN compliant, thus preserving the "no semantic" property of Lanes. A Performer can also be a "group". If Lanes have no meaning, then one Lane can refer to a single subject but also one of its contained Activities can have a "group" as Performer.

The main disadvantage of this solution is that the Performer element is not shown in a diagram, forcing users to look through the properties of the Process to look for the Performer of an Activity checking if it is a collaborative or a single-user Activity.

Use Pools instead of using Lanes

Global Tasks and Call Activities have been defined in BPMN to allow modelers recall already defined (often common) Tasks in different Processes. In a way almost similar to the fourth solution presented above, it is possible to use a Call Activity calling a Collaboration process, instead of calling another Private process as depicted there. The called Collaboration Process can also be the Collaboration view of a corresponding Choreography modeling the shared Activity.

The main disadvantage of this solution lies in the complexity of the process to be modeled. To avoid such complexity, modelers can put much more effort during the planning phase before starting modeling the process, considering whether to model the main process as a Private process calling a Collaboration process or starting directly modeling a Collaboration process.

Extend Global Tasks and Call Activities

Even if Global Tasks and Call Activities have been defined in BPMN to allow modelers recall already defined Tasks in different Processes, it is possible to use this mechanism also inside the same Pool. This is quite a strained interpretation of the given definitions. "A Global Task is a reusable, atomic Task definition that can be called from within any Process by a Call Activity". "A Call Activity identifies a point in the Process where a global Process or a Global Task is used. The Call Activity acts as a 'wrapper' for the invocation of a global Process or Global Task within the execution. The activation of a Call Activity results in the transfer of control to the called global Process or Global Task". The problem with Call Activities lies in the activation of a Call Activity, which results in the transfer of control to the called Global Process or Global Task. This means that a Call Activity can override properties and attributes of the element being called, potentially changing the behavior of the called element based on the calling context. This is the main reason because it is not possible to use Global Task and Call Activities together inside the same Pool to execute the same Task in parallel in a collaborative environment.

This solution suggests instead to extend the Global Task/Call Activity definitions (and their graphical notation as well) by adding new attributes to the Performer class, as in Table 1.

Attribute Name	Description/Usage
cardinality: string = Single { Single | Group | Open }	This attribute defines the number of Performers for a collaborative Activity. The default value is Single, meaning an Activity performed by a single subject. Group identifies collaborative Activities executed by a defined group of subjects,

	while Open is for open activities like conferences, meetings, public discussions or events.
`name: string [0..1]`	This optional attribute defines the name of the Performer, whether it is a single subject or a group.
`leadingPerformer: string`	This attribute defines the subject leading the collaborative Activity.

Table 1: New attributes for the Performer class

It is worth noting that the *name* attribute is optional. The Performer class inherits *BaseElement* attributes without adding any other details, thus the name of a Performer can be specified through the inherited *id* and *documentation* attributes, even if it is strongly suggested to use a separate name qualifier to identify the Performer. From a graphical point of view, a new icon for Tasks and Sub-Processes is proposed. It represents a little chain to highlight the concept of an Activity performed together by a number of different subjects, like in Figure 12. The name given to this new Activity is Chain Task or Chain Sub-Process.

Figure 12: An example of Chain Task

Two different use cases are foreseen. First, it is possible to use the Chain Activity by replicating the same Activity in all the involved Lanes. In this case the Activity related to the `leadingPerformer` should be drawn with a thin border (like Global Tasks) while all the other Activities should have a thick border also displaying the same marker (as for Call Activity definition), as it is possible to see in Figure 13.

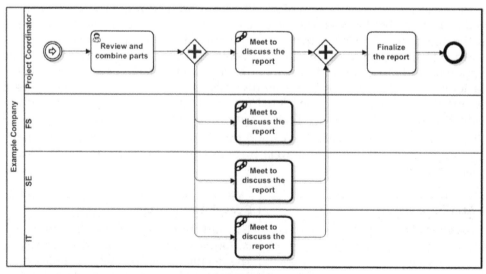

Figure 13: Chain Activities applied in the running example

The main difference from Call Activities is that the semantic of a Call Activity of type Chain acts only as a bookmark for the Global Chain Task, which is the only element responsible for the execution of the Task. That is a Call Activity of type Chain cannot override properties and attributes of the element being called, neither change the behavior of the called element.

In the second use case, instead, it is enough to add a Chain Activity in the Lane related to the `leadingPerformer`. By using the new attributes of the Performers it is possible to specify the cardinality of the involved subjects and the subject leading the Activity. A simplified example of this use case can be seen in Figure 14.

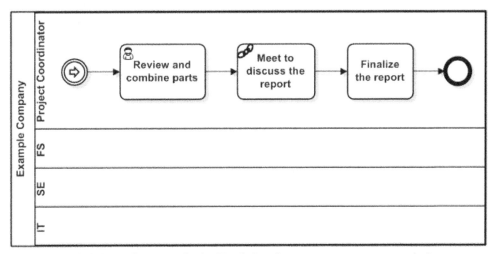

Figure 14: Only one Chain Task in the `leadingPerformer`'s Lane

CONCLUSIONS

BPMN allows modelers to choose the proper granularity level and the more appropriate design methodology to fulfill their representation needs. But BPMN is not a palette of graphical symbols. Instead, BPMN is first of all a leading standard for business process modeling, and even more if considering the high number of new functionalities and features introduced in the version 2.0. Therefore, even if the majority of modelers are approaching BPMN purely as a nice graphical way to document business processes, specifications should be accurately followed. One key point of BPMN concerns the freedom given to the modeler not to follow predefined schemas, but rather to use the notation as a handy but powerful tool.

Unfortunately, this freedom sometimes drives modelers to unforeseen scenarios, as for the need to model collaborative activities inside one Process leaded by only one Participant, thus looking for a solution to use Lanes as sub-Pools with their own "sub-Participants". By looking into literature, academic papers and web communities it is possible to see many examples, common practices and design methodologies, but real scenarios are often much more complex than the examples reported there, and the specifications themselves are a hard reading for BPMN beginners. The first four solutions discussed in this paper come from this context. The other three proposed solutions are tentative attempts to fulfill modelers needs while keeping the diagrams as simple as possible and also valid. Clearly, it is possible to adopt some of the solutions presented in the first part of the paper, at least those ones not contradicting the BPMN specifications. Best candidates are solutions number 3 and 4, followed by solution number 2 which is formally correct, although too complex, while the first solution should be discarded. On the other hand, two of the suggested solutions presented in the second part of the this paper are specifications-driven proposals, while the last one, although complex and hard to implement, could be quite easily understood and used by business users and modelers.

Multi-faceted BPM

Marco Brambilla, Politecnico di Milano, and Stefano Butti, Web Models Srl, Italy

INTRODUCTION

Business process modeling has become the recognized best practice for enterprise-wide application specification. Business process modeling languages and execution environments ease the definition and enactment of the business constraints, by orchestrating the activities of employees and of computer-supported services. In particular, the role of BPMN is recognized as a major leading force towards standardization in the BPM field, enforcing all the software vendors to adhere to (or at least consider) it when shaping their offer. This is definitely a big advantage for the BPM practitioner, since he can rely on unified notation and semantics independently of the modeling tool of choice.

However, turning a business process model into the specification, design and implementation of a software solution for process enactment is a non trivial task: the specified processes can be a mix on new functionality to be developed and interactions with pre-existing systems and the user's activities must be supported through effective and usable interfaces, possibly compliant with the visual identity and interaction style of other corporate applications. Furthermore, the business requirements embodied in the process models, as well as the technical context in which the underlying applications are deployed, are subject to evolution. This may cause severe alignment problems when trying to keep the business process and the application in sync.

We claim that business process models *per se* are not enough for representing the complexity of real world software applications that implements them; therefore other design dimensions must be taken into account in the analysis, design, and implementation of applications.

The gap between process modeling and application development can be alleviated by increasing the degree of automation in the design, implementation and maintenance of applications derived from process models. The automation framework should support the semi-automatic translation of the process model into running applications, be flexible enough to incorporate different architectural and interaction requirements, and apply not only to the initial deployment of the application but also to its evolution and maintenance. An outstanding difficulty in providing such an automation framework is the semantic distance between the process model and the running application: the former dictates roles, activities and business constraints at a very abstract level, irrespective of how these are supported by computing tools; the latter embodies very low-level details, where business, architecture, and interaction aspects are blended together and hard to customize and evolve separately. As an example, the same user's activity specified in the process model could be enacted in a variety of ways: by means of a wizard, by form editing, by using a legacy application interface, and so on.

We propose an integrated design approach to BPM that comprises modeling of business processes, application structure, master data, and user interaction, together with automatic model transformations among them. In this way, it is possible to work at different levels of abstraction and get quick prototypes to be discussed with the customers, but also generate production applications to be delivered as finalized systems. Indeed, the models allow the designers and analysts to work on orthogonal aspects of the design, and to fine tune the final application in several ways, e.g., by integrating the visual identity of the organization, plugging in new components, or connecting the business process to legacy applications via Web Services.

This is in line with and extends the vision of integrated BPM and MDM (Master data management) design proposed by Clay Richardson [6] and studied by several research and industrial entities, such as IBM Research [4, 5] and ISIS Papyrus [7]. We also have been investigating the problem for some years now [3].

The paper presents the different models that we deem essential for complete enterprise application design together with the model transformations among them and the benefits obtained by adopting the approach.

We describe which peculiar aspects of BPMN 2.0 have proven useful in our approach and we explain their role. We also mention which ones we decided not to support and why. We describe the approach at work on design the toolsuite called WebRatio, a model-driven development environment for business processes and web applications. To demonstrate the feasibility and advantages, we show the approach at work on a set of real industrial applications [9].

DESIGN PHASES

We propose a multi-faceted approach to the design of enterprise applications, which is based on the three level conceptual architecture illustrated in Figure 1.

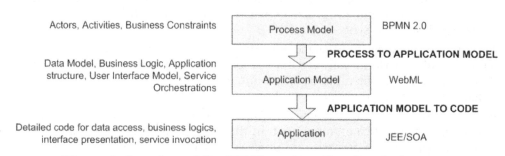

Figure 1. Overview of the BPM-based application design steps

Following the approach of Model Driven Engineering [1] , the business requirements and the application are represented using several models, organized in three levels: 1) the business requirements are expressed as Business Process Models; 2) the application logics and other aspects are expressed in a set of Domain Specific Languages (DSL), capable of representing the managed data, the business logics, the presentation aspects and the interaction with services; 3) the final outcome of the process is an executable application represented by its code. The development is therefore seen as a step-wise refinement of the process model, through two consecutive transformations: the *Process Model to Application Model* transformation translates the actors, activities and business constraints of the BPM environment into a set of data models, navigation models, user interface models and service orchestrations, which specify how the application will serve the business processes. The *Application Model to Code* transformation generates the source code by exploiting technical knowledge on the deployment architecture, platform languages, and visual identity.

The introduction of the application modeling layer increases the complexity of the conceptual architecture, but brings fundamental advantages: there is one place (the application model), where it is possible to reason about the distinct aspects of the application separately; the BPM to Application transformation can be supplied with automatic transformation rules capable of producing alternative ways of encoding an activity, by using different patterns; automatically generated application models can be fine tuned, to introduce usability patterns, without breaking the application compliance to the process model; application evolution can be performed independently of the technical platform, by updating the application model and then regenerating the application code.

RELEVANT MODELS FOR ENTERPRISE APPLICATION MANAGEMENT

Besides the process model, not described in details here because it basically consists of standard design of BPMN diagrams, we propose a set of additional models for describing the various aspect of the application design, that perfectly complement BPMN: the user roles, the application logic, the data structure, and the user interface. In this section we summarize the features and the role of each of them.

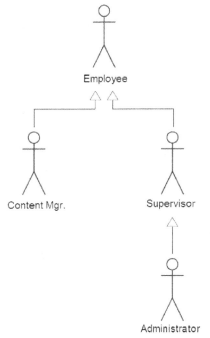

Figure 2. User role hierarchy

Managing user roles

Users are considered as a crucial asset in both business process modeling and application design. In our approach, besides defining the concept of *user role*, which is well known in BPM, we also define a *hierarchy of roles*. Such hierarchy is not representing the organizational hierarchy within the enterprise, but instead is representing the fact that some roles represent a "more powerful" version of other roles, in terms of tasks they can execute within the process. The hierarchy therefore represents inheritance of capabilities among roles. For instance, Figure 2 states that the Content Manager and Supervisor roles can perform all the tasks that can be performed by the generic Employee (plus possibly some additional ones), and in turn the Administrator can perform all the tasks of the Supervisor.

The identification of roles and their dependencies is crucial for the success of the overall design, because it can impact on the correct execution of tasks and on the correctness of the managed data.

Managing data

In terms of data management, our approach provides a tight integration with the business process models, thanks to two main features: the process metadata and the mapping of business objects to the data structure.

The **process metadata** consists of an entity-relationship (ER) representation of all the data structures that are needed for encoding the process descriptions and their executions. Figure 3 shows a simplified model that allows the system to store into a database the process description, according to a simplified and optimized version of the BPDM metamodel [8].

A Process represents a whole BPMN diagram, and includes a list of Activities, each described by a set of input and output ParameterTypes. A Case is the instantiation of a process, and is related to the executed Activity Instances, with the respective actual Parameter Instances. The evolution of the status history is registered through CaseLogEntry and ActivityLogEntry. Users are the actors that perform a task and are clustered into Groups, representing their roles.

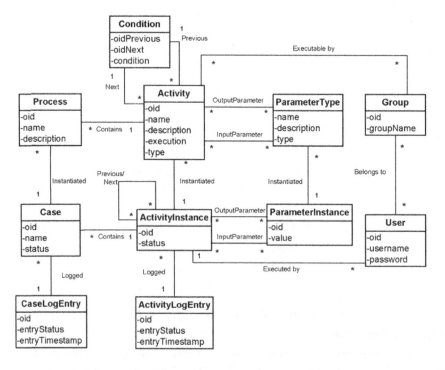

Figure 3. Metadata model describing the BP structure

The metamodel is actually mapped to a concrete database schema that stores the data, which in turn will be used to manage and record the execution of the processes. By modeling explicitly this aspect, we provide the designer with full visibility on the data. Assuming that also the application data are modeled in the same way, this allows explicit integration of the process metamodel with application data models at hand. For instance, if some application data need to be associated with some process concept, the corresponding entities can be simply connected through ER associations.

While several connection options and needs may exist, we identified two typical cases:

- *Activity-isomorphic entities.* In some processes, for any activity A that is part of the process specification, there exists an entity EA that is part of the application data model, such that an instance of EA is created exactly as the effect of successfully executing an instance of activity A. Such entity is activity-isomorphic, and the application can simply test the existence of its instances in order to understand if activities following A can be started.
- *Case-isomorphic entities.* In some cases, the application data model contains a single entity that encapsulates all information about case advancement. Each case is associated with exactly one instance of such entity, and each activity modifies that entity instance to mark activity completion. In this case, the entity is said case- isomorphic. In this situation, the entity will typically include one or more properties aiming at tracking the status of the object. The status of the instances records the case advancement.

The second facility that we provide consists of explicitly **mapping business objects** of the BPM to the concrete data structure of the application. Business objects represent abstract representations of the items that are used in the modeling of the business processes, such as: Invoice, Report, Document, and so on. These objects obviously have a concrete implementation within the data sources of the software applications. The aim of the business object mapping is to grant that the abstract models and the concrete implementations are aligned, and that the business process will manage correctly the respective instances. This phase is extremely helpful for granting quality and coherency of data, according to a MDM vision. Obviously, in some cases the mapping can be trivial (e.g., a business object can map to one single entity into a database), while in general complex mappings could be needed, when a business object actually maps to several entities or even to pieces of information spread through several databases or stored in different formats.

Figure 4 shows some examples of business objects (top left corner), a detailed view of the properties of one of these objects (top right corner), and a sample mapping to a database structure (bottom part of the picture). In the example, the Employee business object maps to the User database entity, while the Report object maps to some data spread through the TechRecord and the Category entities. Notice that the real mapping is more detailed than that, because it involves also the explicit mappings of each property.

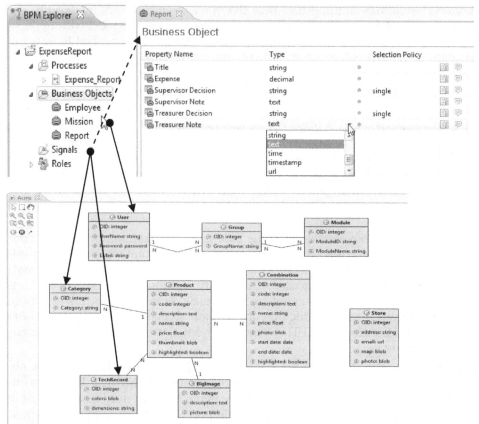

Figure 4. Mapping of business objects to the concrete data schema

Managing application logic

The application logic is described according to the application model, aiming at describing all the user interaction, service calls, and navigational aspects of the designed application. We focus on the Web as the platform of choice for the implementation of the software application, which is in line with the current trends in enterprise application development. Therefore, we adopt the WebML notation [3], a visual language for designing data- and service-centric Web applications, that allows specifying the conceptual model of applications built on top of a data schema. The application model is composed of one or more hypertexts used to publish or manipulate data. Different hypertext models (site views) can be defined (e.g., for different types of users or devices). A site view is a graph of pages, consisting of connected units, representing data publishing components. Units are related to each other through links, representing navigational paths and carrying parameters. Additionally, the WebML application model comprises the definition of Web services (when needed) and their invocations.

Starting from a BPMN specification, an automatic transformation can produce the logical representation of the process metadata and the WebML Application Model, as shown in Figure 5. For each activity in the BPM, a WebML application model is produced: if the activity is a UserTask (as the one highlighted in the example), a browsable hypertext is generated; if the activity is a ServiceTask, a web service invocation is generated.

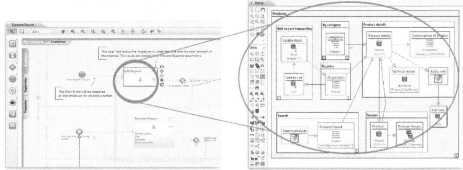

Figure 5. Mapping of BP tasks to application logic models (in WebML)

User interface design

User interface design is an orthogonal aspect with respect to the application logic design. It defines the graphical rules for positioning the elements into the pages and their rendering, together with the management of the user behavior, in terms of clicks and actions that can be performed in the page. We recognize the importance of the graphical and interaction aspects in modern enterprise applications, and therefore we think a specific set of models and tools should be provided for addressing this.

Since the approach is not targeting visual interface experts, the user interface aspect is kept at an abstract modeling level too. This grants designers the possibility of configuring some crucial aspects of the applications, while leaving the details to graphical experts. We provide two facilities for the interface design:

- A *grid model*, in which the designer can decide where to put the contents within the web page template, as shown in Figure 6: starting from a palette of contents (made available from the definition of the application logic), the designer can position them in the main page grid or in specific position within the page template (e.g., the header, the footer, the menu area, and so on).
- A refined *style design* mechanism, which let a more expert user define customized appearance and graphical templates for pages. This allows a designer to obtain applications customized according to the customer visual identity.

The presentation style and the application model are completely independent. Therefore, it is possible to produce applications with completely different styles from the same application model (and thus quickly customize an application to make the customer more familiar with it). Viceversa, it is also possible to apply the same style to many applications, because, once a presentation style has been defined for an application, it can be reused for any other developed application that needs to share the same visual identity.

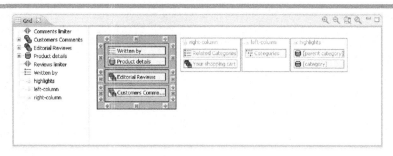

Figure 6. Grid model of an application page

RELEVANT ASPECTS OF BPMN 2.0

The BPMN notation that we adopt for designing business processes supports the visual specification of roles, tasks, and constraints. Precedence constraints are specified by arrows, representing the control flow of the application, and gateways, representing branching and merging points of execution paths. Parallel executions, alternative branches, conditional executions, events, and message exchanges can be specified. Modularization constructs (e.g., sub-processes and link between processes) are available for mastering process complexity.

Some features of Version 2.0 of the language are of extreme importance for the generation of application models, namely: *DataInputs*, *DataOutputs*, and *DataInputAssociations*, which explicitly specify the inputs and outputs of executable tasks; the classification of Tasks in *UserTasks* and *ServiceTasks*; *Non-Interrupting Events*; and a few minor others, such as escalation events, that allow users to redirect tasks and issues to other roles. Overall, the concept of dependency between different models, introduced in BPMN 2.0, is perfectly aligned with a full-fledged MDD approach. At a more detailed level of discussion, we can say that the distinction between *UserTasks* and *ServiceTasks* is crucial for the mapping to the application model, since the activities are mapped respectively to browsable hypertexts with input forms and buttons (UserTasks) and to web service invocations.

With respect to the standard notation, we mandatorily require the specification of DataInputs and DataOutputs for all the tasks of the process, including User-Tasks. Furthermore, we require the designer to specify the *expected actions* on the data within each activity (read, create, update, delete). This is needed for granting that the business process model is rich and complete enough for mapping to a significant application model. If this information was not available, several details of the application model could not be produced, including: the data flow between activities; the input forms into the UserTasks; and the data manipulations within the activities. Furthermore, in our approach we distinguish gateways that require human decisions, to allow their mapping to the user interfaces needed for the human decision making (we call them *UserGateways*).

On the other side, a few important features of BPMN 2.0 that would not be directly beneficial to our approach are choreography and conversation diagrams, as they are more oriented to high level representation of interactions and interfaces and do not impact directly on application development.

MODEL TRANSFORMATIONS AND QUICK PROTOTYPING

Model driven development (MDD) techniques allow for automatic transformation of models. This can be exploited in our setting by devising a set of transformations that produce the process metadata model, a coarse WebML application model, including the primitives for the user interaction and Web service orchestrations, and a draft specification of the user interface too.

Process Metadata Generation

The transformation from BPMN to the process metadata schema consists of an encoding of the BPMN concepts in a relational database structure: the BPMN precedence constraints and gateways are transformed into instances of a relational representation compliant to the metamodel of Figure 3. Each process model is mapped to a Process instance; each activity is transformed into an Activity instance; each flow arrow is transformed into a nextActivity/previousActivity relationship instance; each guard condition is transformed into a Condition instance; and so on. At runtime, the BPMN constraints, stored as process metadata, are exploited by the components of the application model for enacting the precedences among human-executed tasks and executing the service invocations. The choice of adopting a relational encoding ensures a standard and highly performing way of storing control data for the enactment of the project.

Application Model Generation

The transformation from BPMN to the application model considers the type (User or Service) of the gateways and of the tasks, as well as the information on the control and data flows. The generated application models consist of a coarse set of user interfaces and prototype business operations. Process control is encapsulated thanks to the automatically generated logical representation: the computation of the next enabled activities given the current state of the workflow is delegated to a specific WebML component which factors out the process control logic from the site view or service orchestration diagram: this component exploits the information stored in the process metadata to determine the current process status and the enabled state transitions.

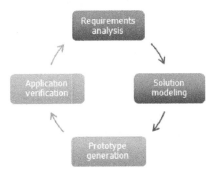

Figure 7. The MDD virtuous cycle

Code generation and quick prototyping

Starting from the application model and the user interface model, a further set of transformations can generate running applications. The benefit of adopting standard modeling notations and a model driven approach for transformation is that the running application will always be aligned to the models that represent its design. Furthermore, several code generation transformations can be devised for addressing different IT platforms. For instance, a code generation transformation can produce standard Java Web applications that can be deployed on any Java application server with no need of proprietary runtime or components (for instance, this is the solution adopted by WebRatio [9]), while other transformations can be developed for deploying on proprietary BPMS solutions.

Thanks to MDD, a running application can be generated at any moment in the development lifecycle. This allows producing a fully functional prototype with simply one mouse click, so as to provide an effective way to discuss the application with the customers and verify the compliance to requirements immediately.

This capability enables the virtuous MDD circle of analysis, modeling, generation and validation, as shown in Figure 7, which greatly facilitates the convergence towards the final solution. This cycle closely resembles to the BPM one, and therefore represents a perfect match at the development process level.

Transformation rules customization

Thanks to MDD, the code generation rules are fully customizable and extensible, to adapt the development environment to the need of any work team. This allows one to get realistic prototypes instead of coarse mockups, and even supports the generation of production applications, to be directly deployed and used. The customization of the rules can apply at two levels: the visual identity and the business logic.

The *visual identity* can be controlled with great precision, thanks to embedding the presentation styles into the generation rules. These rules are based on layout templates, which can be defined in any rendition language, most notably in HTML, as described in section User Interface Modeling.

The *business logic* of the application can be customized too. Indeed, the logic is expressed by the components comprised in the application model. A wealth of useful components are predefined in the WebML language, but additional custom components can be defined and integrated, to obtain any desired behavior (for example, some complex business logic or the integration with a legacy system).

WEBRATIO: A MDD TOOL FOR BPM

The proposed generative framework is implemented within the WebRatio tool [9]. WebRatio is a Model-Driven Web application development tool allowing one to edit BPMN and WebML models and automatically transform them into running applications for JEE and Service Oriented Architectures. The tool comprises the editors for WebML and BPMN models, and implements all the model transformations mentioned above[1].

The one-click publishing function provides immediate generation of a rapid prototype of the BPMN process. This functionality invokes in sequence the two transformations from BPMN to WebML and from WebML to JEE, yielding a dynamic, multi-actor application with a default graphical style. The generator also creates a few exemplary users for each BPMN actor. This allows the analyst to impersonate each role in the process, start a process and make it progress by enacting activities and manual and automatic gateways.

---

[1]See also additional materials available on the companion CD and in the online edition of the book.

The prototypes can be refined at the modeling level by editing the WebML application models and the other design dimensions, including the customized generation rules.

CASE STUDY

The proposed method and tool have been tested in several real industrial scenarios: as an example, we report the outcomes of a project conducted within the leasing division of a major European bank, which needed to reshape its entire software architecture according to a BPM-based paradigm. The resulting pilot application covers 52 business processes, comprising more than 1,100 activities spanning 30 user roles. The development team comprised 14 staff members from 3 organizations, with total effort amounting to 2551 man days, spent in 375 elapsed days. Rapid prototyping let the team deploy 4 major prototypes and 35 minor releases along one year.

We estimated a *spared effort* induced by automatic transformation of BPM models of 20%, only in terms of automatically generated model elements, which therefore did not need to be manually designed. Other experiences [2] confirmed this analysis, by highlighting savings from 17% (in cases where the BPM part was a limited aspect of a larger project) up to 60% (in cases where reduced customization was needed).

However, the biggest advantage we experienced was due to the *quick prototyping* capabilities. We can conclude that, although the customer were able to discuss and refine the process models, they weren't actually able to focus on most of the issues, missing parts and wrong constraints specified in the processes until they were shown some concrete running applications. The continuous prototyping was perceived as valuable and interesting, also in terms of user involvement, although it required some dedication both from customers and analysts: the two basically met once a week in front of an updated prototype for discussing and gathering new information.

Another appreciated feature of the approach was *separation of concerns*, which applied both at the modeling level and at the software architecture layer: process models and the other models were perfectly orthogonal, and this allowed different roles to apply the respective expertise at their best, on the different models. Orthogonalization in architectural sense proved extremely useful too, since it allowed splitting the SOA (Service Oriented Architecture) layer with respect to the lower level banking backend systems (written in Prolog and other legacy technologies) and with respect to the Java Web application layer deployed by WebRatio.

CONCLUSIONS

In this chapter we have presented a multi-faceted approach to BPM, which applies MDD (Model Driven Development) techniques to the design of process-based applications. The development of enterprise applications is seen as a design process that involves several models representing the various aspects of the application. These models are related to each other and can be automatically transformed into the running application.

The benefit of adopting standard modeling notations and model driven approach is twofold: (1) to keep all the models aligned by construction and (2) to grant alignment of the running application with respect to the models that represent its requirements and design.

This paves the path to full-fledged support of BPM and MDM integration. The model driven approach grants further advantages in terms of development productivity (thanks to code generation and quick user feedback based on prototypes) and evolution of the application (thanks to the virtuous model-based development cycle).

REFERENCES

1. Jean Bezivin. On the unification power of models. Software and Systems Modeling, 4(2):171188, May 2005.
2. Marco Brambilla, Stefano Butti, Piero Fraternali, Stefano Borrelli. Lessons learned from applying BPM and MDD practices to large-scale industrial scenarios. In BPM Industrial Experiences, Springer LNCS, Michael Rosemann, Michael zur Muehlen (eds.), 2011, to appear.
3. Marco Brambilla, Stefano Ceri, Piero Fraternali, Ioana Manolescu. Process Modeling in Web Applications. ACM Transactions on Software Engineering and Methodology (ACM TOSEM), volume 15, number 4, October 2006, pp. 360-409.
4. Alin Deutsch, Richard Hull, Fabio Patrizi, Victor Vianu: Automatic verification of data-centric business processes. ICDT 2009: 252-267
5. Christian Fritz, Richard Hull, Jianwen Su: Automatic construction of simple artifact-based business processes. ICDT 2009: 225-238
6. Rob Karel, Clay Richardson. Software AG buys Data Foundations: Business Acumen Meets Data Competency. Forrester blog, October 22, 2010. http://blogs.forrester.com/clay_richardson/10-10-22-software_ag_buys_data_foundations_business_acumen_meets_data_competency
7. Max J. Pucher. Enterprise Architecture Master Data Process Content Relationship Management? On "Welcome to the Real (IT) World!" blog. http://isismjpucher.wordpress.com/2010/10/24/eamdpcrm/
8. OMG. Business Process Definition Metamodel v.1.0, November 2008. http://www.omg.org/spec/BPDM/
9. WebRatio: www.webratio.com

Refactoring BPMN Models: From 'Bad Smells' to Best Practices and Patterns

Darius Silingas and Edita Mileviciene, No Magic, Lithuania

INTRODUCTION

BPMN is already acknowledged as a *de facto* standard for business process modeling. However, it still takes a long journey to raise the maturity of business process modeling practice. The language elements and notation are described in BPMN specification [1], illustrative BPMN examples are given in a supplementary document [2]. The language and basic style guidelines are already covered in BPMN books [3,4]. Despite of it, in practice most business process modelers do a lot of mistakes that make their BPMN models over complex, difficult to understand and maintain. According to the old saying, "it is stupid to not learn from your own mistakes, it is wise to learn from mistakes by others". Therefore, it is important to understand the common mistakes and their identifiers that can be detected automatically or manually in BPMN model. In software development, such identifiers in source code are called 'bad smells' [5]. We suggest reuse of the same term in business process modeling context. When a bad smell is detected in a business process model, the model needs to be refactored to get rid of the bad smell and comply with the best practices. Process patterns provide typical solutions for getting rid of undesired bad smells. Fundamental business process patterns are described in [6]. However, many practitioners find them very abstract and difficult to understand when they are applicable. Practitioners learn best in an example-driven approach. A good combination for learning business process modeling best practices and patterns is explaining a common mistake [7], identifying it by a bad smell, discussing what is a best practice or process pattern to comply with, and exploring how to refactor the model. This paper presents this approach by examining five practical refactoring cases from the extensive authors' BPMN consultancy in banking, telecommunication, defense, and software domains. All refactoring cases are illustrated by BPMN diagrams – original versions containing bad smells and refactored versions compliant with best practices or patterns. The presented business process examples are specified at analysis level, i.e. without properties providing technical details for process automation. For simplicity only a small number of BPMN elements are applied – task, subprocess, exclusive and event based gateways, start, end, intermediate timer or message accept events, and data object. This small set of elements is enough for discussing typical bad smells in the model and demonstrating how to refactor them.

REFACTORING CASE NO. 1: INCONSISTENT NAMING

The first fundamental thing that needs to be reviewed and fixed is BPMN element names. It is quite typical that modelers use nouns for naming activities (especially popular case is ending with management) or use different naming style for the elements of the same type in different places. Lithuanian philosopher Vydunas said that "the language that we speak shapes our thinking". This applies well to the business process modeling context – it is very often that modelers misuse BPMN elements and that is reflected in the naming. The use of inconsistent naming style typically indicates that there is no solid understanding when to use which element while capturing business processes in BPMN. Table 1 examines some typical bad smells in naming and corresponding best practices/patterns.

Table 1. Some Naming Bad Smells and Best Practices

Bad Smell	Best Practice/Pattern
Noun based activity name – indicates that element is an event, data object, or process area as opposed to activity.	**Strong verb + domain specific noun** – emphasizes achieving a discrete goal after performing work.
Gateway named as activity – indicates that a gateway represents a task, which determines the choice.	**Unnamed gateway** – it is merely a branching element that does not perform any work, so it should not be named (except for referencing).
Words and/or in activity name – indicates multiple activities captured in one activity.	**No conjunctions in names** – raise name abstraction level or split into two subsequent/alternative activities.
Long activity name – indicates that details of activity are emphasized instead of the goal; orients diagram towards textual document.	**Short name + documentation** – the name should emphasize the goal, and details of activity can be captured in comments or documentation.

For the experienced business process modeler solving naming conventions may seem to be easy. However, in practice we find inconsistent naming issues in almost every organization that adopts BPMN as a standard for specifying business processes. Unfortunately, you can also find some inconsistent naming cases in BPMN 2.0 specification [1] or its supporting examples guide [2]. A typical case of business process model with bad smells presented in Table 1 and refactoring it is presented in Figure 1.

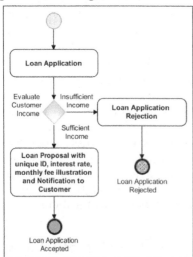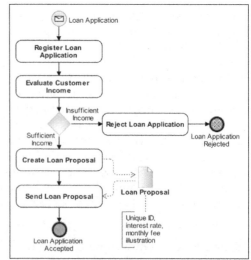

Figure 1. Business process Make Loan Proposal with bad smells in naming and a version refactored to comply with naming best practices/patterns

We analyzed only a few most common naming issues – in practice, you will also face problems with inconsistent naming of events, data objects, participants, messages, etc. For organization that is adopting BPMN as a standard it is highly recommended to establish naming conventions guidelines and regular review models to ensure that these guidelines are followed. For BPMN modeling tools it is rather a difficult task to detect bad smells in naming automatically as such a task would require linguistic analysis. However, some bad smells like too long names can be very easily determined in an automated way.

REFACTORING CASE NO.2: LARGE PROCESS DIAGRAMS

The second fundamental thing that needs to be review is complexity of process diagrams. While BPMN supports modeling processes in multiple levels of details, practitioners very often are used to "everything in one page" style, which impairs overview and makes it difficult to understand and analyze the process. Psychologists have determined that the best number of visual elements to focus on in one diagram is 5±2. In practice this rule is rarely followed. We think that it is quite practical to increase this number to something like 7±4, but consulting various organizations on business process modeling, we have seen extreme cases of business process diagrams with up to 450 (!) tasks. Such large diagrams make it very difficult to analyze them and spot the issues – the value of visualization is lost. In Figure 3, a presented example of a large diagram contains a number of inconsistency issues such as lack of Confirm Seminar activity that is symmetric to existing Cancel Seminar activity, a non-ending loop for registering participants after Decision Deadline, uneven level of details for announcing seminar (the first four tasks) and canceling it (one compressed subprocess), no clear distinction of early and late registration and others. However, it is rather difficult to spot such issues if you are analyzing a large complex business process diagram – you are happy that have managed to read and understand it. It is easy to detect over large diagrams in a modeling tool – you simply have to automate spotting all diagrams that exceed a chosen threshold of maximum number of activities, e.g. 10. A refactored version presented in Figure 2, uses sub processes with additional diagrams assigned for each of them.

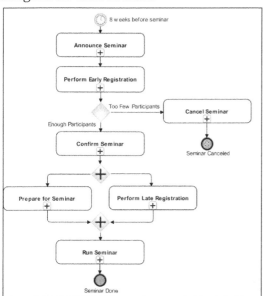 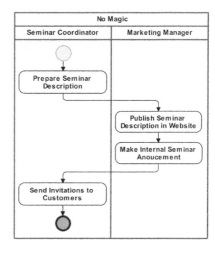

Figure 2. A refactored business process diagram Organize Seminar with 7 sub processes and sub process Announce Seminar specified in a separate diagram

In such an approach, you can decompose a very large business process into a simple process structured in several levels of details. For example, a business process with three levels of details following the rule of up to 10 activities in one level may contain $10^3 = 1000$ tasks.

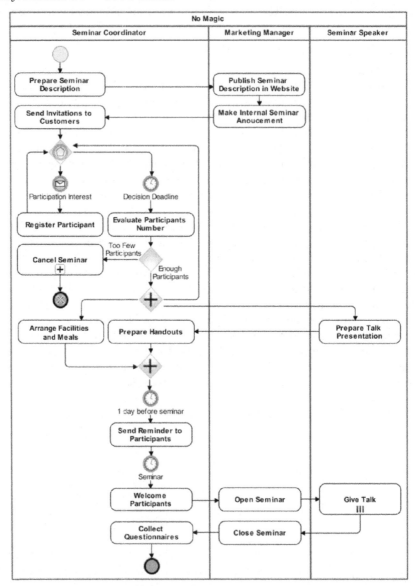

Figure 3. An original large business process diagram Organize Seminar containing a bad smell of 16 activities

REFACTORING CASE NO.3: INCONSISTENT USE OF GATEWAYS

Gateways are very important as they control the branching of a business process sequence flow based on data or upcoming event(s). They also specify a connection point from the sub process end events to the external process. In practice, we can see a lot of issues in using gateways. Very often gateways are omitted and multiple sequence flows go in to/out of an activity, which impairs readability and interpretation. In our opinion, a frequent convention of using a question for a name of a gateway and Yes/No on branched sequence flows is wrong because it makes not possible to connect the names to the names of end events of a preceding sub process (Yes and No are not very good names for the end events). Also, we observe a frequent misunderstanding on how to use event based gateway and workflow patterns related to it. In Table 3, three common bad smells in using gateways are presented together with corresponding best practices/patterns for refactoring them, and Figure 4 show fragments of a business process before and after refactoring. All the mentioned bad smells in gateway usage can be easily determined automatically by a BPMN modeling tool.

Table 2. Typical Gateway Usage Bad Smells and Best Practices

Bad Smell	Best Practice/Pattern
Multiple incoming/outgoing sequence flows – *makes it difficult to understand how many flows are required to come out/in.*	**Always use gateways for branching/merging** – *improves readability of the diagram and explicitly indicates control points.*
Event-based gateway with outgoing sequence flow unconnected to event – *makes it ambiguous when the alternative sequence flow should be taken.*	**Apply** Deferred Choice **pattern** – *all the sequence flows after event-based gateway should be connected to events. Use timer event to model cases when expected event does not happen.*
Gateway unsynchronized with preceding subprocess ends – *shows inconsistency between sub process details and its usage in a larger process.*	**Apply** Internal Business Error **pattern with synchronized end/branch naming** – *makes it very straightforward to consistently use gateways and sub processes.*

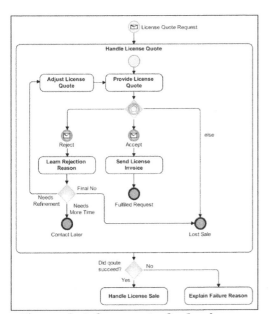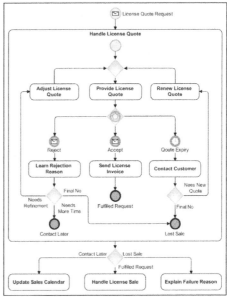

Figure 4. A fragment of a business process Sell Licenses with bad smells and after refactoring them in order to comply with best practices/patterns

REFACTORING CASE NO.4: INCONSISTENT USE OF EVENTS

Events are fundamental elements in BPMN – each process starts with a start event, ends with one or more end events, and reacts to a number of intermediate events happening during the process. While events themselves are not very tricky, deciding at which process level to put the event initiating a process or choosing a proper scope of an intermediate event might done incorrectly. In Table 4, we list two common bad smells with events usage and best practice for refactoring them. Figure 5 gives an example of business processing fragment before and after refactoring. Event-based bad smells can be determined automatically by BPMN tool.

Table 3. Typical Event Usage Bad Smells and Best Practices

Bad Smell	Best Practice/Pattern
Event outside and inside process – *repetition makes it redundant; formal interpretation would require the event to happen twice.*	**Initiating event out of process description** – *it is easier to read a diagram and understand when/why a sub process needs to be performed.*
Repeating events – *complicates diagram and its maintenance.*	**A subprocess with attached event** – *enables to clearly define the scope of an event.*

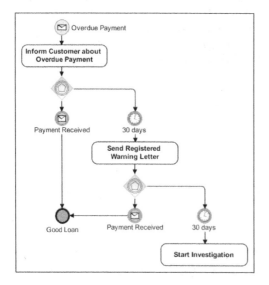
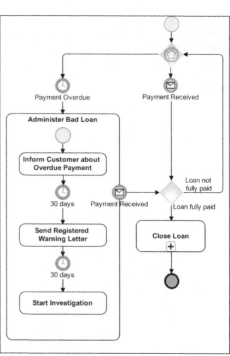

Figure 5. An example of a business process Administer Bad Loan fragment with bad smells in events usages and a refactored version

REFACTORING CASE NO.5: POOR DIAGRAM LAYOUT

Last, but not least, in practice there are many issues with BPMN diagram layout. You can spot many bad smells like different sizes of similar type elements, uneven spaces between elements, long, bended and crossing lines, etc. All of these bad smells in layout do not change the content of the business process but they make a diagram very difficult to read. The generic layout best practices for UML activity diagrams [8] will apply without major modifications for BPMN. Figure 6 represents a typical layout, which contains many of these bad smells and which can be refactored to a good layout that has already been presented in Figure 2. One very important bad smell in Figure 6 is so called *"slalom"* – a lack of consistent direction of flow, which among other things makes it very difficult to differentiate the main and alternative scenarios.

In Western culture, a typical flow should be made either top down or from left to the right. We prefer top down direction because it enables to balance use of space as the activity names' text naturally flows from left to the right, and the sequence flows then progress in a top down direction. Missing a clear direction of flow also indicates that the modeler probably modeled all the details at once, while a best practice is to address the primary 'happy day' scenario first and address alternative scenarios only afterwards. The layout bad smells are tricky for automated detection in BPMN tools – such functionality is possible but it requires a thorough analysis of graphical symbol sizes and positions.

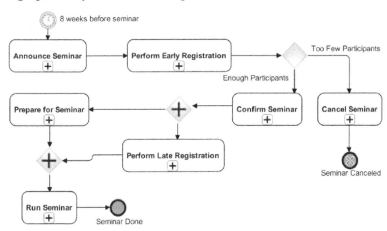

Figure 6. An example of a poor layout diagram for a business process Organize Seminar containing bad smells of slalom, different symbol sizes, uneven spacing and bending lines (see Figure 2 for a refactored version)

SUMMARY

We have analyzed five practical BPMN refactoring cases that are common in practice by presenting original business process samples, specifying bad smells that they contain, suggesting best practices/patterns to comply with, and refactoring the original versions into a better quality business process model. The presented cases deal with mixed style names, large process diagrams, inconsistent use of gateways, inconsistent use of events, and poor diagram layout. We think that such example based approach to analysis of typical mistakes and refactoring them is the most efficient way to teach business process modeling best practices and patterns. It also provides a clear motivation for business process modeling tool vendors to automate detection of bad smells and refactoring work. Both of these two aspects should have major contribution to raising the maturity of business process modeling practice. The presented cases should not be treated as an extensive list but rather as examples of a starting initiative. We hope that this paper will motivate more research and publications on refactoring BPMN models in both breadth (other cases) and depth (more technical details) directions.

REFERENCES

1. OMG. Business Process Model and Notation (BPMN), v2.0 beta2, 2010.
   http://www.omg.org/cgi-bin/doc?dtc/10-06-04.pdf
2. OMG. BPMN 2.0 by Example, v. 1.0, 2010.
   http://www.omg.org/spec/BPMN/2.0/examples/pdf
3. Bruce Silver. BPMN Method and Style: A levels-based methodology for BPM process modeling and improvement using BPMN 2.0. Cody-Cassidy Press, 2009, ISBN-10: 0982368100.
4. Stephen A. White, Derek Miers. BPMN Modeling and Reference Guide: Understanding and Using BPMN. Future Strategies Inc., 2009, ISBN-10: 0977752720
5. Martin Fowler, Kent Beck, John Brant, William Opdyke, Don Roberts. Refactoring: Improving the Design of Existing Code. Addison Wesley, 1999 ISBN-10: 0201485672
6. Stephen A. White. Process Modeling Notations and Workflow Patterns, IBM, 2004
   http://www.bpmn.org/Documents/Notations_and_Workflow_Patterns.pdf
7. R. Laue and A. Awad. Visualization of business process modeling anti patterns. In VFfP, 2009.
8. Scott W. Ambler. The Elements of UML™ 2.0 Style. Cambridge University Press, 2005.

Admission Process Optimization with BPMN (Case Study)

Jack Xue, Butler University and Conseco Service LLC, USA

ABSTRACT

The Business Process Modeling Notation (BPMN) is an increasingly important standard for business process design and optimization and has enjoyed high levels of attention in academic research and business practice. In this paper, experiences are shared from a project that using BPMN to design and optimize an online admission process. This process is optimized by choosing a subset of incoming requests such that the revenue of the service provider is maximized. The admission decision is based on an estimation of requests' service times, and the rewards associated with serving these requests within their Quality of Service (QoS) bounds with respect to limited system resources. Experiments demonstrated the effectiveness of the admission process.

INTRODUCTION

Enterprises are striving on coping with the increasing total ownership costs of their IT systems. In recent years this cost has been reduced through resource pooling and sharing, for example hardware virtualization. If the peak loads of different systems do not occur in the same time, then the aggregated peak-to-average ratio of shared resource utilization is significantly reduced. Therefore, it is possible to only provision resources for a fraction of the combined peaks and services to service the same consumptions. In such a finite service capacity scenario, the service-level agreement (SLA) will specify certain quality of service (QoS) guarantees. Under a SLA, requests would come with associated rewards and penalties. Penalties are incurred when the request is either not serviced (dropped) or serviced outside the QoS bounds (delayed). Rewards are received for servicing a request within QoS bounds. Since the service resource is way less than the peak requirement, it calls for utilizing appropriate Admission Control (AC) measures to reject a subset of requests so that the remaining requests can be served within their QoS bound, which maximizes the revenue of the service provider.

How to intelligently utilize the limited resource to provide services has been a topic for academic study and industrial practice for many years.[1-2] Traditional models of systems that involve customers queuing for service have been made more realistic by incorporating the impatience of these customers. A natural way to incorporate impatience is to assume that each customer independently abandons the queue, if his service has not begun within a certain amount of time.[3] The admission control problem has also been modeled in general graphs

---

[1] D. de Werra, T. Liebling, J. Hêche, Recherche Opérationnelle pour Ingénieurs, PPUR, 2003

[2] Z. Akzin, M. Armony, V. Mehrotra, The Modern Call Center: A Multi-Discipliny Perspective on Operations Management Research, POM 16(6) 665-688, 2007

[3] A. Ward, S. Kumar, Asymptotically Optimal Admission Control with Impatient Customers, Mathematics of Operations Research 33(1), 167–202, 2008

with edge capacities. An online algorithm can receive a sequence of communications requests on a virtual path that may be accepted or rejected, while staying within the capacity limitations. A problem with this objective function is that in some cases an online algorithm with a good competitive ratio may reject the vast majority of the requests, whereas the optimal solution rejects only a small fraction of them.[4] Multi-agent systems (MAS) are also used to resolve the resource sharing problem in which the resource is represented by a resource token and allowed to be passed in the network. An agent receiving a resource token gets the permission to access the resource. If the agent cannot make use of a resource, it passes the token locally on further to an agent that may have better knowledge of specifically who needs the resource. Therefore, no single agent needs to make the whole decisions of where to send a resource but push it to the target agents closer. The common challenge of MAS methods is however the computational overhead of MAS *per se.*[5] It also has been proposed to use a short-term prediction based online admission control methodology to maximize the profit of the service. To effectively handle the variability and diverseness of incoming service requests, the service time of a request is utilized as the most important criterion for making AC decisions. It has been proved that maximizing the number of requests serviced actually minimizes the penalty in an offline setting.[6-7] To further improve this online algorithm in practice, one may leverage the knowledge on the request distribution as well as the detection of the distribution changes.[8]

In the next section, the admission control process modeling is discussed, first mathematically and then in BPMN. In the following section, the optimization of the model is described. Preliminary results are presented before coming to the conclusions.

MODELING

A request denoted as x is represented by a vector $[a_x, s_x, d_x, p_x, b_x, c_x]$. Here a_x stands the arrival time of the request; s_x the service time needed for accomplish this request; d_x the reward if this request can be served within QoS bound; p_x the penalty if the request is dropped or served beyond the QoS bound; b_x the response time bound or the QoS bound; c_x the system resource or the capacity needed to accomplish the request. Denoting C the total capacity or resource that can be utilized in the time interval t, $0 \leq t \leq T$ where T is the upper bound of time interval under consideration. The problem of maximizing of the service revenue by admitting a subset of requests is to find a schedule

$$Y(t) = \left(y_{x,t} \right)_{t \in T}^{x \in X} \quad (1)$$

[4] N. Alon, Y. Azar, S Gutner, Admission Control to Minimize Rejections and Online Set Cover with Repetitions, ACM Trans. on Algorithms, 6(1), 1-13, 2009

[5] Y. Xu, P. Scerri, Token based resource sharing in heterogeneous multi-agent teams, PRIMA 2009, 113-126, 2009

[6] A. Siberschatz, P. Galvin, G. Gagne, Operation System Concepts, Addison-Wesley, 7th Edition, 2004

[7] A Verma, S. Ghosal, On Admission Control for Profit Maximization of Networked Service Providers, WWW2003, May 20-24, 2002 Budapest, Hungary

[8] X. Xue, Adaptive detection of distribution changes in medical information systems, PAMM, 2080019-20, December 2007

for all requests such that the overall revenue is maximized, viz,

$$\max \sum_x \left[d_x \sum_t y_{x,t} - p_r \left(1 - \sum_t y_{x,t} \right) \right]$$

$$s.t. \quad \sum_x c_x y_{x,t} \le C, for \; \forall t \in T \qquad (2)$$

$$\sum_t y_{x,t} \le 1, for \; \forall x \in X$$

Here

$$y_{x,t} = \begin{cases} 1, \text{if request } x \text{ is scheduled at time } t \text{ and } (t + s_x - a_x) \le b_x \\ 0, \text{otherwise} \end{cases} \qquad (3)$$

The request x is rejected if $\sum_t y_{x,t} = 0$.

This scheduling problem is a NP-hard even in the offline situation (i.e. all requests are known and T is a constant at the time of scheduling) and hence no optimal solution can be found effectively. Therefore the goal becomes to find an online algorithm that makes decision on rejecting or accepting a request without knowledge of future requests. This online algorithm will sub-maximize the revenue, denoted as $w(t)$ and defined in Equation 2.

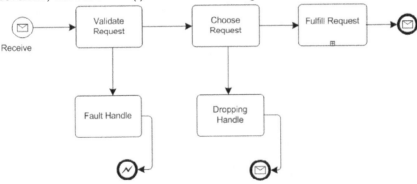

Figure 1. Admission Control Process with BPMN

The mathematically modeled admission control process can be presented with BPMN as shown in Figure 1, for illustrating the workflow and for BPEL mapping. Once a request is received, it will be validated. If the request is invalid, a fault handler will send a fault response to the caller. Otherwise, the online algorithm will decide if this valid request should be dropped or fulfilled. In case it decides to drop this request, the dropping handler will generate an informational response to the caller. Otherwise the request will be forwarded to the process of fulfillment which will generate a conformational response to the caller.

OPTIMIZATION

All online optimization algorithms actually share the same generic framework as shown in List 1, which simply considers the set of available and new requests at each time step and chooses a request x which is then served and removed from the set of available requests.[9-10] Function AVAILABLEREQUEST(X, t) returns the set of requests available for service at time t and function SERVEREQUEST(x, t) simply serves x at time t. Function CHOOSEREQUEST returns a request over the interval [t, $t+\Delta$] by sampling the arrival distribution $\Theta(t)$. *In this study, a greedy and a local optimal algorithm were tested.*

```
ONLINEOPTIMIZATION(T) {
        Y←∅; w←0;
    for t in T do Θ(t) ←NEWREQUESTS(t) {
            X←AVAILABLEREQUESTS(X,t)∪Θ(t);
            x← CHOOSEREQUEST(X,t)
            SERVEREQUEST(x,t);
    }
}
```

List 1. The online algorithm for admission control

Using the online optimization algorithm in the task of Choose Request, a feasible solution of the admission control problem as specified in Equation 1 is guaranteed. Moreover, the optimality of the solution, as defined in Equation 2, is approximated owing to that the optimal solution of the original problem is a HP-hard even in the offline situation.

The proposed admission control process as shown in Figure 1 can be further enhanced by utilizing the knowledge of the request sample space as well as the detection of the changes of sample distribution, which leads to a new BPMN model as shown in Figure 2.

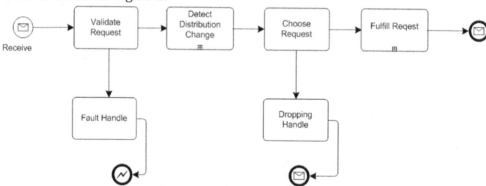

Figure 2. Enhanced admission control process

The process of Distribution Change Detection (DCD) is to help CHOOSEREQUEST() better predicting the requests may come in a near future. Mathematically, the number of requests received by the admission control process is the signal in a stochastic process (SP), $\{x_i\}$, $i \geq 0$. If the random variables are distributed independently and normally and their means and variances are different, an independent normal process can be characterized by the mean and variance vectors, $\Theta(\mu_i, \sigma_i)$. To better predict the future requests, the distribution changes in mean or variance are required to be identified as soon as possible. If the given distribution family contains only two distinct members and moreover, its mean

---

[9] R. Bent, P. Van Hentenryck, Online Stochastic Optimization Without Distributions, AAAI, 2004

[10] P. Van Hentenryck, R. Bent, Online Stochastic Combinatorial Optimization, MIT, 2009

changes but not its variance, a larger than expected mean is discriminated by two simple hypotheses

$$H_0 : \mu = \mu_0, \quad H_1 : \mu = \mu_1, \quad \mu_1 = (1 + \Delta_\mu)\mu_0 \qquad (4)$$

The tests of the hypotheses are subject to an operating characteristic function (OCF) with parameters a and β, and $a + \beta < 1$. At any step, when $n>0$, H_0 is either accepted or rejected according to the lower or the upper inequalities

$$b < z_n < a, \quad z_n = \sum_{i=0}^{n} \ln \frac{f_{\mu_1}(x_i)}{f_{\mu_0}(x_i)}, \text{ and } b = \ln \frac{\beta}{1-\alpha}, \quad a = \ln \frac{1-\beta}{\alpha} \qquad (5)$$

Here, $f_{\mu_0}(x_i)$ and $f_{\mu_1}(x_i)$ are the probability mass functions (PMFs). Since PMFs are normal distributions,

$$z_n = \frac{\mu_1 - \mu_0}{\sigma^2} \sum_{i=1}^{n} x_i + \frac{n}{2\sigma^2} (\mu_0^2 - \mu_1^2), \text{ and } \begin{cases} b < z_n < a, \text{ continue} \\ z_n \le b, \text{ accept } H_0 \\ z_n \ge a, \text{ reject } H_0 \end{cases} \qquad (6)$$

Equation 6 is used to detect the status changing to a new value. After n steps, z_n is accumulated to a and therefore an alert is sent to Choose Request. To continue detecting distribution mean drifting, z_n is reset and another sequence is started. However, if the signal continues drifting in the same direction, this strategy will repeatedly generate the same type of unnecessary alerts. If z_n is left alone and preceded in the current sequence, it will be deeply saturated and consequently the algorithm's sensitivity will be reduced. To avoid this situation, a is used to cap z_n, and the values of z_n and z_{n-1} are used, viz,

$$\begin{cases} \text{if } z_n \ge \alpha \text{ and } z_{n-1} < \alpha, \text{ then issue an alert, set } z_n = \alpha, \text{ continue the sequence} \\ \text{if } z_n < \alpha \text{ and } z_{n-1} \ge \alpha, \text{ then issue a recovered notice, set } z_n = 0, \text{ start a new sequence} \end{cases} \qquad (8)$$

Equations 5-6 are used to detect and report the mean changes in the normal process. Accordingly, the algorithm for detecting and reporting the variance changes is formulated for the same process.

PRELIMINARY RESULTS

The experiments simulate a messaging service using empirical workload from the distributions generated as described in [8]. Reward was proportional to the service time of the request and penalty was proportional to the average service time. Each experiment was repeated until statistical stability was achieved and the computed means are reported in Table 1.

The Greedy algorithm is the simplest format of online algorithm which each time returns a request x if the capacities constrain (the first condition in Equation 2) is satisfied at time t by serving this request. With such an algorithm the ratio of request serviced, which is defined as

$$\rho = \frac{1}{m} \left| (y_x)^{x \in X} \right| \qquad (9)$$

is marginally acceptable, where m is the total number of request received. The local optimization (LO) algorithm returns a request x that satisfies Equation 2. here X are all known requests at time t, without any "forward" thinking. The experiments show that by using LO the ratio of request serviced improved 10 percentile, which is significant from the perspective of operation.

DCD can be used to further improve the admission control process. DCD has two functions. It can forecast in a near future which kinds requests may appear, thus provide an opportunity to let the online algorithm has some "forward" think by selecting a request to not only good for the current value of revenue but also "reserve" some capacity for the future requests. Also if the distribution of sample space changed, it can signal the online algorithm. The experiments show that leveraging this adaptively forward thinking, the proposed admission control system can further improve the ratio of request serviced by 4 percentile. As expected, the DCD has no effect on Greedy algorithm as it is by-design not forward looking.

Using the mean of total revenue from Greedy algorithm to normalize the mean of total revenue (NMTR) from other algorithms, one can find the LO dramatically improve NMTR as the results of maximizing the revenue at each step. Again, the DCD has no effect on Greedy algorithm in maximizing revenue. However, DCD can further improved LO in achieving a higher NMTR.

All these improvements come with a price which is the system response time – the more complicate the algorithm, the longer the response time is. Using the mean of response time from Greedy algorithm to normalize the mean of response time (NMRT) from other algorithms, it is demonstrated that LO has a 10% delay and LO+DCD a 30% delay compared to that of Greedy.

	P	NMTR	NMRT
Greedy	0.80	1.00	1.00
LO	0.90	1.25	1.10
Greedy+DCD	0.80	1.00	1.00
LO+DCD	0.94	1.35	1.30

Table 1. Experimental Results

CONCLUSION

This paper demonstrated the process of using contemporary optimization technologies in conjunction with BPMN to carry out the design and optimization of a business process. The preliminary experimental results presented in this paper showed that the diagrams of BPMN helped in understanding the perspectives of optimization. More specifically, after one uses BPEL to map a business process designed with BPMN into web services, the optimal algorithm needs to be carried over all the way first as a part of Key Performance Indicator (KPI) and Notes and then as a part of pseudo code. Unfortunately, there is no existing tool can directly map the optimization algorithm into web service coding and web server configuration. Thus heavily manual work is still the only means.

Organizationally, this is always a challenge in deciding who should design the optimization algorithms and who should map them into enterprise services. Moreover, these optimization algorithms need to be parameterized based on the hardware, software and network environments. Therefore, it is called for the new generation of business analysts, system engineers and programmer to work together in order to design, implement and operate an optimized business process.

Workflow Patterns with BPMN 2.0

Vishal Saxena, Roubroo, USA

INTRODUCTION

Over the past few years, workflow patterns have become a touchstone of workflow standards and products. The Workflow Patterns initiative is a joint effort of Eindhoven University of Technology (led by Professor Wil van der Aalst) and Queensland University of Technology (led by Professor Arthur ter Hofstede) which started in 1999. The aim of this initiative is to provide a conceptual basis for process technology. In particular, the research provides a thorough examination of the various perspectives (control flow, data, resource, and exception handling) that need to be supported by a workflow language or a business process modeling language. The results can be used for examining the suitability of a particular process language or workflow system for a particular project, assessing relative strengths and weaknesses of various approaches to process specification, implementing certain business requirements in a particular process-aware information system, and as a basis for language and tool development. These workflow patterns cover a majority of use cases that BPM modelers would need. Most workflow standards have been evaluated against these patterns.

In this paper I would present how these workflow patterns can be modeled using BPMN 2.0. We will use simple real life examples to illustrate the patterns. Further, we will focus on specific constructs in BPMN 2.0 that let the users extend the workflow patterns if required. Our initial intent is to target the various control flow patterns. Let's start off with Basic Control Flow patterns, then we move to Advanced Branching and Synchronization Patterns followed by State based control flow patterns and towards the end we will cover Recursive and Termination patterns. In order to maintain the interest of the audience, some of the not so common patterns will not be covered in this version of the chapter.

BASIC CONTROL FLOW PATTERNS

We start off with some basic control flow patterns. These will introduce some of the common gateways that will be used later. More importantly, these will lay the ground for more complex patterns later in the chapter.

SEQUENCE

The simplest of control flow patterns is the sequence flow where a task in a process in enabled after the completion of a preceding task in the same process. In BPMN, this pattern can be modeled using a simple set of sequence flows connecting activities.

Example: Verify Account

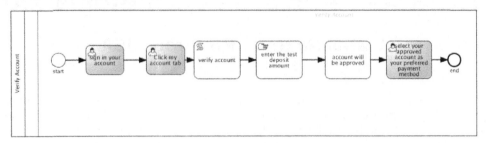

In this example Verify Account, the activities are executed in a linear sequence. The user first signs into the account, then clicks on my account tab and then verification of account happen and so on. This is a fairly common and easy pattern.

PARALLEL SPLIT

Another simple control flow pattern is when two or more task sequences can execute in parallel. In BPMN this can be modeled using an AND gateway. Another option is to model this without a gateway with multiple outgoing sequence flows. When there are multiple outgoing sequence flows from an activity, it is treated as AND split.

Example: Dinner Plan

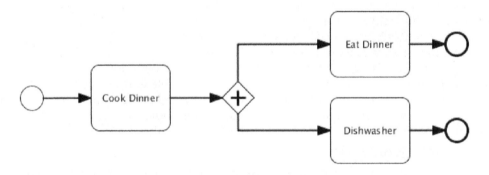

In this example Dinner Plan, after cooking dinner, the individual can eat dinner while the dishwasher is running. Once the dinner has been cooked, these two activities can happen in parallel.

SYNCHRONIZATION

This is a common pattern where two or more control flow sequences merge. In this pattern, the subsequent tasks are executed only after both sequence flows have executed. For multiple incoming tokens, there is only one outgoing token i.e. only after all incoming sequences have finished execution, will the control flow pass to the subsequent activity.

Example: Dispatch Goods

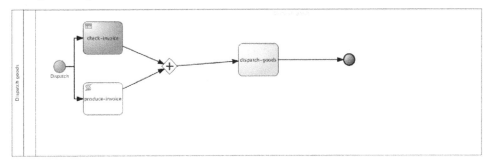

In this example, the tasks to check a received invoice and produce invoice happen in parallel but dispatch goods will only happen after the produce invoice and check invoice have both finished

EXCLUSIVE CHOICE

This is yet another common pattern where the control flow is transferred to one and only one outgoing branch from the activity. This is based on data/conditions. These conditions are evaluated at runtime. In BPMN this pattern is supported by a construct called XOR gateway. There may be more than one outgoing sequence flows from the XOR gateway but one and only one will be enabled at runtime.

Example: Check Results

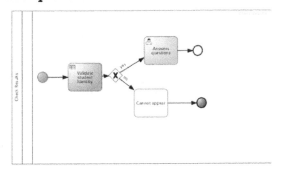

In this example, the XOR gateway decides if the student identity has been validated or not. If identity is validated, the student can proceed and answer questions; otherwise the student cannot appear in the examination.

SIMPLE MERGE

Simple merge is a pattern in which two or more distinct branches are merged without synchronization. Each enablement of an incoming sequence results in enabling of the subsequent activities. If there is more than one enablement, the subsequent activity will be executed more than once. In BPMN, this pattern is supported by a converging XOR gateway.

Example: Grocery Shopping

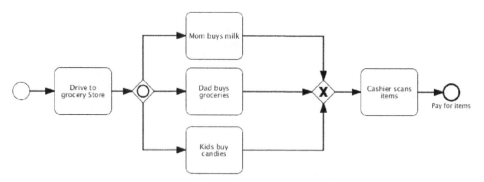

In the grocery shopping example above, every member of the family bringing in items to the checkout counter will result in the cashier scanning the items as they arrive. Mom buying milk, Dad getting groceries and kids getting candies may happen in any order but each time one of the these items arrive, the cashier will scan the items. There would be a problem if there are other customers besides this family waiting in the line for sure!

ADVANCED BRANCHING AND SYNCHRONIZATION PATTERNS

Next we discuss some advanced branching and synchronization patterns. These patterns cover more complex branching and merging concepts. These are fairly common in business processes in real life and support for these is critical to model and support realistic business use cases.

MULTI-CHOICE

This pattern gives the ability to diverge a single thread of execution into multiple concurrent threads based on conditions. In BPMN, this pattern can be modeled using an IOR split gateway or it can also be modeled using conditional sequence flows.

Example: Respond to Emergency

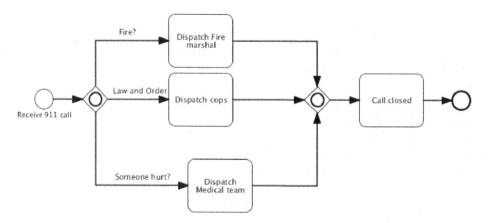

In this example, the response to an emergency call may be dispatching of none, one or more of the three services: fire marshal, police and medical response team, based on the kind of emergency. It is important to note that none of the conditions may evaluate to true and therefore it is advisable to have a default branch with IOR gateways. In this example, we have used an IOR gateway. Alternatively, this can be modeled using three conditional sequence flows.

STRUCTURED SYNCHRONIZING MERGE

The structured synchronizing merge pattern provides a way to merge multiple branches emanating from a specific multi-choice construct into one single outgoing branch. There is an implicit synchronization. This can be considered the counterpart construct for the multi-choice split. In BPMN, the easiest way to model this construct is by using a synchronizing IOR gateway.

Example: Respond to Emergency

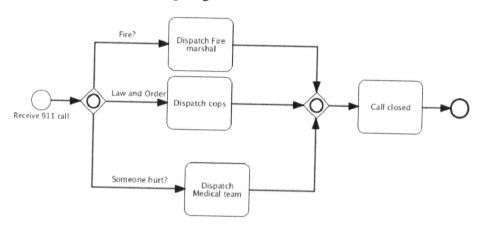

In the example above, respond to emergency, the second IOR gateway synchronizing the closure of the call is an example for the structured synchronizing merge pattern. Depending on which of the three services were dispatched, the call can be closed only after *all* the dispatched services report closure. The second IOR gateway waits for all initiated services to finish, this is the BPMN construct supporting the structured synchronizing merge.

MULTI-MERGE

The multi-merge pattern results in merging of distinct branches into a single branch without synchronization. Each and every active branch would result in activation of downstream activities. In BPMN, this pattern is supported by XOR merging gateway. This gateway will pass the tokens as they arrive to the subsequent activity. The difference between simple merge and multi merge is that it allows for multiple incoming sequences to be active at the same time and it is not necessary for the converging gateway to be safe.

Example: Rank the sprinters

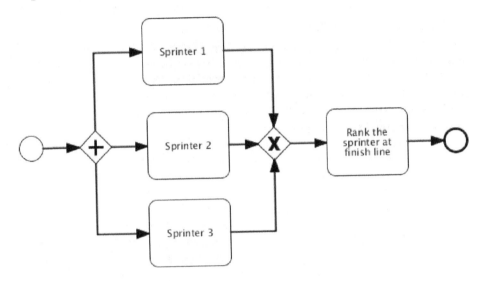

In this example, as the sprinters 1, 2 and 3 crossed the finish line they are ranked by the ranking task. Each time a sprinter crosses the finish line, the ranking tasks will record the relative rank.

THREAD-SPLIT AND THREAD-MERGE

The thread split and thread merge patterns allow a process to spawn a specific number of threads and also consume a number of tokens. The thread split pattern is supported by a multi-instance activity with the specified number of instances. Alternatively, it can also be supported by specifying the number of tokens on the outgoing sequence flow from a task.

The thread merge pattern is supported by the start quantity attribute on the task. This will ensure that a specific number of tokens must arrive for the task to start.

Example: Request for Proposal

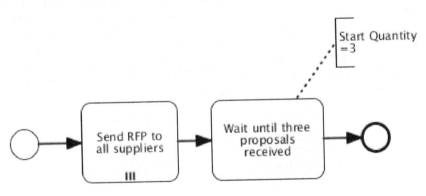

In this example, the request for proposal is sent to all suppliers in parallel. However, the immediate next activity has a start quantity specified as three, which implies that it can execute only after three tokens arrive on it. This is one way of achieving tread split and merge.

STATE-BASED PATTERNS

State-based patterns let user model processes that are aware of the state of the process and also the data associated with the current state of execution. The process may also interact with the environment to define the behavior in state-based patterns.

DEFERRED CHOICE

The deferred choice pattern is where the process chooses one of the branches based on interaction with the external environment. In BPMN this can be achieved using event-based gateway. Another use case would be choosing the value of a process data state or look up the data state from an external source.

Example: Shipment

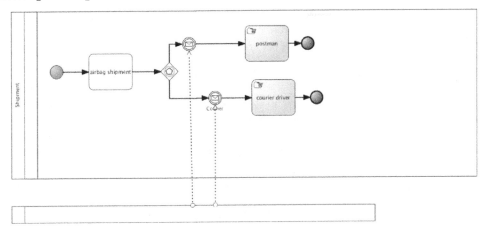

In this example, once the package is ready, it waits for an external event. The external event will either be a pickup by a courier or pickup by the postman. Based on which event occurs first the subsequent activity will be initiated. Alternatively, this pattern can also be supported by using a user task and its outcome to determine which one, of the two alternative paths, gets chosen.

INTERLEAVED ROUTING AND PARALLEL INTERLEAVED ROUTING

The interleaved routing patterns relax the sequencing requirement for activities within a process. There is a partial ordering requirement among a set of tasks for Interleaved parallel routing though. However, they both mandate that only one activity should be active at any given point of time. In BPMN this pattern can be supported by a sequence of ad hoc sub-processes. Further there has to be a notion of state awareness to fully support this pattern as execution environments need to restrict that only one activity should execute at any given point of time.

Example: Ready for School

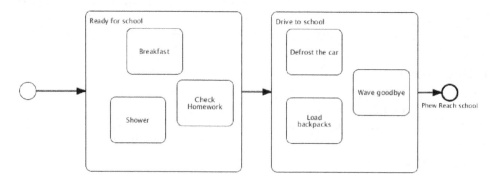

In this example, getting ready for school is a bunch of ad-hoc activities in the morning. The drive to school however, cannot happen unless the kids are ready for school.

ITERATION PATTERNS

Another common class of patterns is iteration patterns. These patterns allow users to model processes where same activities need to be repeated unless a condition specified becomes true. Although there are three iteration patterns, viz. Arbitrary cycles, Structured Loop and Recursion, the most common workflow pattern is structured loop and we cover it here.

STRUCTURED LOOP

The structured Loop is one of the most commonly used iteration pattern. This gives the user ability to execute a task or a set of tasks repeatedly based on a pretest or post-test construct. The loop structure has a single entry and exit point. In BPMN, structured loops can be created by simply connecting XOR gateway with an upstream activity.

Example: Structured Loop

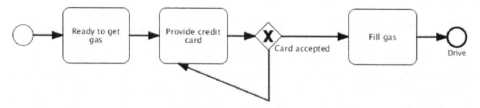

In this example, unless one of the credit cards is accepted, the user cannot get gas. The user does have a choice to provide any number of credit cards until one of them gets accepted.

TERMINATION PATTERNS

Process termination patterns are very important to guarantee usability of standard and product. It is important to let processes terminate if a specific activity is reached. There are two kinds of terminations explicit and implicit.

IMPLICIT TERMINATION

The implicit termination pattern is the most commonly used construct for terminating process instances at any given point in the process. This pattern keeps the diagrams free from clutter as users can terminate the process in case of an error at any given point in the process without having to traverse all the way to a common end event. In BPMN, this is supported by the ability to add end events at any given point in the process.

Example: Loan Flow Implicit Termination

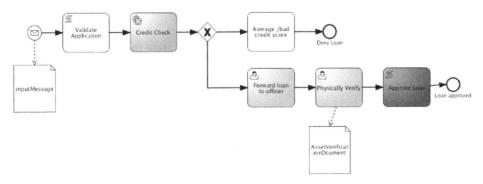

In this example, the sequence of good credit score ends on a different end event as opposed the sequence pertaining to bad credit score.

EXPLICIT TERMINATION

As opposed to implicit termination, explicit termination pattern expects the process to always reach a specific end node. This provides a well-defined successful completion point of a process instance. In terms of usability, the explicit termination pattern mandates a single end event. This is supported by BPMN using a single end event.

Example: Loan Flow Explicit Termination

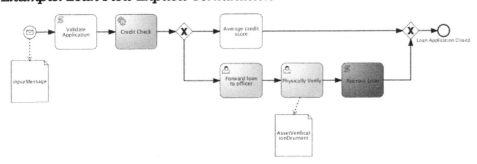

In this example, we redraw the same loan flow example with a single end event. The sequence of good credit score and the sequence pertaining to bad credit score both *must* end at the same end event. This will lead to making diagrams hard to read especially when the diagrams get big.

CONCLUSION

In this chapter we tried to cover some of the common control flow patterns using BPMN 2.0 constructs. There are more than one ways to model any given pattern. For example, an organization might standardize on gateway based patterns or conditional sequence flow pattern. It is more of choice of method and style which option to use for any given pattern.

However, it is advised to have a standard practice across the organization in terms of choosing the method and style. A good understanding of these basic control flow patterns will help you evaluate the everyday business activities you are trying to map into the business process. Also it will enable you to model clear, consistent and comprehensible models which can be executed. I hope this understanding will help bridge the proverbial business IT divide.

Analytics for Performance Optimization of BPMN2.0 Business Processes

Robert M. Shapiro, Global 360, USA
Hartmann Genrich, GMD (retired), Germany

INTRODUCTION

We describe a new approach to process improvement based on the combined use of statistics and simulation to study the structural aspects of process models. Past efforts to use simulation focused on resource optimization have led to some significant successes when coupled with Workforce Management scheduling technology[1], but that approach has not been particularly successful in making structural improvements in the actual processes. The difficulty of preparing satisfactorily detailed schedules, combined with the structural complexities introduced in particular by the event and looping structures in BPMN, requires a fresh look at the problem.

We have developed a tool, the Process Analytica Performance Analyzer, which can do basic timeline analysis of a BPMN model. It is aligned with Bruce Silver's modeling methodology[2]. Not a resource schedule simulation engine, but an analysis engine that is much simpler to use but gives good results for a broad class of processes. Most simulation tools are too focused on the resource bottleneck problem but not so useful (and too hard to use) for the much more common process structure problem, in which resources spend a small fraction of their time on process tasks.

Extensive use is made of spread-sheets both to prepare simulation inputs and work with the analysis. Our major target is business analysts who will be comfortable with the spread-sheet approach. This is a much easier and more efficient way of setting up simulation runs and doing analysis.

Intermediate and Boundary Event simulation properties include probability of occurrence and time of occurrence. Like all simulation parameters, they can be expressions, not just constants. Timer Event is determined by the duration parameter (in combination with the Activity's duration). Error Event on a Subprocess boundary is triggered by an Error End Event in the Subprocess.

Inputs and outputs for Tasks are similar to what is done in typical Lean process improvement/redesign projects. Inputs for Tasks include: PT (processing time) is the active time per instance, with no interruptions; LT (lead time) is the additional time, after starting to work on it, for interruptions. Also important, is the batch time (BT), since work is often batched and forwarded N times a day instead of immediately. The Wait time (WT) is the time before the performer begins work on it. In BPMN terms, the Task has started but the performer has not started work on it yet.

---

[1] Integration of Workforce Management with a Business Process Management Suite, Robert Shapiro, 2008 BPM and Workflow Handbook.

[2] BPMN Method & Style, Bruce Silver, 2009

REQUIRED INPUTS TO THE ANALYSIS

There are three inputs to the analysis:

- A BPMN business model, serialized in either the XPDL format or the BPMN2.0 format.
- An EXCEL Workbook containing the statistical performance characteristics of all the processes in the model.
- An EXCEL Workbook containing the arrival patterns for the work (work items) to be processed.

We discuss the details of these inputs in what follows.

BPMN Business Model

There are a number of modeling tools now available for creating and editing BPMN models. Prior to the completion of BPMN2.0, the only standardized serialization of BPMN models was the xml format defined in XPDL2.1[3]. With the completion of BPMN2.0 there is now a second standardized serialization. The analysis tool accepts either format.

The BPMN2.0 specification[4] defines four types of conformance, namely *Process Modeling* Conformance, *Process Execution* Conformance, *BPEL Process Execution* Conformance and *Choreography Modeling* Conformance. Here we focus on *Process Modeling*. Within Process Modeling there are subclasses. Our focus is the Analytics subclass which we believe is most appropriate for business analysts studying the structural characteristics of business processes. For a complete definition of the Analytics subclass refer to the BPMN2.0 specification.

In addition to the ability to load BPMN models in either serialization, the analysis tool contains an editor which allows visualization of the model and the ability to modify it if need be in the course of studying performance.

The behavioral interpretation of the BPMN model uses certain special features described in **BPMN METHOD & STYLE**.

- Exclusive Data-based Decision Gateways can be linked to End Events in an immediately preceeding Sub-Process by the Names used. The exit path in the Sub-Process then determines which Gate is chosen for Sequence Flow out of the Gateway.
- Error Events on a Sub-Process boundary are linked to Error Events in the Sub-Process.

Statistical Performance Characteristics

The performance characteristics for a model are contained in a single Excel Workbook. A template for the Workbook is generated by the analysis tool based on the model. For each Process or Subprocess in the model there is a set of Sheets. The set consists of three types of Sheets:

- Flow Nodes
- Routes
- Properties

In the discussion that follows we will refer to one sample model which we depict here.

---

[3] XPDL2.2: Incorporating BPMN2.0 Modeling Extensions, 2010 BPM & Workflow Handbook and also XPDL2.1 – Integrating Process Interchange & BPMN http://www.wfmc.org/

[4] Business Process Model and Notation Version 2.0, June 2010, OMG Document Number: dtc/2010-06-05 Standard document URL: http://www.omg.org/spec/BPMN/2.0

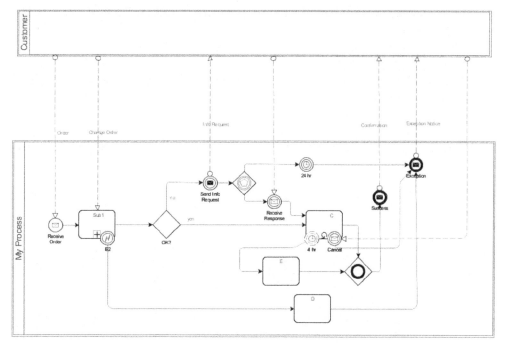

Analysis Example

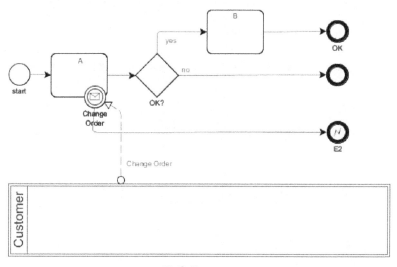

Sub Process

Flow Nodes Sheet

The Activities, Gateways and Events for a Process or Sub-Process are listed as rows on this sheet. Some of the information (columns) are determined by the model and cannot be changed. Other information characterizes the performance. The specifics of the behavior depend on model details.

- Activity: All activities can have Looping or Multi-Instance specifications
- Task: Tasks can have Wait Time, Processing Time, Batch Time and Lead Time specifications.

- Event: All Intermediate and Boundary Events can have a Time-of-Occurrence specification
- Events other than Timer can have a probability specification.
- Exclusive Event-Based Gateways can have a routing rule specification.

Since the intended user of the tool is a Business Analyst rather than an IT professional, these specifications are all done without requiring knowledge of a scripting language (such as JavaScript).

The specification is done by filling in a preformatted Sheet. This is the most efficient way of supplying the simulation specific information. A section of the Sheet for the Sub-Process is depicted in the following diagram:

Name	Id	Node Type	Trig/Result	Duration
<78>	78	end event/None	None	
A	70	task		10.0 (min) with spread: 10 %
B	73	task		20.0 (min) with spread: 10 %
Change		boundary		
Order	81	event/Message	Message	
E2	80	end event/Error	Error	
OK	76	end event/None	None	
OK?	72	exclusiveData gateway		
start	69	start event/None	None	

Flow Node Sheet (partial)

The left four columns are determined by the BPMN model and cannot be changed.

In addition, the tool also supports modification of any specification by user-invoked dialogs. We illustrate with diagrams that show an abbreviated version of the sheet and a dialog for editing the Task specification:

Flow Nodes

Name		Id	Node Type		Duration	Wait Time	Probability	When
<78>		3	end event/None					
A		3	task		10.0 (min) with spread:...	4.0 (min)		
B		3	task		20.0 (min) with spread:...	4.0 (min)		
Change Order		3	boundary event/Message				5.0%	0.0 (min)
E2		3	end event/Error					
OK		3	end event/None					
OK?		3	exclusiveData gateway					
start		3	start event/None					

Abbreviated Sheet Panel

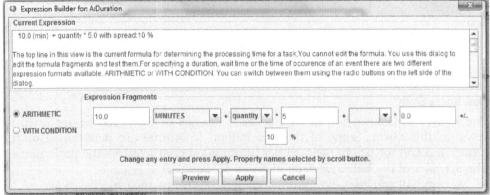

Dialog for Specifying Task Processing Duration

Routes Sheet

The Routes specification determines the rule to use in choosing the exit gate for Sequence Flow out of an Exclusive Data-Based Decision Gateway. The following Sheet fragment shows the specification for the Gateway in the Sub-Process:

Gateway Name	Id	Routing Type	Route Name
OK?	72	defaults	no
			yes

Route Sheet (partial)

In this case the default logic reverts to choosing the exit gate at random. The user could have designated the use of Weights to bias the choice, or the use of Conditional Expressions to select the Gate based on testing properties of the Work Item. If the gateway were preceeded by a sub-process, then if an End Event of that subprocess was labeled (in the BPMN modeler) 'OK' it would control the Gate selection, choosing the 'Yes' Gate only if the subprocess terminated with that End Event.

Properties Sheet

The Properties specification allows the user to define Work Item properties specifically for the analysis. BPMN2.0 uses Data Objects and associated constructs for this purpose. XPDL provides Data Fields. These, if present in the model, provide initial definitions for the Properties specification. The user may extend or override these.

The properties are used in other specifications to allow the handling and behavior of work items to depend upon the values of their properties. This is illustrated in the Dialog for Specifying Task Processing Duration (above) where the value of the 'quantity' property affects the duration calculation. Properties are also commonly used in the condition expressions for routing logic and the time-of-occurrence of Events. The Arrival Patterns supply the property values for Work Items. The following is a snippet from the Properties Sheet:

Property Name	Data Type	Value
quantity	INTEGER	5

Route Sheet (partial)

Arrival Patterns

The Arrival Patterns for executing a model are contained in a single Excel Workbook. A template sheet for the Workbook is generated by the analysis tool based on the model. The template sheet is also influenced by the Properties Sheet just discussed.

Name	ProcessId	Arrival Time:yyyy-MM-dd HH:mm:ss	How Many	quantity
Monday Q20	2	2010-10-25 09:00:00	20	10
Monday Q10	2	2010-10-25 09:00:00	10	5

Arrival Sheet (partial)

ANALYTICS GENERATED BY THE SIMULATION

Applying the statistical specifications to the Arrival Patterns generates a collection of analysis tables and charts. These are all available for interactive use within the tool and for export to EXCEL spreadsheets for independent analysis, depiction and transfer to other tools used by Business Analysts. Here we mention some of the most useful Charts.

History Chart

This chart is an interactive window into the paths taken by all the arriving work items through the BPMN model. Controls allow the user to determine the level of detail, the focus in terms of processes and flow nodes selected, the time frame etc.

The work item paths can be grouped in a variety of ways and a path pattern analyzer uses heuristics to identify the set of unique patterns generated by the complete arrival set.

The representation is based on Gantt charts[5]. The selected set of flow nodes is depicted on the left edge and each flow node that a work item traverses has one or more horizontal bars depicting the start and end times for each occurrence of that node. Parallel paths, critical paths and slack time (synchronization delays) are all depicted. Multiple occurrences of the same activity (e.g. from use of the BPMN Multi-Instance attribute) are folded into a single bar, but can be unfolded as well.

The following chart shows a bird's eye view of the example model, depicting detail only for the top level process, with single bars for each sub-process. The particular path is for a work item that encounters a boundary interrupt during the 6th looping repetition of Task 'C'. (In this example there is no parallelism: parallel paths are associated with parallel gateways and non-interrupting boundary events).

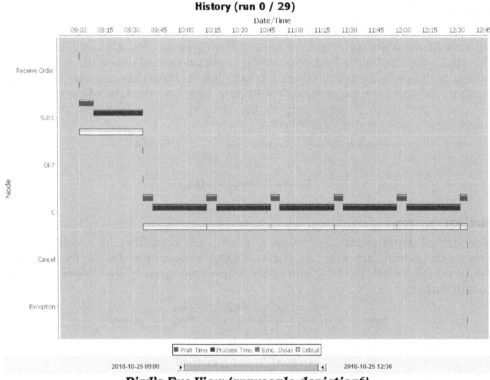

Bird's Eye View (grayscale depiction[6])

---

[5] http://en.wikipedia.org/wiki/Gantt_chart

[6] The Analytics tool uses colors to distinguish the different kinds of bars.

History Filters

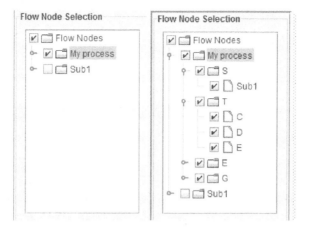

On the left is the setting for the Bird's Eye View. On the right is an Expansion to show scope of selection. Flow node types are S=Sub-Process, T=Task, E=Event, G=Gateway. The node names appear after the page icon.

Run Selection establishes the criteria for grouping paths.
- End States: Groups by the End Events in the top level process.
- Behavior: Groups by the path patterns heuristics which the user can adjust.
- Data fields: Groups by property values of the Work Items.

This ends a brief description of the History controls. We expect that real use by Business Analysts will aid in fine tuning our approach and adding other views that can aid in understanding the behavior of a model. In concluding this section we show one more history chart with some parallelism due to a non-interrupting boundary event.

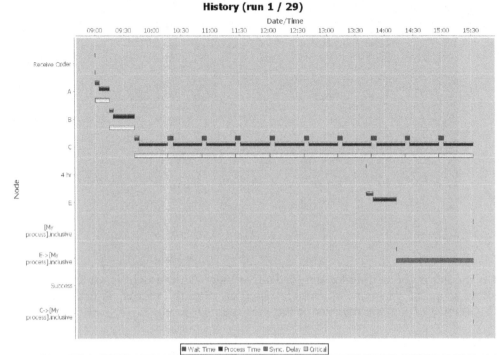

History (run 1 / 29)

Parallel Paths due to non-interrupting Boundary Event

Process Cycle Time

This chart depicts the minimum, maximum and average cycle times for groups of work items and the number of work items in each group. We anticipate broadening the ability to specify the grouping criteria to match the capabilities in the History filters described previously. We are also complementing the choice of presentations to include a Histogram format.

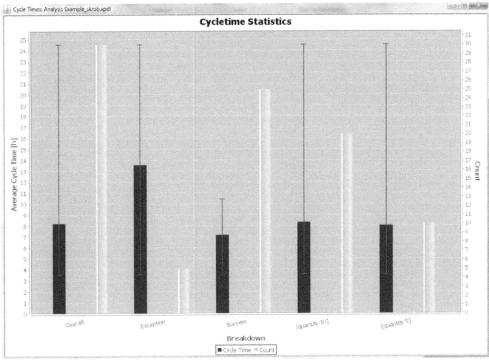

(Grayscale Depiction)

Workload Wait Time and similar charts for Task Specific Durations

These charts make extensive use of color so the depiction in this paper is curtailed.

The Workload chart presents the processing time associated with every Task as a collection of lines, one for each task. The Y axis represents the processing time in a time period and the X axis represents clock time.

The user can determine which tasks to include and which subset of the work items to include, using the same filtering techniques available in the History chart. The user can also choose the size of a time period and the scale for the Y axis.

These controls allow viewing the overall picture of task processing in a single screen, or detailed examination of any time segment. Here is a view generated by our example model:

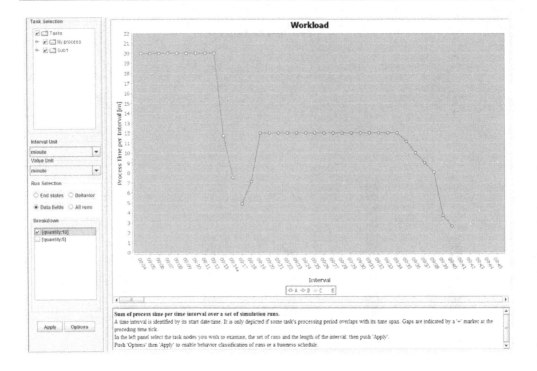

The same viewing technology is used for Wait Time and other Task-related metrics. The data is all exportable to EXCEL.

It should be noted that the Workload statistics is important for determining the resource requirements for a BPM enactment system. It also feeds into the analysis of costs and their allocation. Workload and Wait Time data, combined with critical path information, play an important role in optimization.

Task, Event and Exclusive Data-Based Decision Statistics

These Tables present basic information about the Tasks, Events and Decision Gateways.

History	Process Statistics	Task Statistics	Event Statistics	XOR Statistics				
row ▲	Name	Process	Frequency	Interrupt Fre...	Waittime	Processtime	PT min	PT max	Slacktime
0	C	My process	7.43	0.01	300.722	1,775.785	0	1,800	0
1	E	My process	0.53	0.00	484.666	1,440	1,440	1,440	0
2	<34>	My process	1.60	0.00	0	0	0	0	1,556.774
3	D	My process							
4	A	Sub1	1.00	0.00	240	598.698	540	660	0
5	B	Sub1	0.50	0.00	240	1,229.268	1,080	1,320	0

History	Process Statistics	Task Statistics	Event Statistics	XOR Sta
row ▲	Name	Process	Type	Frequency	Processtime
0	start	Sub1	S	1.00	0
1	<78>	Sub1	E	0.50	0
2	Receive Re...	My process	I	0.43	0
3	4 hr	My process	B	0.53	0
4	Success	My process	E	0.83	0
5	24 hr	My process	I	0.07	0
6	Send Info ...	My process	I	0.50	0
7	Exception	My process	E	0.17	0
8	E2	My process	B		
9	Cancel	My process	B	0.10	0
10	E2	Sub1	E		
11	Change Or...	Sub1	B		
12	Receive Or...	My process	S	1.00	0
13	OK	Sub1	E	0.50	0

History	Process Statistics	Task Statistics	Event Statistics	XOR Statistics
row ▲	Name	Process	Frequency	Branch Frequencies
0	OK?	Sub1	1.00	[<78>:0.50, B:0.50]
1	OK?	My process	1.00	[C:0.50, Send Info Request:0.50]

THE SIMULATION ENGINE AND PERFORMANCE ANALYZER

Engine Architecture

The engine incorporates a novel approach to reduce the amount of time performing a simulation for a large number of work items. Instead of proceeding in strict time order, as the typical discrete event simulator would, the engine follows pathways into the future and if subsequent events cancel a pathway, the log events generated on that pathway are erased. Future experimentation will determine whether this offers any real benefits.

It should be noted that analysis of the log events generated by simulation consumes more CPU power and memory than the simulation proper. That limits the benefits obtainable from a speedup in the engine.

Environment

The Performance Analyzer is currently embedded in the Sketchpad[7] desktop application for creating and editing BPMN models. In principle, it could be divided into two independent web-based facilities. The simulation facility, fed with a BPMN model (using either XPDL or BPMN XML formats) and the two EXCEL Workbooks, would generate a stream of log events for the analytics facility. The analytics facility would deliver the results of analysis (charts, data) to the Business Analyst.

This is a long-term objective. In the meanwhile it is critical that Business Analysts use the tool and provide the feedback necessary to refine the approach and improve the user interface.

Future Extensions

Previous work by the authors focused on Automatic Optimization[8], using a discrete event simulator[9] and sophisticated analysis of historical data generated either by an enactment engine or by the simulator. We are incorporating these ideas so that our tool will be able to generate suggestions for process improvement.

SUMMARY

We have described an ongoing effort to provide performance analysis and business process optimization tools to Business Analysts who currently do this kind of work without building sophisticated process models or simulation of such models. We believe that a sub-class of BPMN2.0 and a tool like the Process Analytica Performance Analyzer could be of value to this community.

---

[7] Sourceforge Open Source project: http://sketchpadbpmn.sourceforge.net/

[8] The AutoOptimizer, Robert Shapiro and Hartmann Genrich, 2009 BPM & Workflow Handbook

[9] The Cape Visions 'Vision Forecaster', used by FileNet/IBM, Fujitsu and Global 360.

Making a BPMN 2.0 Model Executable

Lloyd Dugan, IES, Inc., and
Nathaniel Palmer, SRA International, Inc., USA

INTRODUCTION

The very notion of an executable BPMN model can generate very different reactions. On one hand, BPMS vendors and implementers may agree, since the majority of BPMS platforms run models represented by BPMN. Yet their agreement belies the significant use of embedded business logic and proprietary extensions to make models executable. Process modelers, however, may question whether making a BPMN model executable is even worth pursuing. They might argue that the proper use of BPMN surrounds other purposes than simply creating BPMS applications. Yet this position often stems from a lack of appreciation for what makes models executable, which involves technical concepts perhaps of little interest to modeling purists. What is often missed in the "pure model" versus "executable model" argument, however, is that the same techniques that make BPMN models executable can in fact make models better.

Too often tension exists between the developer and analyst perspectives, resulting from the lack of a common semantics and heuristics set capable of depicting process activities in a way relevant to both parties. One resolution of this is to employ a modeling method able to support models through the round-trip lifecycle from design-time to run-time and back with minimal lossiness. This approach is described as a "model preserving strategy," which is in contrast to the traditional approach of interpreting and recreating models, such as in the handoff from a business analyst to a system analyst. The weakness of this latter, and still today most common, approach is that inevitably, meaning becomes lost with each translation. Further, round-tripping is nearly impossible, given the enormous effort required to transform the executable model back to the original format (essentially the process code re-engineering). The benefits of a model preserving strategy should be obvious, yet support for true round-tripping between pure modeling and BPMS *execution* environment is lacking in most environments, even those based on the BPMN standard. More common today is to rely on scripting languages and proprietary extensions to the BPMN standard to enable executable BPMS-based applications.

The advent of BPMN 2.0 provides a breakthrough in bridging the communication divide through two notable advances. One is an expanded iconic set offering more procedural and message-level behavior than before. The other, and most controversial, is a new serialization format containing implementation details for an executing platform. This chapter proposes a set of minimum characteristics for an executable BPMN 2.0 model as well as modeling guidelines that ensure modeled elements map to executing components. This approach applies to all areas of BPMN modeling, but is also necessary for leveraging the emerging class of BPMS environment where processes orchestrate services within a Service Component Architecture (SCA) composite.[1] The result is a design pattern for implementing BPMN processes that is particularly applicable to applications that run as services and leverage SOA components.

Yet the advent of a serialization format does not alone resolve the issues otherwise surrounding executable models. Well-designed models require the first principles of modeling to ensure that design-time BPMN constructs follow the necessary characteristics of an executable model. This is particularly important for environments that purge the BPMS layer of most (if not all) core business logic, instead orchestrating invoked services that components of capabilities. In the examples that follow, this approach is illustrated by using specific task types and swimlanes to map to SCA components. Also presented is the recommended approach for mapping an XML expression of BPMN, either the serialized version of BPMN or XPDL, to and from an XML expression of an SCA composite.

MARKET OVERVIEW FOR BPMN AND SCA REALIZATION

With most of the BPMS market having moved away from proprietary notational sets, BPMN today represents the most common approach to configuring process definitions within target execution environments. BPMN modeling evolved out of a desire to represent business processes in a standard way that allowed differing levels of articulation and abstraction to be realized for different audiences. Historically, however, translating BPMN diagrams to an executable framework has been plagued with the challenges and risks described previously. Partial realization of BPMN 1.1 to date has meant that not all associated BPMN constructs were supported and that those that were supported possessed some limitations as a result of how the enabling platform permitted their configuration.

Few BPMS vendors have offered the BPMS platform along with SOA-implementing technologies (e.g., BPEL) as is necessary to support true, SOA-style deployments of BPMS applications. Rather, the majority of BPMS platforms only supported consumption of external Web services within modeled process activities or exposure of modeled processes as Web services for external consumption. Admittedly the BPM/SOA relationship is better realized among Java EE platform vendors, due in large part to tighter integration between the application server and the BPMS environment. Yet, the use of BPMS applications as components within SCA composite deployments is still rare, as SCA remains relegated to the province of deep Java programming with extensions only available for BPEL.

A common characteristic among all BPMS platforms is the assumed control of both data flow and message flow. This often results, however, in a disconnect between design-time and run-time constructs, as service invocations by definition lack transparency. This is the core concept of loose-coupling and service-orientation – the properly designed service describes how to access it and what it provides, but not how it achieves the result. The BPMS defines when the service is invoked, what it gives the service, and what it gets back, hence abstraction and orchestration, and the purging of business logic (e.g., that which is performed by the service). Although this is an accepted pattern within the BPMS community, business analysts will seek to design the process holistically. The translation between design and execution is immediately lossy. Similarly, while a BPMN model designed in the BPMS platform offers strong expression and realization of basic workflow design patterns, (e.g., sequence, parallelism, conditional flow, etc.), it typically fails to support the expression and realization of message exchange patterns (MEPs) that could otherwise be clearly expressed with BPMN.

The BPMN specification prior to version 2.0 had yet to recognize the different constituencies that BPMN served. In practice, this resulted in the BPMS vendors deciding which constructs to support (as well as how to support them) and the process modelers deciding which constructs to use (as well as how to use them).

In the case of the former, this led to inconsistencies across BPMS platforms of what an executable model should look like, as different BPMS vendors utilized their own unique subset of BPMN elements. Though XPDL is available and supported by many BPMS platforms as a model interchange format, it does not impose any specific notation. In the case of the latter, the lack of a standard usage pattern has led to an "80/20 rule" (or more accurately 90/10) in which the majority models are built with a limited number of available BPMN elements.[2]

Another factor that has complicated the development of executable process models is the misunderstanding of BPEL as an executable expression of BPMN. The limitation is that the full equivalence of BPMN cannot be expressed in BPEL, thus BPMS platforms cannot fully interpret and execute BPMN models as BPEL script. In addition, BPMS applications and BPEL processes typically execute in separate application server containers, making simultaneous translation and execution problematic to implement. The result has been confusion and disagreement over what BPMN was and/or what it should be doing, with different and entrenched camps forming and pursuing very different agendas.

Against the backdrop of all of these developments, the OMG still managed to develop the BPMN 2.0 specification, which purported to make executable process models possible. In an earlier era, this might have been characterized as simply another attempt to realize visual programming as a development paradigm, fulfilling the long-standing yet unfulfilled promise of computer-aided, software engineering (CASE) tools. However, CASE tools never escaped reliance on a significant level of coding, mostly because the modeling techniques lacked sufficiently rich semantics to make truly executable process models.

Where the emerging class of BPMN 2.0-compliant environments transcends what was offered by either CASE tools or previous generations of BPMS environments is through the ability to fully present both a visual and executable model using a single environment for all BPM functions and SOA components. This advance allows design-time constructs to map cleanly and with little or no intermediating translation to run-time equivalents. In addition, assembling SCA components into executing composites now explicitly includes BPMS applications (BPMN processes) as well as SOA-implementing technologies (BPEL, human workflow, business rules engine, and local service bus). The Oracle 11g platform, for example, now permits BPMN constructs to not only define process sequences, but also to call out (and render explicitly in the model) the service components that support BPMN tasks and events. Unifying BPM and SOA technologies makes it possible to achieve enterprise-wide solutions as sets of services rather than as disparate systems, which can be codified into design patterns for such solutions.

CREATING AN EXECUTABLE BPMN MODEL

The BPMN 2.0 specification adds new execution-oriented design elements, offering a notional definition of what makes a model executable. While an important development, this is still insufficient for establishing the parameters of a well-designed executable model. Such criteria must come from a methodological context to ensure that the resulting model exhibits the desired features and contains elements that explicitly map to implementing components.

BPMN 2.0 Requirements

The first set of requirements is implicit. The model must be syntactically correct with respect to the BPMN 2.0 notational specification, meaning that only BPMN 2.0 constructs are used and that connections or relationships among constructs are correct. Since executing BPMS platforms will assume the span of control, a model must be a collaboration diagram, shown as collapsed pools, (for participants other than the main one) and a process diagram within its own pool for the BPMS platform, (as the main participant) containing swimlanes for the BPMS engine and any user roles engaging with the application.

The second set of requirements is explicitly stated in the BPMN 2.0 specification and represents one of its more innovative breakthroughs.[3]

The designer tool in which the model was created must support the BPMN execution semantics required by the Process Execution Conformance Class Type, which includes using only those elements and attributes defined as belonging to the Common Executable Conformance Sub-Class (as a sub-class of the Process Modeling Conformance Class). Execution details must be incorporated as model attributes and information that are contained in a serialized XML expression of the model, which is presumably how an executable model would be exported to and imported from an implementation platform.

Other requirements dictate how processed information, service invocation interfaces, and business logic are to be expressed in the model:

- The data type definition language used must be XML schema documents (XSDs), which ensures conformance of exchanged messages to desired message structures
- The service interface definition language used must be WSDL, which means service invocations are either for or as Web services
- The data access language used must be XPath, which standardizes the scripting language to be used where/when it is needed.

These requirements help formalize what the handoff from an analyst to a developer would be with respect to a BPMN model moving to be executable. It is a beneficial (and presumably intended) result that the requisite BPMN constructs map reasonably well (albeit not 100%) to subset of commonly used elements.[4]

First Principles of Process Modeling

The term "first principles" means that "[for] a formal logical system, that is, a set of propositions that are consistent with one another, it is probable that some of the statements can be deduced from one another…[but] a first principle is one that cannot be deduced from any other…[and] all propositions can be deduced from a set of definitions, postulates, and common notions…all three of which constitute "first principles.".[5] In the case of process and service modeling, these are principles that represent irreducible concepts and approaches that transcend a specific use within a modeling technique or by a supporting modeling tool and that get at the heart of what must be analyzed in creating an abstract representation of a set of executable activities.

These principles amount to modeling conventions and other guidance to follow, which can be considered a set of best practices. The principles put forward here emerged from attempts to integrate process and service modeling under a unified approach and are focused on making a model more suitable for execution. Similar principles can be espoused for models that are not seeking to be executable, and attempts to formalize such principles will encourage their use and help to ensure more consistency in the creation of good models.[6]

The principles stated below cover the different levels of describing the expected behavior of the to-be-designed system's functionality. This covers the "what" of the functional requirements to be satisfied, the "how" of the operations to be executed, and the "what-how" of characterizations that fall somewhere in between.

THE "WHAT" OF FUNCTIONAL REQUIREMENTS:

Functional Decomposition from a To-Be Business Architecture:

Modeled activities consist of functions and processes that reflect a to-be business architecture that is functionally decomposed into appropriately named activities with similar or homogenous operations, rules, and data at successively lower levels.[7] This decomposition ends with functionally pure process primitives that do not need to be decomposed further for modeling the processing of transactions. Functions and sub-functions should be named with nouns or noun phrases to indicate the ongoing nature of the modeled activities without start and end points. Processes and sub-processes should be named with verbs or verb phrases to indicate the instantiation of the modeled activities with start and end points.

Incorporation of Relevant Business Factors:

Processes are broken down based on applicable business factors, consisting of one or more specific functional requirements or business alignment considerations (e.g., a business driver, need, or metric that is affecting an organization). These factors are explicitly accounted for by specific elements within the model. These modeled elements isolate the business factors to allow for the direct capture, monitoring, and reporting of business performance information as the modeled processes are instantiated, (e.g., showing compliance with applicable regulation or legislation), helping to ensure that the developed application has a tight alignment with the business value for such a system.

THE "WHAT-HOW" OF TWEENER FUNCTIONAL REQUIREMENTS/OPERATIONS:

Rationalization to Leverage Reusable and Callable Components:

Modeled processes have been rationalized to consolidate similar activities and data into reusable and callable sub-processes. Such sub-processes are candidate services to be orchestrated or otherwise leveraged within the process model. This approach effectively picks up where decomposition leaves off, fulfilling the latter's true raison d'être.

Explicit Recognition of Process Transaction State Transitions:

Inter-process and intra-process transaction state transitions are distinctly represented and determined within the modeled processes. State transitions are moments in a process sequence when meaningful state is changed or created. Accounting for these transitions helps to ensure that transaction processing activities are sufficiently broken apart such that the workflow stages are explicitly realized. State values move from the initial null (blank) value through and among one or more interim values to one or more terminal values that may be final.

Application of Cohesion and Coupling Programming Principles:

Cohesion describes how closely related the elements are to each level of decomposition, (i.e., cohesion is a measure of relatedness of sub-processes), while coupling describes how closely related each element in the decomposition is to elements that are not siblings.[8] The term "strongly coupled" means having many dependencies and/or strong dependencies that require detailed knowledge be shared among activities for a flow to occur, while the term "loosely coupled" means having few dependencies and/or weak dependencies that require little knowledge be shared among activities for a flow to occur. Modeled processes should show higher cohesion and looser coupling among the higher levels of the model and lower cohesion and stronger coupling within the lower levels of the model.

Separation of Execution Responsibilities By Actors and Roles:

Modeled activities are separated by appropriate pools for participants and by swimlanes for roles within a pool to accurately reflect different scopes of responsibility. Accounting for these different scopes helps to ensure that transaction processing activities are sufficiently broken apart such that executing operations are unambiguously performed by a specific and single resource.

Application of Design Patterns and Use of Design Primitives:

Established design patterns for workflows and message exchanges are represented within the model, typically using standard design primitives from best practices for each. Workflow patterns dictate the flow of work, information, and decision-making in a process sequence.[9] MEPs formalize how interfaces are realized among different participants.[10] Primitives are the smallest, functionally pure activity that processes a limited number of inputs into outputs and leaves the organization in a consistent state (after execution) while it also provides a meaningful business result.[11]

THE "HOW" OF OPERATIONS:

Satisfaction of Transaction Processing Context and Integrity Needs:

A transaction is a formal relationship between two or more participants that is communicated among them and binds them to a stable, persistent outcome.[12] Modeled activities define the context for managing the transaction being processed, including where persistence of the state of the transaction is required by the system, and when error handling and compensation are needed. The resulting modeled transaction should exhibit ACID properties[13]:

1) **Atomicity** wherein the input/output of the processing of the transaction completes or is completely undone if there is error, (e.g., an edit or validation test is failed), which would be achieved via error-handlers that correct, roll-back, or compensate for initial state changes made in processing the transaction;

2) **Consistency** in that the persisted result is a consistent change in state;

3) **Isolation** in that the state being changed is insulated from any change attempted by other processes;

4) **Durability** in that the change is assured.

Finally, the transaction processing operation that persists the transaction's state should yield the same result every time it is tried, which makes it idempotent.[14]

Abstraction of Executing Service Components and Mapping to SCA:

Modeled activities to be abstracted as executing service components have been so designated and appropriately configured for the implementing platform, including SCA wiring. A Business Rule Task is abstracted to a Business Rules Engine (BRE) that is invoked as a type of decision service. A User Task is abstracted to a Human Workflow (HW) that realizes a user interface. A Call Activity maps to a BPMN sub-process wherein the modeled elements and activities are to be executed by the component that implements them. Thus, a Call Activity abstracts to another BPMN process that is implemented by the BPMS, a BPEL process that is implemented by a BPEL Engine, or a Local Service Bus (LSB) process that is implemented by an LSB. A Service Task is abstracted to an external reference service as a WSDL invocation. This can include anything that can be so exposed, e.g., a Notification Service that provisions the sending of an e-mail message, which would be an alternative to using a Send Task in the same way.

Reconciliation of Process vs. Service Component Granularity:

Granularity refers to the "fineness" or "coarseness" of a modeled activity.[15] It describes the fine-grained or coarse-grained characteristic of the operations executed by an activity, the data being communicated and/or manipulated by an activity, or a combination of both. Metaphorically speaking, an activity that is more fine-grained is like a basic Lego block. Granularity conflicts emerge in service modeling when the service requester has processing and information needs that are not directly addressed by the component provisioning the service. To keep the service requester loosely coupled with respect to the service, the service itself must reconcile the input/output aspects of the service by using components that further abstract the underlying sources of granularity conflict, incorporating transformational business logic to smooth out such conflict, or some combination of both. More accurately understood as EAI middleware than a true BPMS platform, a BPEL or LSB process is well suited for this purpose, since the problem these technologies tackle is one of integration.

METHODOLOGICAL CONSIDERATIONS

A BPMN model is compliant with these first principles when the modeled activities conform to the described conventions and guidelines. Application of these principles must occur within a methodological context that both directs and constrains the analysis that creates a process model, including a BPMN model. Most modeling efforts are top-down in orientation, which is a reasonable way to capture the business requirements that an automated solution must satisfy. Yet, when an application implements a modeled process is intended to orchestrate or otherwise leverage services, there must be a bottom-up perspective that informs the modeler when new or existing functionality may be invoked, as well as what functionality must be built or modified to resolve granularity differences between the to-be process and the services coming from legacy systems, to-be built systems, or some combination thereof. This alternative perspective must be identified and analyzed in parallel with the top-down analyses, and any tensions in perspectives are resolved within the designed process models, particularly at the lower levels, as shown in Figure 1 below.

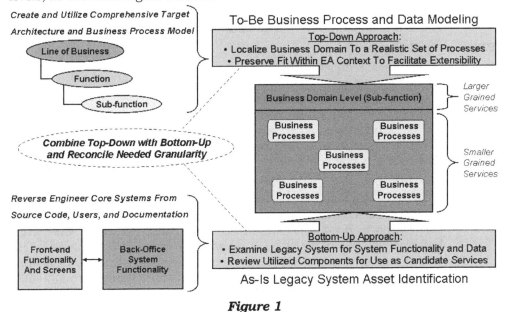

Figure 1

While the principles of top-down process modeling are widely and (usually) well understood by modelers, the same is not the case with respect to the legacy system analysis that bottom-up modeling requires. (This is likely the result of an aversion to such thinking as being too programming-like or implementation-specific, which is not as legitimate a claim when dealing with services.) Fortunately, strong techniques for modeling legacy systems exist that require only a limited form of reverse-engineering to identify the input/output relationships among different types of programs. One such approach focuses on classifying programs as Root programs that call other programs, Leaf programs that are called by other programs, or Node programs that can either be called, call other programs, or both.[16] Figure 2 below shows how this approach can be used to isolate the behavior of a legacy system. Using this technique is part of identifying the relationships among legacy systems, which is necessary to identify the points where these programs may be invoked as services, as well as to define the data requirements that such invocations must satisfy.

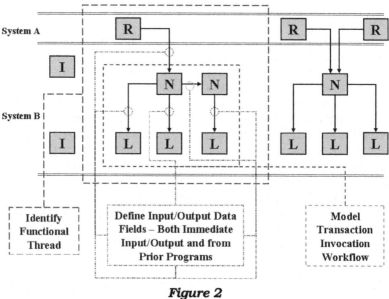

Figure 2

BPMN vs. SCA Composite

A BPMN model is a representation of modeled processes, which represents a process-oriented view of orchestration, but an SCA composite is a representation of service composition, which represents a wiring-oriented view of orchestration. Thus, a BPMN model is focused primarily on showing sequence flow, but the SCA composite is focused foremost on showing message flow in an SCA composite diagram.[17] A BPMN model abstracts invoked components, but an SCA composite makes explicit those same components and how they connect with each other. With the dual maturation of BPMN and SOA, SCA components implementing services have become more or less standardized, as summarized in Table 1 below.

BPEL	BPEL is used for situations in which management of a workflow is not needed, (which would be handled by the BPMS), but where some level of orchestration of activities is otherwise required. For example, it is used to implement synchronous message exchange through calls and responses, as well as asynchronous message exchange through callbacks or by dehydrating while waiting for responses. It is also leve-

	raged to enforce transactional integrity through compensation activities within a BPEL process and the interaction with system interfaces.
BRE	A BRE instantiates a simple or complex rule set as a standalone decision service. It is used for situations in which it is better to embody the rule set within a single service call rather than as several modeled activities. A BRE has no responsibility for managing a transaction other than to return a result based on the evaluation of its data.
LSB	An LSB routes messages and does rudimentary transformations while interfacing with service requesters and service providers. An LSB is a light-weight version of an Enterprise Service Bus (ESB) and is used when the routing and transformation logic is simple, leaving BPEL or even BPMN to address more complex routing and transformation logic. An LSB process is generally not concerned with transactional integrity, since this was the province of the service to which a message would be routed (and where, for example, a business transaction or a system transaction would require such treatment).

Table 1

How a BPMS implements the execution of SCA components is part-and-parcel of how the BPMS realizes BPMN. This is easily shown by examining a simple request/response MEP. Expressed as a design primitive, this is shown as message flows between two pools wherein throwing and catching message events are mirrored and reversed between a requester and a responder, as shown in Figure 3 below.[18] This representation allows for no distinction between a composite component that is invoked and a participant external to the composite that is called.

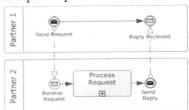

Figure 3

This expression is too verbose for the actual BPMS platform, which cannot show in its own designer tool the provisioning process flow, since it is outside the BPMS platform's span of control. Instead, the BPMS platform will design and realize the upper half of the modeled sequence as shown in Figure 4 below, which shows the service invocation as configuration in a service task to make a WSDL invocation.[19] However, this representation still equates all invocations with message flows.

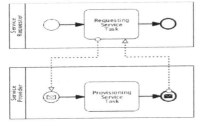

Figure 4

What is needed is a set of conventions that will ensure that a set of BPMN models will explicitly map to implementing SCA components, as proposed in Figure 5 below. This layered abstraction fulfills evolutionary potential of BPM to be a true orchestration engine wherein the BPMS contains little if any core business logic, having abstracted such functionality to loosely-coupled service components.[20]

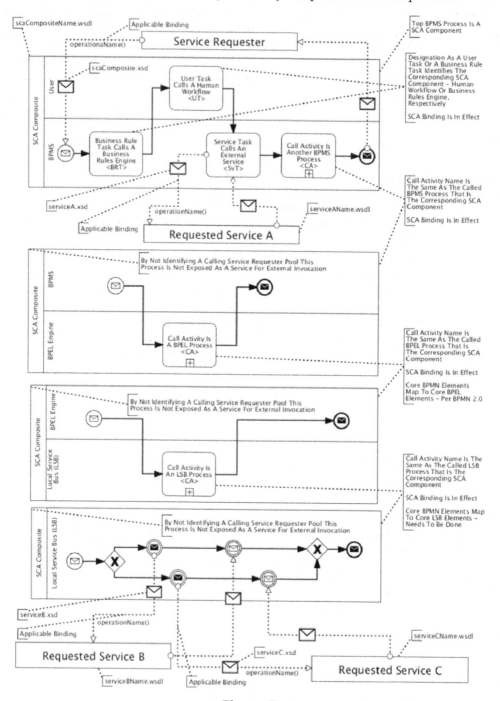

Figure 5

The SCA composite that maps to the collected set of the BPMN models above is shown in Figure 6 below, illustrating service composition and wiring.

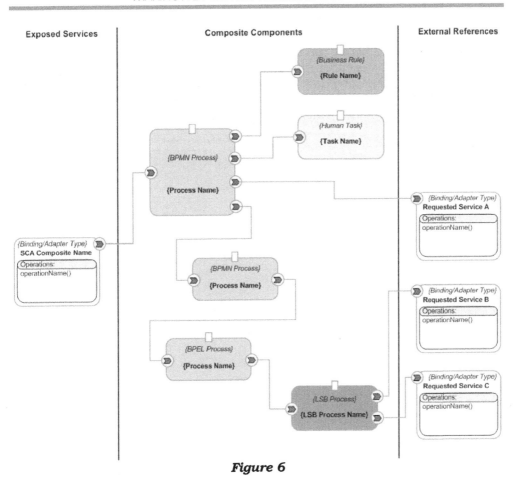

Figure 6

SAMPLE MODEL AND DESIGN PATTERN

Application of the modeling principles presented here can be illustrated through a sample model created for just such a purpose. What follows below are a series of BPMN collaboration and process diagrams that collectively map to an SCA composite diagram that wires together the various service components*. The model shown here is for a deployable construct that interacts with service requesters, service providers, and its own components in an entirely synchronous request/response MEP.

The sample model below passes a syntax check and conforms to the Process Execution Conformance Class Type. It consists of activities that either abstract to implementing components that contain the actual business logic or are simple script tasks that only manage transaction data. The resulting design pattern is something that is mostly stateless (save for two instances of persisting state in a database), but explicitly manages the status of the transaction such that the construct can correctly and resiliently respond in a completely synchronous manner with any entity invoking it. As oxymoronic as it sounds, this is a "stateless state machine" that is deployed as a service and created as an executable BPMN model.

---

* A fuller set of artifacts and explanatory material for this model are provided on the **BPMN 2.0 Handbook CD** available from the Publisher, Future Strategies Inc. www.FutsStrat.com.

BPMN Model

As shown in Figure 7 below, the top-level BPMN model shows a process for quali-
fying a candidate who is either evaluated by a recruiter or interviewed by a potential employer. Qualify Candidate has two child processes: Pre-screen Candidate
and Interview Candidate. The inbound message that triggers the top-level process
is checked for conformance with the XSD and then routed for processing.

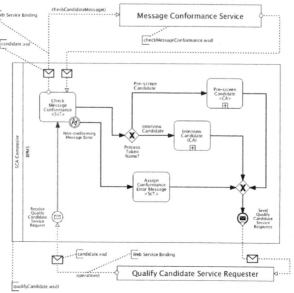

Figure 7

Each of the two call activities maps to corresponding sub-processes. Pre-screen
Candidate is used by a recruiter to evaluate the suitability of a candidate for a
subsequent interview and to schedule that interview, as shown in Figure 8 below.

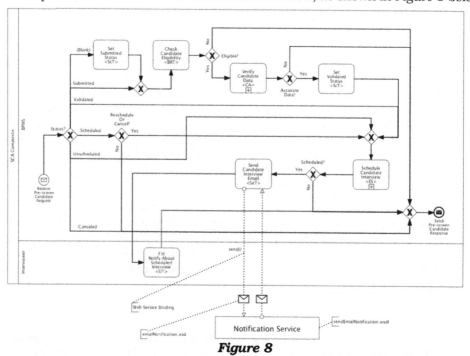

Figure 8

Interview Candidate is used by an interviewer to score a candidate to recommend a hiring decision and to override a negative recommendation if desired, as shown in Figure 9 below. Note that each sub-process uses the same call activity, Verify Candidate Data, to check certain data against an authoritative source.

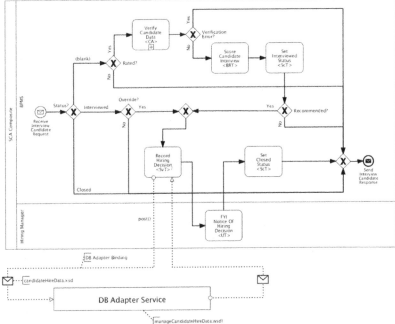

Figure 9

The embedded sub-process for Schedule Candidate Interview is expanded in Figure 10 below, which reveals the internal activities for persisting scheduling data via SQL over a database adapter service rather than natively via SQL over JDBC.

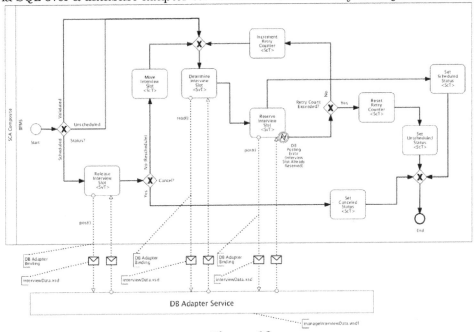

Figure 10

While the call activity for Verify Candidate Data is a BPMS process, it performs a call activity, Check Authoritative Sources. Implemented as a BPEL process, the latter is shown in the BPEL swimlane in Figure 11 below.

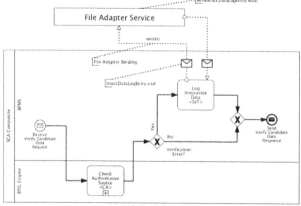

Figure 11

The elements modeled therein conform to the BPEL Execution Conformance Class Type. While the call activity for Check Authoritative Sources is a BPEL process, it performs a call activity, Route Data Verification Request. Implemented as an LSB process; the latter is shown in the LSB swimlane in Figure 12 below.

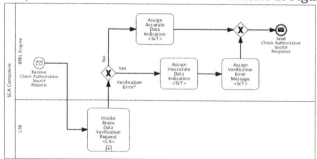

Figure 12

The elements map to the standard functions of an LSB (e.g., simple routing of messages) per Figure 13 below. Though such a mapping as is proposed here must still be formalized (as has already been done for BPEL) the elements used in the diagram below align well with the design primitive for the request/response MEP shown earlier, since it only manages message flows.

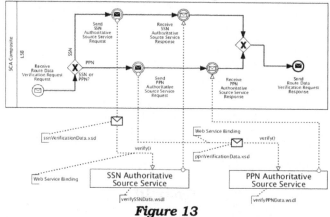

Figure 13

The conformance of this sample model to the modeling principles presented here is described in Table 2 below.

THE "WHAT"
Functional Decomposition from a To-Be Business Architecture

A to-be enterprise-wide business architecture decomposes through functions and processes:
• HR Management function at the top level decomposes into multiple sub-functions, including Hiring – not shown, but is assumed
• Hiring sub-function decomposes into multiple processes, including Qualify Candidate – not shown, but is assumed
• Qualify Candidate process decomposes into multiple sub-processes:
  • Pre-screen Candidate – invoked by a Recruiter
  • Interview Candidate – invoked by an Interviewer
• Pre-screen Candidate sub-process consists of elements that do not decompose further except for the called sub-process Verify Candidate Data and the embedded sub-process Schedule Candidate Interview
• Interview Candidate sub-process consists of elements that do not decompose further, except for the called sub-process Verify Candidate Data

Incorporation of Relevant Business Factors
Qualifications are tracked against the eligibility rule for the job being sought
Accuracy of select candidate data is checked against authoritative sources, and occurrences of inaccurate data are recorded in an error log
THE "WHAT-HOW"
Rationalization To Leverage Reusable and Callable Components
Pre-screen Candidate and Interview Candidate sub-processes each need to verify the accuracy of candidate data, which occurs at different times for each sub-process, thus the same Verify Candidate Data is called as a reusable sub-process wherein similar activities and data are consolidated
Explicit Recognition of Process Transaction State Transitions

The value of Candidate Status in the triggering message is moved through different statuses:
• Pre-screen Candidate sub-process transaction state transitions:
  Blank – null value at time of initial submission
  Submitted – first assigned value at initial submission
  Validated – interim assigned value if data is validated
  Scheduled – interim/terminal assigned value if interview is scheduled
  Unscheduled – interim assigned value if interview is unscheduled
  Canceled – terminal assigned value if interview is canceled
• Interview Candidate sub-process transaction state transitions:
  Blank – null value at time of initial submission
  Interviewed – first assigned value at initial submission
  Closed – terminal assigned value after hiring decision is recorded

Table 2

Application of Cohesion and Coupling Programming Principles
Pre-screen Candidate and Interview Candidate sub-processes fit logically into end-to-end sequences within the Qualify Candidate process to show high cohesion, but each executes independently to show loose coupling
Activities within each sub-process are logical only within the context of that sub-process to show low cohesion with respect to other sub-processes, but high coupling within each specific sub-process

Separation of Execution Responsibilities by Participants and Roles
Participants are in separate pools to indicate separate scopes of control, which are represented by collapsed pools for all but the main pool: <ul><li>Qualify Candidate Service Requester calls the process as a service, which is represented by proxy in a collapsed pool for both the Recruiter (for the Pre-screen Candidate sub-process) and the Interviewer (for the Interview Candidate sub-process)</li><li>SCA Composite for the Qualify Candidate Service (the actual application)</li><li>Message Conformance Service that checks the XSD conformance of inbound triggering messages – not needed if an interceding ESB is used</li><li>DB Adapter Service for SQL operations against the Interview/Hire DB</li><li>File Adapter Service for the file writing operations for the Error Log</li><li>SSN Authoritative Source Service for validating candidate SSN data</li><li>PPN Authoritative Source Service for validating candidate PPN data</li><li>Notification Service for sending interview email via an SMTP server</li></ul>
Roles within the SCA Composite for the Qualify Candidate Service are represented as swimlanes for the implementing SCA components: <ul><li>BPMS – for the top-level and called BPMN processes (Qualify Candidate, Pre-screen Candidate, Interview Candidate, and Verify Candidate Data)</li><li>BPEL Engine – for the called BPEL process (Check Authoritative Source)</li><li>LSB – for the called LSB process (Route Data Verification Request)</li><li>Human Workflow Roles (for non-interrupting user tasks as interfaces):<ul><li>Interviewer (for the FYI Notice of Scheduled Interview User Task)</li><li>Hiring Manager (for the FYI Notice of Hiring Decision User Task)</li></ul></li></ul>

Application of Design Patterns and Use of Design Primitives
Each process or sub-process shows established workflow patterns of sequence, split, and join
Each interaction with and within the entire construct is a synchronous request/response MEP: <ul><li>Each invocation of the Qualify Candidate Service process is synchronous request/response, shown as the exposed service in the associated SCA composite</li><li>Each call of a service component is either synchronous request/response (for BPEL and LSB processes) or the functional equivalent (for BPMN processes and Business Rule and Human Workflow tasks), shown as wired components within the associated SCA composite</li></ul>
Each call of an external service is synchronous request/response (for adapter services or external Web services), shown as external references in the associated SCA composite

Table 2 (cont'd.)

THE "HOW"

Satisfaction of Transaction Processing Context and Integrity Needs

The core transaction is defined by an XSD and consists of a set of Candidate data that is being messaged and processed throughout the modeled activities

Process activities performed by the BPMS are mostly stateless with respect to the transaction, though these activities manage the status of the transaction through the workflows

State is persisted when the Candidate interview is scheduled and when the Candidate hiring decision is made, using the two-phase commit feature of the database used by the Database Adapter to ensure transactional integrity and to obviate any need for compensation, which collectively makes the transaction ACID

Conformance for the inbound request message is checked against the applicable XSD, with the error noted in the response message

Posting of scheduled interview data for a Candidate may error out if another instance has already posted such a record, which routes to another attempt to look up an available slot

Through the use of status checks and routing, the service tasks that persist, either scheduling or hiring data, can only post a set of data once, even if requests are subsequently submitted after processing, which makes the processing idempotent

Abstraction of Executing Service Components and Mapping to SCA

Appropriate modeled activities have been designated as being implemented through abstracted service components:
- Call Activity (CA): Pre-screen Candidate, Interview Candidate, and Verify Candidate Data BPMS sub-processes; Check Authoritative Source BPEL sub-process, and Route Data Verification Request LSB sub-process
- Service Task (SvT): Check Message Conformance, Write Inaccurate Data Log Entry, Determine Interview Slot, Record Scheduled Interview, Release Scheduled Interview, and Send Interview E-mail
- Business Rules Task (BRT): Check Candidate Eligibility, and Score Candidate Interview
- Human Workflow User Tasks (UT): FYI Notice of Scheduled Interview (for the Interviewer) and FYI Notice of Hiring Decision (for the Hiring Manager)

Reconciliation of Process vs. Service Component Granularity

The Check Authoritative Source BPEL process works to smooth granularity differences in the processing of data returned via the subordinate calls to the relevant authoritative sources for verifying Candidate data based on social security number (SSN) or a passport number (PPN), which implements the SOA design pattern for smoothing over data exchange known as "contract denormalization" [21]

An LSB process routes outbound messages, based on whether the Candidate data contains an SSN or a PPN, and shown as a wired component in the SCA composite with wires to the services invoked from the authoritative sources

Table 2 (cont'd.)

SCA Composite

The corresponding SCA composite diagram for the collective set of BPMN models is presented below in Figure 14. It shows the composition and wiring of service components within the SCA composite that is the construct to be deployed.

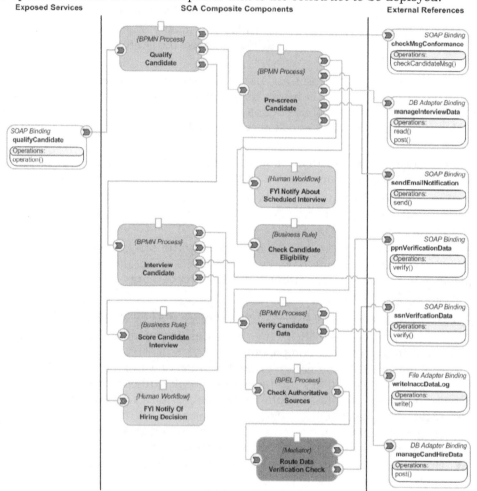

Figure 14

This representation shows how process decomposition and reuse in BPMN models look in an executable configuration. It also gives these concepts meaning within an execution context and should guide process modelers in the creation of executable models. Similarly, the use of BPEL and LSB processes and user interfaces realized as human workflows, all represented as modeled elements, gives those concepts meaning within an execution context and should also guide process modelers in the creation of executable models.

XML REPRESENTATION AND NEXT STEPS

A serialized expression of a BPMN model is claimed by two different realizations: XPDL, which is pushed by the WfMC, and BPMN XML, which is pushed by the OMG. [22] With the advent of BPMN 2.0, the latter realization will likely prevail as BPMS vendors seek to support the specification. This means that it will become the means by which implementation detail is inserted into an executable model. This already includes things like operation name and a place for XPath expressions, but could also include more of the information that the SCA composite XML file contains, which includes component type and binding type.

With some tweaking, such a conversion needs only an XSLT transformation to make it work. [23]

ENDNOTES

---

[1] Most literature on SCA still speaks to Java programmers, but it is hoped that literature about SCA as a means of designing systems around typical SOA technologies will be forthcoming. Two informative books on SCA are SOA for the Business Developer: Concepts, BPEL, and SCA, by Ben Margolis with Joseph L. Sharpe, MC Press (2007) {ISBN 1-58347-065-4}, and Understanding SCA, by Jim Marino and Michael Rowley, part of the Independent Technology Guides by Pearson Education, Inc., Addison Wesley (2010) {ISBN 978-0-321-51508-7}.

[2] This controversial result is but one of many important findings in, *How Much Language is Enough? Theoretical and Practical Use of BPMN* at http://www.stevens.edu/ses/documents/fileadmin/documents/pdf/MIZU-JARE-BPMN-CAiSE-2008.pdf, authored by Assoc. Prof. Dr. Michael zur Muehlen of the Stevens Institute of Technology and Dr. Jan Recker of the Queensland University of Technology.

[3] See the BPMN 2.0 links at http://www.bpmn.org/.

[4] See a summary and BPMN histogram from the study referenced in Endnote [2] at http://www.bpm-research.com/2008/03/03/how-much-bpmn-do-you-need/.

[5] This definition of the term is taken from the Wikipedia, which can be read at this link: http://en.wikipedia.org/wiki/First_principles.

[6] See two different but kindred takes on BPMN modeling guidance in the forthcoming paper *Primitives: Design Guidelines and Architecture for BPMN Models* by Michael zur Muehlen of the Stevens Institute of Technology, Dennis Wisnosky of the Office of the Deputy Chief Management Officer of the U.S. Department of Defense, and James Kindrick of Jacobs Technology Inc. to be presented at the Australian Conference on Information Systems, and *A Design Methodology for BPMN* by Michele Chinosi and Alberto Trombetta of the University of Insubria, Varese, Italy in the 2009 BPM & Workflow Handbook – Spotlight on Government, edited by Layna Fischer, Future Strategies Inc. (2009) {ISBN 978-0-0777527-9-9}

[7] For a contrarian take on functional decomposition's limitations to be avoided, see BPMN Modeling and Reference Guide, by Stephen A. White, PhD and Derek Miers, Future Strategies Inc. (2008) {ISBN 978-0-9777527-2-0}, pp 195-198.

[8] Because the terms are not universally understood, look at these links from Wikipedia for definitions that are based on at least a partial consensus: http://en.wikipedia.org/wiki/Cohesion_(computer_science) and http://en.wikipedia.org/wiki/Coupling_(computer_science).

[9] See the seminal paper on this topic in *Workflow Patterns* by Wil van Der Aalst, Arthur H.M. Hofstede, Bartek Kiepuszewski, and Alistair P. Barros (2003) at http://is.tm.tue.nl/staff/wvdaalst/publications/p108.pdf, published in *Distributed and Parallel Databases* 14 (1): pp. 5--51. doi:10.1023/A:1022883727209, and a comparison of modeling notations for workflow patterns in *Process Modeling Notations and Workflow Patterns* by Stephen A. White, IBM, February 2005 at http://www.bpmn.org/Documents/Notations_and_Workflow Patterns.pdf.

[10] Among system architects, these message exchange patterns are typically known, but not always by the same names, so what one may call Re-

quest/Response, others call Request/Reply, and what one may call One-Way, others may call Fire-and-Forget. Here is a link to the Wikipedia definition as a common reference that is based on definitions for SOAP-based patterns from the World Wide Web Consortium (W3C): http://en.wikipedia.org/wiki/Message_Exchange_Pattern; this does not include other patterns of note in system design, including one often known as Publish/Subscribe: http://en.wikipedia.org/wiki/Publish/subscribe.

[11] A deep exploration of design primitives and patterns of design primitives, built around BPMN, has been worked up by a team from The Stevens Institute of Technology lead by Dr. zur Muehlen to prepare guidance for the Department of Defense's DoDAF standards through the sponsorship of the Business Transformation Agency (BTA) – see: http://www.bta.mil/products/bea/products/2009-03-03_Primitives_Guidelines_OV-6c for_DoDAF_Journal.pdf for the design primitives and http://www.xpdl.org/nugen/p/gseonklyf/a/2009-06-03_BPMN_Primitives_for_XPDL_Workshop.pdf for the patterns.

[12] See BPMN Modeling and Reference Guide, pp. 183 - 190 on the Transaction Sub-Process, which provides a good working definition of transaction in BPMN.

[13] See Enterprise SOA: Service-Oriented Architecture Best Practices by Dirk Krafzig, Karl Banke, and Dirk Slama, part of the Coad Series from Pearson Education Inc., Prentice Hall (2005) {ISBN 0131465759} pp. 122-127.

[14] See Enterprise SOA: Service-Oriented Architecture Best Practices, pp. 140-141.

[15] The terms granularity and fine/coarse-grained are not universally understood, but see Wikipedia at http://en.wikipedia.org/wiki/Granularity for one view.

[16] This terminology, which predates the SOA movement, is taken from a seminal work on modernizing legacy systems called *Incremental Modernization of Legacy Systems* (Technical Note CMU/SEI-2001-TN-006) by Santiago Comella-Dorda, Grace A. Lewis, Pat Place, Dan Plakosh, and Robert C. Seacord, July 2001.

[17] SCA composite diagrams are variants of UML package diagrams, and a common notation is used in most of the SCA literature. However, the notation used by Oracle, and replicated in Visio, provides a richer visual expression than UML.

[18] See the BTA studies referenced in Endnote [12] on design primitives.

[19] The realization of service invocation out of a service task shown here is based on how Oracle 11g realizes it, which is as a configured call to the WSDL for the service being requested, but it is nonetheless representative of such realizations.

[20] Though more of a historical reprise than something yet to be realized, as this paper would suggest, an evolution of BPM was succinctly characterized by Keith Swenson, Chief Architect and VP of R&D at Fujitsu Computer Systems Corporation in a presentation at the Process and Architecture 2008 Conference; see http://www.slideshare.net/TransformationInnovation/bpm-workflow-in-the-new-enterprise-architecture-368078?src=related_normal&rel=1703138.

[21] See http://www.soapatterns.org/contract_denormalization.php.

[22] See the two XML formats claiming to be serialized expressions of BPMN models at http://www.wfmc.org/xpdl.html or http://www.xpdl.org/ for XPDL, and at "BPMN 2.0 By Example at" http://www.bpmn.org/ and with sample files at http://www.omg.org/spec/BPMN/2.0/examples/ZIP.

[23] The **BPMN 2.0 Handbook CD** available from the Publisher contains more material on this topic. www.FutsStrat.com

Bespoke Enterprise Architecture: Tailoring BPMN 2.0 using Conformance Classes

Dennis E. Wisnosky, Office of the Deputy Chief Management Officer, Department of Defense, and Michael zur Muehlen Ph.D.,
Center for Business Process Innovation
Stevens Institute of Technology, USA

INTRODUCTION

Government agencies have to fulfill their missions while being fiscally responsible and responsive to customer needs, both internal and external. Understanding the agencies' end-to-end processes and mission threads is essential to ensure that both performance and compliance objectives are met. Increasingly, Enterprise Architectures are used to document end-to-end business operations and to prove compliance to rules and regulations. Enterprise Architecture covers the creation of analytical or prescriptive models of organizations to understand, manage, or change the enterprise (Ross et al. 2004). The models that describe different architecture facets are typically organized according to the views they describe, such as process, data, rules and organization models, among others. For organizations that engage in multiple architecture projects, a systematic organization of these views is essential; only if the views and their representations are consistent across different projects can an organization efficiently identify organizational and technical interfaces, streamline cross-functional operations, and assert compliance to rules and regulations.

A number of obstacles to consistent architecture efforts currently exist: Divergent viewpoints, different frameworks, multiple modeling methods, and inconsistent interpretations of individual methods. This paper reports on the development of a methodology for the creation of architecture models that are centered around BPMN and is based on the use of conformance classes and design patterns.

MODELING VIEWPOINTS

Enterprise modelers have a choice of competing viewpoints when they describe an organization. Depending on which artifact they place at the center of their considerations they may organize their models around a process, one or more business objects, events, resources, or policies and directives. As a consequence, models that originated from different starting points may have different levels of detail, content, and context.

Data architects focus on the information objects that exist within the system architecture. Their approach to architecting begins by identifying central artifacts and their properties, relationships, constraints, and then moves on to the methods that may alter the state of each artifact. The first model created during a data-centric analysis tends to be a conceptual data model. The modeling language of choice is often UML, since the UML class diagrams offer a strong support for data modeling with anchor points for dynamic system properties through the use of other methods (Dobing and Parsons 2006). Other methods such as Entity-Relationship Models and Object-Role Models are popular as well.

Process-centric approaches start with the consideration of end-to-end processes, and contain detailed models of sub-processes, and generalized models of value chains as required. These processes are then refined with input-output relationships, and supplemented with the data that is being consumed and produced by these processes and their activities.

A **process architect** will place the dynamic behavior of a system at the center of his or her considerations. The Business Process Modeling Notation (BPMN) has become a method of choice for many organizations. It provides a rich set of constructs to depict activities and their dependencies, as well as the event-based behavior of processes. While it provides linkages to data objects that are produced and consumed over the course of a process, a modeler will need to create separate data models that depict the relationships among these data objects (and those that are not explicitly linked to a process).

Rules architects will begin with the identification of core axioms and concepts, define properties of these concepts, the relationships between concepts, and then define restrictions on properties and relationships (structural rules), as well as allowable and prohibited operations (behavioral rules). Compared to data and process modeling, fewer representational standards exist for the documentation of business rules, as many emerging rules standards focus on formats for the interchange and enforcement of rules (e.g., the W3C Rules Interchange Format) as opposed to the visualization of rules. The OMG Semantics of Business, Vocabulary and Rules (SBVR) standard proposed a Structured English representation for rules, which is well suited for the description of policy and rule statements, but is not directly executable. While the definition of structural rules can be compared to the definition of a data model, the definition of behavioral rules describes the process space inverse to how a process modeler would describe it: While a process model captures all possible execution paths of a process instance (thus defining the solution space), a rules model describes the constraints that a process instance must comply with (thus limiting the solution space).

Event architects focus on the response of a system to its context. They begin by classifying sources of events, sensory features of the system at hand, and the patterns and rules that are used to filter, classify, and react to the occurrence of certain events. Similar to process architectures, an event architecture focuses on the dynamic properties of a system, but views the system as reacting to its environment, rather than proactively shaping its environment. The emergence of Complex Event Processing platforms has given prominence to an event-based analysis of organizations (Taylor and Raden 2007), and the Business Process Modeling Notation contains symbols for a variety of event types, allowing for a convergence of event- and process-based views.

Organization architects begin with a look at the resources of the system at hand—the information processing units, be they human or technical. From this viewpoint the system architecture centers on a set of capabilities (i.e., processing abilities or functionalities) that can be invoked by sending information to the different processing stations.

Depending on the original viewpoint, certain architecture artifacts represent first-class objects while others are derivative objects, whose structure is affected by the design of the first class objects. In other words, there is a path dependency that develops during the construction of architecture models.

ARCHITECTURE FRAMEWORKS

Multiple alternative frameworks for the organization of architecture viewpoints exist: The Federal Architecture Framework (FEAF), the Department of Defense Architecture Framework (DoDAF, see U.S. Department of Defense 2009), the Open Group Architecture Framework (TOGAF), the Architecture for Integrated Information Systems (ARIS), the Zachman framework (Zachman 1993), and others. These frameworks, while often overlapping, do not share a canonical set of views on the enterprise. Furthermore, frameworks with many views, such as DoDAF, require an architect to choose which views a particular architecture should contain, and which ones can be omitted. DoDAF in particular is supplemented by instructions such as the Joint Capabilities Integration and Development System (JCIDS), which outlines the viewpoints that have to be documented in large system development projects. Out of the 53 possible architecture models outlined in the DoDAF 2.0 specification, the JCIDS process requires the delivery of 15 models at milestone reviews, among them the OV-6c Event-Trace Description. While the OV-6c view was originally designed to accommodate UML Sequence Diagrams, an increasing number of projects in the Department use this view to capture process models.

Multiple Methods

Even within the same architecture view, multiple modeling methods can be used to document the enterprise. For process models, methods such as Flowcharts, IDEF, Event-driven Process Chains and BPMN are well established for the creation of process models. Both modeler experience and existing tool support will influence the choice of modeling method in a particular project. If no method is prescribed a modeler will choose the method he/she is most familiar with, or that is best supported by the toolset chosen for modeling. This can lead to incompatible architecture models created by different modelers in different tools.

Modeling Individualism

Even if modelers all use the same notation, for example BPMN, there are different ways to express the same semantics. One particular example is the conditional sequence flow element in BPMN—a modeler can represent a decision in the process using an exclusive or inclusive OR gateway symbol, or he/she can express the same semantics using conditional sequence flow elements. The example below shows two process fragments that are semantically equivalent, but the casual reader would have to read the transition conditions for the conditional sequence flow example on the right to determine whether this is an exclusive or inclusive OR split. The gateway on the left signals this semantic through the use of the X symbol.

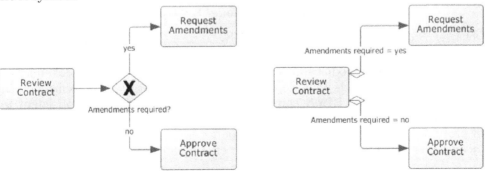

Implicit and Explicit Gateways in BPMN

PROCESS-ORIENTED ENTERPRISE ARCHITECTURE IN THE DEPARTMENT OF DEFENSE

The Business Mission Area of the US Department of Defense (DoD) is responsible for the business and financial infrastructure of the department. Due to the large number of systems that support logistics, financial transactions, contract management and other applications, data integration and compliance management are critical issues to ensure the continual functioning of the department's processes. In order to manage these integration issues better, the DoD began to specify the Business Enterprise Architecture (BEA)[1] as a means to prioritize improvement efforts, understand the impact of systems modernization projects, and to create an end-to-end representation of the core processes of the Business Mission Area in 2005.

The BEA is organized in six core areas that cover financial management, supplier management, materials management, facility management, human resources management and procurement. Each of these areas is documented through a series of business processes modeled in BPMN. In addition, business rules, data standards, system interfaces, and other models are maintained in views that conform to the DoD Architecture Framework (DoDAF 2.0) (U.S. Department of Defense 2009). Overall the BEA contains several hundred models and is updated annually. At the time of this writing version 7.0 represents the most current release.

From a process management perspective two types of models in the BEA are of particular interest: The end-to-end business process models (DoDAF view OV-6c), and the functional decomposition of activities (DoDAF view OV-5a). While the process models are created in BPMN, the models describing functional decomposition and the activity inputs and outputs were created using IDEF0. Other views are described in tables, entity-relationship diagrams and custom notations. The figure below shows a typical BEA process model.

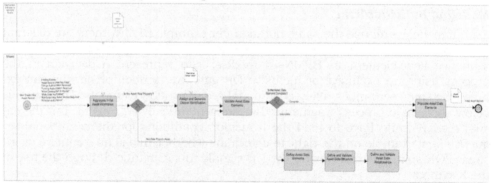

BEA Process Model Excerpt

CREATING AN ENTERPRISE ARCHITECTURE STANDARD

Our analysis of the process models in the BEA uncovered that over time modelers had created various modifications to BPMN at the behest of their stakeholders, leading to BPMN models that were not aligned with the BPMN specification. In addition, the available BPMN constructs had been used in an inconsistent fashion. For example, while some modelers used gateways to denote splits and joins in processes, others used conditional sequence flow to create splits and multiple incoming sequence flows into activities to create joins. As a result the same se-

---

[1] see http://www.bta.mil/products/bea.html

mantic content looked different depending on who created the model. This problem was exacerbated by the frequent turnover of process modelers, as each generation of modelers introduced their personal style into the resulting diagrams.

In May 2008 the CTO and Chief Architect of the Business Mission Area launched a project (the Primitives project) to investigate three questions:

- How can the Department of Defense enforce a consistent representation of architecture descriptions (i.e., ensure the diagrams created by different modelers will look similar)?
- How can the Department of Defense leverage existing standards for architecture descriptions (i.e., no new notation)?
- How can the Department of Defense enforce that the resulting models are interchangeable between platforms (i.e., create process model portability)?

Primitives – A Practical Set of Modeling Guidelines

The Primitives design guide consist of three parts: A subset of the BPMN 2.0 symbols (the graphical part, as pictured below), a collection of design patterns for the use of these symbols, and design rules that cover design aspects not covered by the patterns or the symbol set.

The development of our BPMN modeling guidelines began with an analysis of the modeling habits present in the existing BEA models. We identified the most commonly used BPMN symbols, and combined this information with a previous study of the application of BPMN as a baseline for the development of a BPMN subset (zur Muehlen and Recker 2008). We stripped out the least used BPMN constructs and limited the use of others where equivalent representation could be achieved by other means. For example, we outlawed the use of conditional sequence flow and mandated the use of gateways for splits and joins.

The resulting primitives are best characterized by the elements that were removed from the BPMN 2.0 symbol set: Transaction and Compensation elements were eliminated because their technical nature is several levels of abstraction below the models we encountered in practice. The Multiple Gateway element and the multiple event type were removed because in practice modelers used these symbols to cover up situations where the actual flow logic of the process had not been thoroughly analyzed. We originally intended to eliminate error events and escalation events, but in practical tests we found that stakeholders responded well to a visual distinction between error situations and changes in the priority of a process due to external circumstances. Similarly, while the link event symbol is merely a graphical embellishment (it is used to improve the visual appearance of a diagram) and was a candidate for elimination, modelers and model users found it very useful in practice. In essence, the symbols that were removed from the BPMN 2.0 set were either too technical, too ambiguous, or did not find sufficient use in practice.

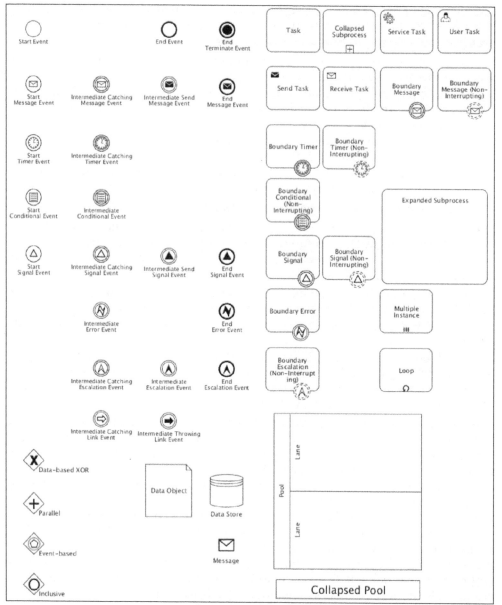

BPMN Primitives Subset

While the popularity of symbols provided one data point for the elimination of BPMN constructs, this assessment was based on established modeling practices, many of which had flaws that had grown over the years. The team decided it was important to encourage good design principles through the inclusion of specific symbols, such as the new non-aborting attached events in BPMN 2.0.

To assist modelers in the construction of primitives-compliant models we paid particular attention to syntactical errors that modelers had made in the BEA processes. We created reference patterns that would represent the intended semantics correctly, and added them to a library of patterns that was complemented by design patterns from the Workflow Patterns library (van der Aalst et al. 2003). The example below shows a description for one of the low-level patterns, the event-based choice.

Event-based Gateway Semantics

After completion of Activity A the Process will halt until one of the subsequent events occurs. In the sample diagram above, the process will halt until either a message is received or a timer expires. If the message is received first, Activity B can start and the timer is disabled. If the timer expires first, Activity C can start and the message receiver is disabled.

Only one outgoing sequence flow from the Event-based Gateway can evaluate to true at any given time, thus the Event-based Gateway behaves like an XOR-Gateway, and the separate process paths can later be merged with an XOR-Join.

Rationale

A process may have to react to changes in its environment. Intermediate catching events are listeners that sense environmental changes (arrival of messages, expiration of timers, presence of signals etc.). If a process will react to just one out of a set of environmental changes the Event-based Gateway reflects this situation.

Design Guide

The Event-based Gateway reflects a wait state in the process – no processing will occur until the occurrence of one out of multiple events.

If a subsequent activity can be triggered by different events, merge the multiple alternative triggers with an XOR Join Gateway.

If the event trigger is based on contextual information that is not easily captured by timer, message, or signals, a conditional intermediate event symbols should be used. The underlying contextual conditions can then be represented by a rule written outside of the BPMN diagram.

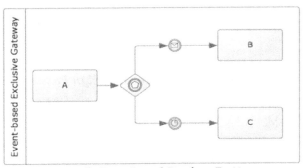

Sample Low-Level Design Pattern

To determine if the resulting subset of BPMN symbols was sufficient for use within the DoD, we applied the constrained BPMN vocabulary in the design of processes outside of the BEA, namely the Joint Close Air Support (JCAS) process, and several governance processes. Beyond the elementary patterns (e.g., how to model a process split) we found a number of recurring situations with specific semantics—reviewing and approving a document, collaboration between two parties, voting on an issue etc. These patterns were captured in a high-level pattern catalog that is meant to be extensible, work that is currently ongoing. The example below shows a description for a high-level pattern, the modeling of state-like activities.

State-like Activity Pattern

Sometimes a modeler may need to represent an activity that will complete upon the expiration of a timer or the manual completion of the activity. To represent this situation the modeler can attach a timer event to the boundary of the activity—once the timer expires the execution of the activity will cease and the sequence flow originating from the timer event will be followed. If the activity completes prior to the expiration of the timer a regular sequence flow from the activity will be followed. The sequence flows from the timer event and the regular sequence flow may be merged using an unsynchronized join (XOR Join), but can be kept separately if different downstream activities result from the different modes of activity completion.

State-like Activity Pattern

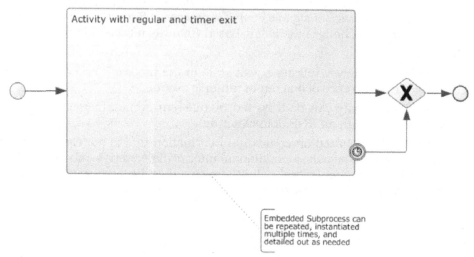

Activity with regular and timer exit

Embedded Subprocess can be repeated, instantiated multiple times, and detailed out as needed

Sample High-Level Design Pattern

BEYOND MODELING – MODEL EXECUTION AND EXCHANGE

The tailoring of the BPMN vocabulary in the Primitives project was a big step towards ensuring a consistent representation of processes created by different modelers. However, the design of such a subset is only feasible if a modeling tool supports it. Many enterprise architecture tools allow administrators to create custom method subsets (for instance ARIS, Mega, System Architect and others), but the interchange of the resulting models is hampered by the absence of formal interoperability tests and compliance standards.

The most ambitious goal of the architecture standard effort was the design of executable architecture, i.e., models that can be taken from an architecture tool to an execution platform. For example, BPMN up to version 1.2 did not specify any means by which a vendor could claim conformance with the standard unless all BPMN elements were supported by the tool. While this approach is feasible for diagramming tools, execution tools that instantiate and automate BPMN processes (i.e., BPMS) often support just a subset of the BPMN syntax. This is often due to the limitations of the underlying execution infrastructure. If an execution engine cannot interpret a non-aborting attached timer event then its development environment will most likely not contain that symbol.

Such limitations are often apparent in the area of organization modeling. A BPMS typically assumes full control over all elements of the process model that is created in the BPMS design environment. In BPMN this means that all process elements reside within a single pool, as the pool element represents one coherent unit of control. As a consequence, many BPMS do not support multiple pools, and thus do not support message flow symbols, as message flow can only occur between elements in different pools.

BPMN PRIMITIVES AND THE BPMN 2.0 STANDARDIZATION EFFORT

In early BPMN versions a vendor that supported just a subset of BPMN had little guidance which elements should be supported in future releases – in BPMN 1.0 through 1.2 there was just a core set and the full set of the language, and a big gap in the middle. Vendors that did not support the full set of BPMN constructs often added proprietary symbols to approximate the missing functionality of their models, but did not have intermediate milestones.

The official BPMN 2.0 specification contains three conformance subclasses that describe subsets of the BPMN vocabulary for different uses, Descriptive, Analytical and Common Executable (Object Management Group 2010). The first subset, *descriptive*, contains a very limited vocabulary in order to facilitate model understanding by a broad group of stakeholders. The second subset, *analytical*, adds more refined modeling elements such as different event types and exceptions. The third level, *minimum executable*, focuses mainly on the attributes of BPMN elements that need to be maintained to support the execution of a BPMN process.

The subset defined as part of the Primitives project provided key input for the design of the analytical conformance subclass. Using the different subclasses vendors can formally claim conformance to a defined subset of the BPMN vocabulary. This in turn will lead to clearer BPMN serializations based on these subsets, which should make it easier to exchange models between different tools. This is one significant step toward our goal of executable architectures.

The DoDAF BPMN Subset (i.e. the primitives) is a user-driven, practically validated subset of BPMN that ensures a high level of expressiveness, while leaving out many of the constructs that can either lead to inconsistent representations for the same semantics or that are so technical that the vast majority of IS and systems engineers will not miss them. It is a yardstick for vendors that may still have gaps in their own coverage of BPMN constructs and it gives members of the training community a target set for higher-level BPMN certifications.

Future DoD Architecture

The initiative to create BPMN-based DoD Primitives for symbols, design rules and patterns represents the beginning of the Department of Defense's 21st Century Enterprise Architecture work. The goal of this work is to deliver human-readable architecture, machine-readable architecture, executable architecture, and the long-term re-use of authoritative data. The Department categorizes all of these efforts as Semantic Web technologies. Today, a series of Proof of Delivery (PoD) projects under the name Enterprise Information Web (EIW) are delivering business capabilities every 90 days based upon ontologies derived from common vocabularies that were discovered though building end-to-end business process models with the BPMN conformance class described in this chapter.

REFERENCES

Dobing, B., and Parsons, J.: How UML is used, Communications of the ACM, 49, 109-113 (2006).

National Institute for Standards and Technologies. "Integrated Definition for Function Modeling (IDEF0)." Gaithersburg MD, 1993.

Object Management Group. "Business Process Model and Notation (BPMN 2.0)." Framingham, MA, 2010.

Ross, J. W., Weill, P., and Robertson, D.: Enterprise architecture as strategy: Creating a foundation for business execution, Harvard Business Press, (2006).

Taylor, J., and Raden, N.: Smart (Enough) Systems: How to Deliver Competitive Advantage by Automating Hidden Decisions, Prentice-Hall, (2007).

U.S. Department of Defense. "DoD Architecture Framework Version 2.0. Volume 1: Introduction, Overview and Concepts." Version 2.0, Washington DC, 2009.

van der Aalst, WMP, ter Hofstede, AHM, Kiepuszewski, B, and Barros, AP. "Workflow Patterns." *Distributed and Parallel Databases* 14, no. 1 (2003): 5-51.

Zachman, JA. "A Framework for Information Systems Architecture." *IBM Systems Journal* 38, no. 2/3 (1999): 454-70.

zur Muehlen, Michael, and Recker, Jan. "How Much Language is Enough? Theoretical and Practical Use of the Business Process Management Notation." *Conference on Advanced Information Systems Engineering (CAiSE '08)* (2008).

Section 2

Guide to the Business Imperative for BPMN

Best Practice Guidelines for BPMN 2.0

Gerardo Navarro Suarez, Jakob Freund and Matthias Schrepfer
camunda services GmbH, Germany

INTRODUCTION

In practice modeling projects often tend to be quite large. Adopting BPMN 2.0 eases the creation of process models for business and technical projects. However, the creation of models in large modeling projects is still not a trivial task. The introduction of modeling guidelines guides and supports modeling projects. This article introduces an approach to establish such modeling guidelines for individual modeling projects using BPMN 2.0 as modeling notation. The article discusses the concept of modeling guidelines and shows why their application can help to apply BPMN 2.0 in practice. A framework for the creation of guidelines is described in detail. Real-world examples illustrate the use of modeling guidelines and constitute the effectiveness of best practice guidelines.

WHAT ARE MODELING GUIDELINES?

Modeling guidelines are documents which collect and provide best practices for modeling projects. In the context of modeling guidelines, best practices are techniques, methods or examples to support process modeling. If applied in modeling projects, best practices illustrate effective ways to capture real-world scenarios in process models. These best practices derive from experience as well as from academic research. Modeling guidelines cover best practices in form of instructions or rules which should be followed while modeling business processes in BPMN 2.0. Modeling guidelines guide and influence process modelers to use best practices for process modeling. Additionally, best practice guidelines can be used to enforce specific instructions in projects.

WHY DO WE NEED BEST PRACTICE GUIDELINES?

Modeling projects usually require the creation of several process models. These models often tend to be quite complex and large. This complexity must be dealt with by process modelers who map real-world process into process models. In real projects, modelers often lack knowledge in process modeling. Thus, they need guidance for the modeling process in order to create high quality processes. Best practice guidelines compensate these issues by guiding modelers with examples. Best practices assist modelers especially while mapping real-world processes and knowledge into process models. Furthermore, best practices help to manage and govern modeling projects especially if many models need to be created. Best practices further contribute to achieve higher quality of process models. Process modelers are advised to use modeling and visualization styles that are superior to others. This leads to more sophisticated model representations which in turn positively affect the readability and understandability of the created process models. The number of errors in process models decreases due to the increased comprehensibility. Model viewers understand the models faster and better. In addition, the purpose of process models, most often the communication between project stakeholders, is achieved at a higher degree.

CONTENT OF BEST PRACTICE GUIDELINES

Modeling projects differ in their purposes and goals. Due to this the contents of best practice guidelines also varies. The establishment of modeling guidelines requires the availability of the scope definition of the modeling project. The guideline content should be based on this definition so that users can apply the guideline to support the project-specific goals. In practice the guideline content is divided into categories. These categories assist organizations to develop individual guidelines. Best practice examples are put into categories based on their scope. In the following we introduce and define the categories that best practice guidelines should contain. Examples illustrate the application of guidelines.

BPMN 2.0 Symbol Set

The specification of BPMN 2.0 defines the symbols to be used for creating process models. The specification describes the syntax and semantics of all symbols. In practice, process modelers are free to choose symbols to map real-world situations into process models. Therefore, we recommend you to define the symbol set which you want to use within projects. Based on the scope of the modeling project the set of symbols should be chosen. An agreed set of symbols helps to avoid misinterpretations of symbols and supports the harmonization of process models. The symbol set in modeling guidelines is divided into two sub-categories: symbols and artifacts. Both categories are defined as follows.

BPMN Symbols

As mentioned before the BPMN 2.0 specification defines the symbols. Due to the large amount of symbols in BPMN 2.0 some elements are seldom used in actual modeling projects. The large set of BPMN symbols might be too large. Then a subset of symbols might be convenient. The restriction decreases the number of symbols which helps process modelers to focus on the actual modeling goals. However, for creating such subsets the project purposes and goals must be known. Thus, the symbol subset can differ among projects. The category contains all specified BPMN 2.0 elements except the so-called artifacts. To illustrate the application of symbol sets we describe how to define such subsets.

BPMN Symbols – Examples

A subset defines the BPMN 2.0 symbols which can be used in modeling projects. The elements of a subset must be suitable to capture all situations of the project in process models. The subsets must be designed carefully so that they fit the projects. The BPMN 2.0 specification already provides three predefined subsets, so called conformance sub-classes: descriptive, analytic, common executable. The descriptive and the analytical sub-classes focus on process elements and a small amount of attributes. The common executable sub-class concentrates on executable process models. It contains all BPMN 2.0 symbols and a large number of attributes of process elements to prepare models for their automatic execution. In case these classes do not meet the purpose of modeling projects, individual subsets can be created. Establishing such subsets works as follows. Symbols of the specified BPMN 2.0 symbol set that are suitable for the project are taken and grouped as subset.

In order to illustrate the application of symbol subsets, the following example is used: The goal of a modeling project is to create process diagrams with the objective to document processes suitable for the management level of an organization.

To actually model such high-level processes, the full symbol set of BPMN 2.0 is not needed. Thus, we define a small subset that contains the necessary symbols. The subset reduces the amount of symbols and helps the process modeler not to get lost in details. The modeling guideline for the project describes the symbols of the subset. In Figure 1 the subset is depicted. The subset is suitable to create models that are intuitively understandable to the management level without showing too many details of the processes.

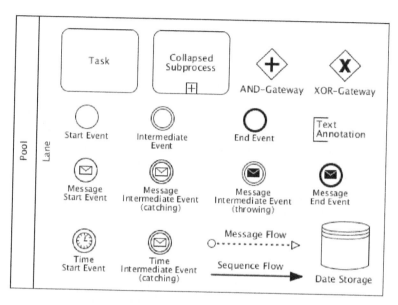

Caption 1: A Symbol Subset for Documenting High-level Processes

BPMN Artifacts

The BPMN 2.0 specification defines so-called artifacts. Artifacts can be used to provide additional information within process diagrams. They are connected to flow elements, e.g. tasks, with the help of associations. The specification allows the user to create customized artifacts which can be added to the standard symbol set. The specification defines the syntax of using artifacts so that the semantics of process diagrams is kept correctly. Modelers are free to define customized artifacts and use them within process models.

For individual modeling projects, customized artifacts are useful to highlight certain meanings within process models. The definition of customized artifacts helps to emphasize specific information in models. In such cases it improves the comprehensibility of process models. Customized artifacts help to present situations visually in a clearer and more precise way. The definition of artifacts must be based on the project purposes and chosen on individual basis. However, if artifacts are customized, their semantic meaning must be defined properly.

BPMN Artifacts – Examples

Figure 2 shows a process model where two customized artifacts are used. An artifact depicts an IT system, e.g. Salesforce or a SAP system, and is associated to task A. The second artifact expresses an organizational role and is associated with task B. Both artifacts add additional information to the model. The IT system expresses that task A uses the system to fulfill the task. The role associated to task B expresses that an additional participant takes part in task B.

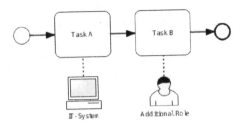

Caption 2: Two Customized Artifacts

Modeling Styles

The category of modeling styles contains rules that are generally known and accepted. These rules apply to all modeling projects. This type of styles does not rely on specific modeling situations or contexts. Modeling styles are also not dependent on actual modeling goals and purposes. The styles assist process modelers by guiding them with general instructions on how to create process models more effectively. Modeling styles restrict the freedom of process modelers to draw models as the modelers must apply the style definitions. These restrictions support the governance and standardization of process models. Modeling styles influence the modeling behavior of modelers which often leads to an increase in the comprehensibility of process models.

Modeling Styles – Examples

In order to illustrate the use of general modeling styles we propose three examples and explain them in detail.

- You should model in a structured and symmetric way.
- You should decompose models with a large number of activities.
- You should use as few symbols in models as possible.

The first modeling style deals with structured and symmetric modeling. A process model is structured and symmetric if every split gateway has a respective join gateway of the same type. This modeling style leads to formations in process models that are known as blocks. Process models that incorporate block structures are easier to understand due to their increased comprehensibility. Empirical studies showed that people have difficulties to understand unstructured process models because they expect every split gateway to match its respective join gateway. Furthermore, it is more likely that unstructured process models contain more errors, e.g. deadlocks or livelocks. It must be mentioned that certain situations cannot be captured symmetrically. In such cases process models incorporate unstructured parts.

The next two figures present a scenario that is modeled in a structured and an unstructured way. Figure 3 shows the structured and symmetric process model. Notice that every opening gateway has its corresponding closing gateway. Figure 4 shows the same situation in an unstructured model. The model in Figure 4 is less comprehensible as model viewers do not recognize the model structure easily. Therefore, process modelers are advised to model as symmetric as possible.

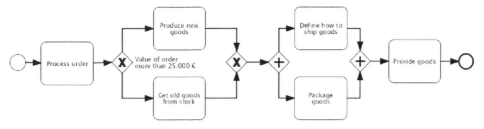

Caption 3: Structured Process Model

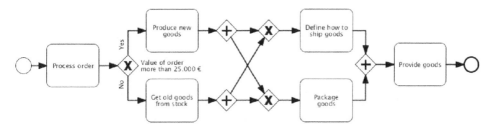

Caption 4: Unstructured Process Model

The second modeling style limits the number of elements in process models. Empirical studies showed that the larger a model the more difficult it is to understand. The size of process models is thus directly connected to the understandability and error probability of a process model. Therefore, the modeling style advices to decompose process models when the number of process elements reaches a certain limit. The limit depends on a number of factors, however, we recommend to set it lower than 50. Large models should be decomposed into smaller ones with the help of sub-processes.

The third modeling style advices modelers to use a few elements as possible in process models. This style is based on similar reasons as the second one. However, as few elements as possible means that a process modeler should only use BPMN 2.0 symbols if really needed. There should be no superfluous elements in models. Process models should only contain elements that focus on the control flow in the model or those that add value to the model, e.g. in the form of additional information. Although the modeling style sounds trivial, in practice this style is not always met by modelers.

Layout Styles

The layout of process models is important when it comes to read and comprehend the model content. Models with improved layouts are easier to read than those whose layouts are obfuscated by means of visual cues, e.g. color or line width. Layout styles define rules that influence how modelers draw process models. Modeling notations do not define how to place elements within process models. Modelers are generally free to place symbols anywhere within the modeling canvas. Layout styles restrict this freedom by enforcing rules that define how process models should be visualized. Layout rules do not change the graph structure of process models so that the semantic meaning of them remains the same. Layout styles can be divided into two groups: general and optional layout styles. General layout styles should be applied to all modeling projects. Optional layout styles are recommendations to further improve visual representations. They should be followed but they are not mandatory. In practice there are a number of rules in both categories.

Layout Styles – Examples

In the following two examples for layout styles are shown. To illustrate the use of layout styles, there will be one example for each category. One general style concerns the representation of the exclusive gateway (XOR). The specification allows the user to draw the gateway with and without an internal marker. Although it advises to use only one representation within a single process model, process modelers can change their style according to their modeling behavior. In practice this can lead to different layouts which might confuse model viewers. Therefore, it is advisable to stick to the representation of the exclusive gateway with internal marker (shown on the left side of Figure 5). Enforcing this general layout style leads to the harmonization of process models with respect to this visual cue.

Exclusive gateway with marker   *Exclusive gateway without marker*

Caption 5: Representation of the Exclusive Gateway

An optional layout style is to enforce rules for the drawing of sequence flows between symbols. BPMN 2.0 does not define the way of drawing sequence flows. Process modelers are free to choose the way to draw the flows. Figure 6 shows several but not all ways for connecting two symbols with a sequence flow. All representations are semantically equivalent but they differ in placing the flows. In modeling projects where a large number of models is created, the enforcement of best practice rules for placing sequence flows in models contributes to increase their comprehensibility. For this optional layout style we recommend the following two rules.

- Incoming sequence flows should enter a symbol from the left, top or bottom side.
- Outgoing sequence flows should leave a symbol from the right, top or bottom side.

Organizations should introduce general as well as optional layout styles to control and harmonize the visual representations of process models to increase their comprehensibility.

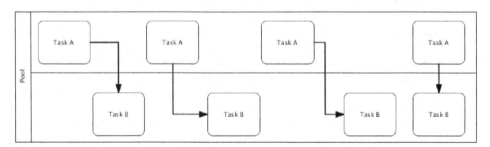

Caption 6: Drawing of Sequence Flows between Symbols

Modeling Alternatives

Process modeling is a task where humans usually judge real-world situations and map them into models. The mapping often leads to different representation of the same situations. Although the representations differ, the information of the models is semantically identical. The differences occur due to the freedom of process modelers to use symbols from the given symbol set and to connect them according to the underlying syntax. Especially in large projects with a lot of modelers the representations for one situation usually differ. If modelers use different symbols, the visualizations of the models change which immediately affects the comprehensibility of the underlying models. If there are no rules or recommendations, modelers base their decision on intuition which is often known to be wrong, especially for novice modelers. In order to govern situations where alternative process models represent the same information, organizations should provide best practices for certain situations.

The category of modeling alternatives presents those best practices. It describes the alternatives and recommends the best one for a specific situation. The recommendations can be used in several contexts. The best practices guide process modelers to choose the best representation for specific situations.

Modeling Alternatives – Examples

In order to illustrate the concept of modeling alternatives two examples are given. The first example deals with non-interrupting message events. The second one shows alternatives for the modeling of conditional flows.

Figure 7 depicts a sub-process that has a non-interrupting intermediate event attached to its boundary. The event is triggered by an external event. Figure 8 displays the same situation but uses different BPMN 2.0 symbols. In Figure 8 an event sub-process is modeled which starts the event handling if it is triggered by the external event. Both alternatives are identical from a control flow perspective. Therefore, modelers can choose between the alternatives. Organizations should focus on one alternative and enforce it in all process models if possible.

It must be noted that the alternatives differ in their data handling if they are executed in process engines. The event handling in Figure 7 runs in the scope of the main process. Thus, the event handling cannot access the data used within the scope of the sub-process. In Figure 8 the event sub-process runs in the scope of the sub-process. It has full access to the data used by the sub-process. With respect to reusability, the two alternatives can differ. If sub-processes are marked as call activity, the alternatives differ. Process modelers must be aware of these details and take appropriate actions. The figures shown below are identical with respect to usability as sub-processes are not marked as call activity. The modeling guideline should definitely point out these details to advice the readers.

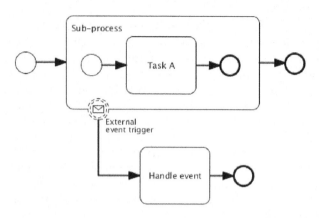

Caption 7: Sub-Process with Non-Interrupting Message Event

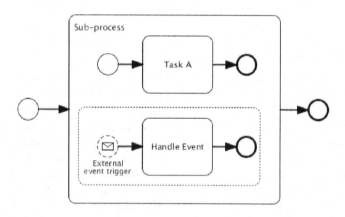

Caption 8: Sub-Process with Event Sub-Process

The second example is concerned with the modeling of conditions. Figure 9 depicts a common decision using an exclusive gateway. The gateway decides on the path that is activated based on the outcome of the decision. The same situation is modeled differently in Figure 10. The decisions to activate the outgoing paths are made separately with the help of two conditions. For each path a condition is attached and shown as small diamond leaving the task A. Both situations are semantically equivalent if the conditional flows in Figure 10 incorporate the same conditions as in Figure 9. However, in order to comprehend this information the model viewer has to understand the semantic meaning of the conditional sequence flows. It is advisable to use the alternative shown in Figure 9 as this version is easier to comprehend. Organizations should choose this alternative and enforce it for all process models.

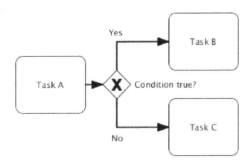

Caption 9: Exclusive Gateway

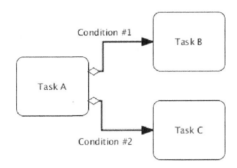

Caption 10: Implicit Decisions with Conditional Flows

Design Patterns

Design patterns are based on specific situations or contexts which should be captured in process models. Design pattern rely on these contexts or situations. Patterns can only be used if the real-world scenario matches the context of the pattern. Thus, process modelers have to check whether they can use design patterns for a given situation. Design patterns describe best practices for specific situations. They show the most intuitive and comprehensible version to model. Best practices are especially useful at the beginning of modeling projects. They help novice modelers to become familiar with process modeling. In certain situations design patterns are also applicable to other contexts. However, process modelers must check these situations to ensure the proper application of design patterns. Modelers must have modeling expertise to perform such checks. With the help of design patterns organizations influence and improve the way modelers capture situations in process models.

Design Patterns – Examples

Design patterns are applicable for specific contexts. The use of design patterns is illustrated in two examples. The first example focuses on the modeling of a meeting where several people participate. Although the context seems trivial, capturing this situation often leads to different process models. Figure 11 shows a design pattern to model such situations. The PreSales Consultant triggers a meeting which is held by the Account Manager. Although the task "Perform Meeting" is shown in the lane of the Account Manager, additional resources participate in the meeting. These additional roles are shown as customized artifacts and associated with the meeting. In total, three roles participate in the meeting as shown in the example. The pattern can be reused for other meeting situations or collaborations. It shows an effective way to capture the situation in the model.

Another possibility to capture the meeting in a model is the creation of lanes for all meeting participants. All participants execute the task "perform meeting" in parallel. This representation requires a lane for each participant, the duplication of the meeting task as well as the parallel execution of the task and the corresponding synchronization. Summing up, the design pattern shown in Figure 10 is a superior representation of the meeting context and easier to comprehend.

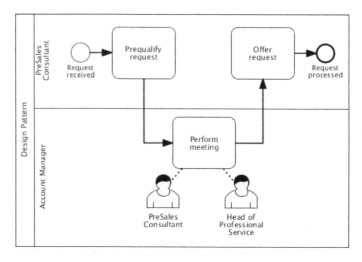

Caption 11: Modeling Meetings

Another example for a design pattern is the use of business rule tasks. Modelers can represent rules explicitly in models as shown in Figure 12. However, in case the rules get updated, extended or deleted, the whole process models must be changed in order to capture the changes. Thus, the process model in Figure 12 should be used with care when depicting business rules. A better representation for business rules is shown in Figure 13. The computation of the discounts is done in the task "Compute discount". The task is marked as a business rule task as described in the BPMN 2.0 specification. The marking means that the rules are stored in an external container, e.g. a file or a table. It must be mentioned that the container is not shown in Figure 13. The model in Figure 13 is easier to read and comprehend than the one in Figure 12. Additionally, business rules can be modified or changed without changing the process models. This becomes especially important if processes contain several business rule tasks. Process models that explicitly capture rules in the model tend to get large and complex. Additionally, model viewers face difficulties to focus on individual rules. The pattern shown in Figure 13 is recommended to avoid these drawbacks. The pattern for business rules can be applied to similar situations where rule tasks are applied.

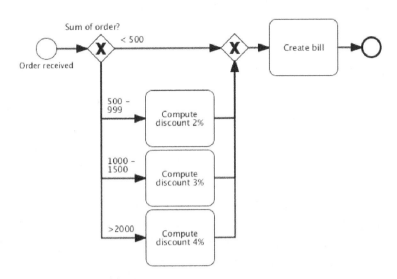

Caption 12: Business Rules explicitly modeled

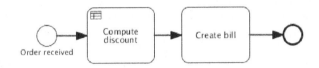

Caption 13: Business Rule Task

Naming Conventions

Process models exhibit the control flow of processes. In order to add semantic information to symbols, e.g. tasks, they get labeled. The naming usually relies on the process modeler and his naming style. The semantic information given by labels is important when it comes to the verification of process models. The verification checks how well process models capture real-world scenarios. Thus, labels should be present in models. The quality assurance of name tags is important for verification tasks. It is advisable to propose naming conventions to guide the labeling of process elements. The standardization of name tags assists the governance of models.

The labels of process elements are typically chosen according to their actual types. Name tags of tasks differ from those of events. The labels of tasks are chosen with the help of the verb-object style. This style enforces modelers to choose a verb together with a business object. The verb-object style is known to be less ambiguous and easier to understand. Naming conventions describe the styles to propose labels for different element types.

Naming Conventions – Examples

Labeling process elements is an important feature. In practice, the names of elements are often chosen freely which can lead to misinterpretations. Figure 14 shows how labels for different process elements can be chosen. The upper part of the figure depicts labels that can be understood well. The lower part illustrates the same element types but shows labels which should be avoided. Organizations should describe how labels for elements are chosen.

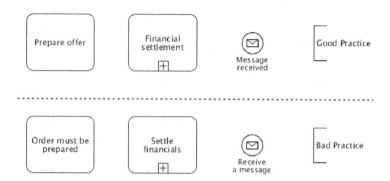

Caption 14: Naming Conventions

HOW TO DEVELOP BEST PRACTICE GUIDELINES?

Best practice guidelines should be individually developed for modeling projects. Each modeling project has its own characteristics, purposes and goals. Modeling projects can largely differ in their purpose, e.g., process automation projects vs. process documentation. Thus, these differences should be taken into account when developing best practice guidelines. It is important to tailor best practices to the unique purposes of process models and the project roles involved. Of course, certain best practices can be used in all modeling projects but must still be checked. The introduction of modeling guidelines should be done by expert modelers who do have large expertise and experience. Best practice guidelines should also be updated if new best practices arise or existing ones change due to project-specific requirements.

In order to develop best practice guidelines you can use the framework described in this paper. Along with the categories you should focus on your individual modeling project and collect best practices to meet your goals. The categories capture characteristics of modeling projects that influence the modeling behavior and, thus, the creation of process models. The categories guide the development of best practice guidelines. The content of the categories should be proposed by the organization and process modelers involved in the project. We suggest to define modeling guidelines before the actual modeling in projects takes place. This avoids misinterpretations especially at the beginning of modeling projects. Modeling guidelines can be updated

SUMMARY

The establishment of modeling guidelines for specific modeling projects requires proper planning. Guidelines should contain best practices that fit the purposes and goals of the actual projects. The introduction of modeling guidelines enables organizations to govern and manage process models as well as process modeling more efficiently. Best practice examples guide process modelers to create models that meet agreed specifications. Especially novice modelers are supported by modeling guidelines. Best practice guidelines further assist the validation of process models which in turn helps to avoid semantic problems in models.

In this paper we presented a framework to develop best practice modeling guidelines. The framework is suitable to establish guidelines that meet the individual purposes of modeling projects. Best practice guidelines for BPMN 2.0 incorporate best practices that often also fit for BPMN 1.x. Existing guidelines for BPMN 1.x can be reused while creating guidelines for the BPMN 2.0. We recommend an agile development of modeling guidelines. The management and enforcement of best practice guidelines plays an important part in modeling projects. If organizations introduce best practice modeling guidelines for their modeling projects, they have to keep their guideline up to date. If they do so, they gain effective measures to manage their modeling projects more successfully.

Making BPMN 2.0 Fit for Full Business Use

Tobias Rausch, Harald Kuehn, BOC AG, Marion Murzek, BOC GmbH, Austria and Thomas Brennan, BOC Ltd, Ireland

ABSTRACT

Addressing users throughout the business is one of the key goals of BPMN 2.0. At the same time "BPMN is constrained to support only the concepts of modeling that are applicable to business processes. This means that other types of modeling done by organizations for business purpose is out of scope for BPMN." [OMG, 2010]. While this is understandable when defining a standard, it is essential for organizations to have support for BPM scenarios such as work instructions, organizational analysis, process costing, ICS/ERM etc.

This paper shows how BPMN 2.0 could be extended with business relevant concepts to support business-analysis (e.g. creating risk reports by assigning risks/controls to tasks). This will be demonstrated by looking at different real-life scenarios and how BPMN processes are linked with organizational data, (IT) resources, information, risks and controls and thereby allowing rich business analysis, reporting and simulation. The application of the proposed extensions will be illustrated using the BPM tool ADONIS [BOC, 2010].

There has been much discussion about BPMN's first letter and this paper illustrates how users are offered both a standard for describing process models and support of their key business application scenarios.

INTRODUCTION AND CONSTRAINTS OF BPMN

In defining the scope of their specification the OMG writes about having developed "a standard Business Process Model and Notation (BPMN)" and that "the primary goal of BPMN is to provide a notation that is readily understandable by all business users from the business analysts that create the initial drafts of the processes, to the technical developers responsible for implementing the technology that will perform those processes, and finally, to the business people who will manage and monitor those processes" [OMG, 2010]. The second important goal of the notation is that XML execution languages (as e.g. BPEL) can be visualized.

From a notation point of view focusing on process modeling, it can be concluded that the BPMN specification fulfills these goals. Despite the fact that there are ongoing discussions [SINU 2010, SWEN 2010] about the final result and degree of achieving these goals – this discussion is being left to others and in particular the users for a final judgment.

However when looking at BPMN in terms of providing a framework and means for business professionals and analysts to go beyond modeling process flows and implement typical (business-driven) Business Process Management (BPM) scenarios such as work instructions, organizational analysis, process costing, or ICS/ERM, the specification has clear constraints.

This is pointed out on page 22 in the specification itself: "BPMN is constrained to support only the concepts of modeling that are applicable to business processes.

This means that other types of modeling done by organizations for business purpose is out of scope for BPMN." [OMG, 2010]

Also various books on BPMN 2.0 have explicitly stated this. For example Bruce Silver in his book "BPMN Method & Style" states that "BPMN really just describes processes in terms of their activity flows. That alone encompasses quite a lot, but admittedly more information is needed to do BPM. [...] Business architects and other BPM practitioners never cease to remind me that process modeling, as defined by BPMN, is only one component of the business modeling needed to properly describe, analyze, transform, and optimize a company's business processes." [SILV, 2009]. He then continues by listing half a page of information (such as controls, products, policies, organizational structure and roles, activity resources, IT systems, Services, Data, etc.), beyond what is captured by BPMN, but needed to support business professionals or as he calls it "support a process manager in an enterprise BPM program".

In terms of defining a standard like BPMN these limitations are certainly understandable and might be even necessary, as trying to cover and provide standards for all possible aspects of business modeling and associated scenarios would certainly take more than one life-time of a human being and possibly have negative effects on the wide acceptance and adoption of BPMN.

Nevertheless business users will not restrict themselves to process flow-charting only and have obvious requirements in having their BPM scenarios supported, i.e. they need a means to overcome the lack of such concepts in BPMN – business modeling and analysis is more than BPMN!

This chapter aims at contributing to this point and showing how both the BPMN standard for describing process models and support of key business application scenarios can be provided.

This will be done by showing the core elements of model-based BPM and what typical requirements and scenarios business professionals have, beyond the modeling of processes. Based on this the subsequent sections take a look at different, selected use cases for business modeling and analysis and how BPMN 2.0 can be extended and/or integrated to support these real-life use cases.

We then propose concrete extensions to BPMN 2.0 derived from these use cases, and how the BPMN meta-model can be embedded in a wider business modeling and analysis environment (and meta-model).

The paper concludes with expectations on the application of BPMN 2.0 and an outlook towards future work and research.

CORE ELEMENTS OF BUSINESS PROCESS MANAGEMENT

Within a model-based management approach the following four core elements can be identified when referring to BPM [JKBK, 2004]. Business professionals involved in BPM normally have to deal with aspects related to all of these core elements.

A corporation defines itself by its *products*. A product can be either a tangible asset such as consumable goods, motor vehicles, raw materials and pharmaceuticals or intangible assets such as licenses, patents, professional services and consulting services.

Business processes describe how the products will be designed, produced, offered, sold, delivered, and maintained. We distinguish external processes and their value exchange with the market, internal (private) processes executed within an enterprise and inter-organizational processes which are executed by cooperating with business partners.

For the execution of its business processes a company requires two main resources: on the one hand, *organizational resources* such as employees who execute the tasks and sub-processes based on their skills, experiences, and organizational rules. And on the other hand, *technical resources* such as information technology (IT) and information systems (IS) which build the backbone for handling all related information properly.

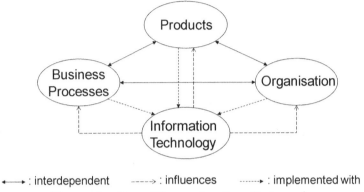

←——→ : interdependent   ----→ : influences   ......→ : implemented with

Figure 1 – Core Elements of an Enterprise

So, process flow-charts and therefore BPMN diagrams are an essential part of information needed by business professionals. But additional aspects represented by the other core elements have to be taken into account as well.

TYPICAL REQUIREMENTS AND SCENARIOS OF BUSINESS USERS

While process modeling is key to understanding the intra- and inter-organizational business processes of an enterprise, Business Process Management does not stop there. It takes these business processes as a starting point for various application scenarios and strives to satisfy the needs of all the different parties involved in BPM. The following figure shows typical application scenarios originating from business' requirements.

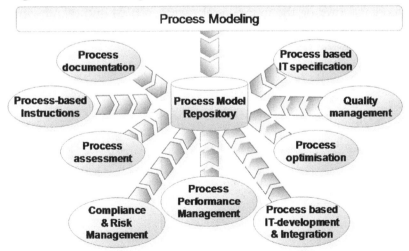

Figure 2- Business Process Management application scenarios

As you can see all of them are developed from and have references to business process models and continually build on their content with additional information needed for the different scenarios and their stakeholders. However they all go beyond process modeling and are required to capture and provide information for various groups inside (and possibly outside) the organization.

The next figure shows the typical stakeholders and their interests and requirements towards BPM and information in an Integrated Management System [BOC, 2010].

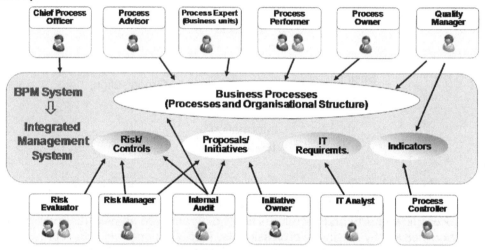

Figure 3 – Stakeholders and their BPM association

Now, what does this mean for BPMN? Through its defined meta-model BPMN 2.0 provides "three basic types of sub-models within an end-to-end BPMN model: Processes, Choreographies and Collaborations (a view of Conversations)" [OMG, 2010, page 23].

The central diagram for business processes (private and public) is what is commonly called the Business Process Diagram (BPD).

The following figure shows how the BPD can be embedded in a wider business modeling context covering the four core elements of BPM and thereby integrating BPMN into a full BPM modeling and analysis environment.

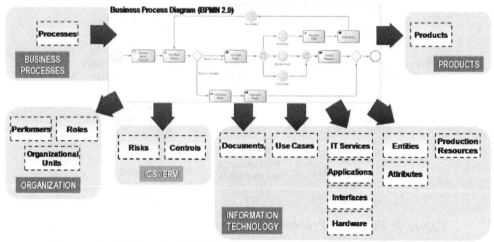

Figure 4 – BPD embedded in a business modeling environment

Next to the four core elements of BPM in an enterprise you will see that additional elements providing mechanisms to document an ICS by assigning risks and controls to processes have been added in the figure above. Building and documenting an ICS has become increasingly important, in particular as legislation has been tightened after the big financial scandals in the early 2000s and has further intensified following the latest economic downturn and failure of financial services institutions. Therefore identifying risks, relating them to business processes where they can occur and designing proper controls has become more or less a fifth core element to be found in most organizations.

The next sections will provide use cases for business-driven analysis and show how and where BPMN has been extended to make it fit for full business use in these chosen use case scenarios.

USAGE OF BPMN WITHIN BUSINESS ANALYSIS SCENARIOS

Within this section we will show how BPMN could be used and integrated with additional business information for selected BPM use case scenarios.

The scenarios selected are:
- Organizational analysis and work instructions
- Building an Internal Control System (ICS), Enterprise Risk Management
- Process costing, Simulation
- Test-case management

These are typical use case scenarios involving various stakeholders from the business and providing answers to their different needs.

In each of the following sub-sections we will briefly present the goals of the use case scenario, the stakeholders and the business roles involved. We will explain the requirements and expected results and how these can be achieved by extending BPMN. Where appropriate to support the presented information we will illustrate the proposed extensions using the BPM tool ADONIS.

Organizational analysis and work instructions

Having a clear picture of organizational responsibilities and making them transparent is one of the key issues of Business Process Management. It is also the basis for distributing precise and correct work instructions to the work force, as needed by larger organizations across all industries.

Typical roles involved in these tasks are business analysts, process experts from the business and stakeholders also include the process owners, the quality management team and internal auditing.

An essential starting point for process design and all activities related to BPM is a process map (company map, process landscape). A process map allows an organization to identify their processes, to classify and cluster them (e.g. into management, core and supporting processes) and to define a structure and a clear scope of the processes. It is also an essential medium to create a common picture and understanding of the company's processes, for assigning process owners, to understand end-to-end processes properly and for defining interfaces and possible service levels. All in all there is this "golden rule": do not start any BPM task/initiative without having an agreed upon process landscape in place!

In BPMN 2.0 Conversation Diagrams can be seen as a first step towards a more high-level process based view of an organization, but do not provide the elements typically used for creating structural diagrams.

Therefore it is suggested and highly recommended to include a level "above" the BPMN elements that provides references to the BPMN elements, such as the Business Process Diagram.

The following figure shows an example of a process map: such a map can have several levels and will lead to the concrete BPD of a process (references to BPDs can also be seen in the graphics of the processes in the map).

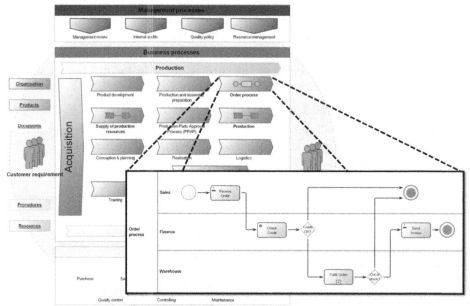

Figure 5 – Example of a Process map referencing a BPMN Business Process

Looking at a concrete business process there are some typical key elements needed to describe a process from a business point of view and to store enough relevant data to perform organizational analysis and provide work instructions.

BPMN by its nature of focusing on the execution of processes provides some means for assigning input and output data (sets), data structures, documents and resources as well as interfaces needed for the execution. Therefore the following extensions are suggested:

- In the Start event:
  - Process owner, inputs, referenced products and required applications/IT-services (to cover at least the four core elements)
  - Critical success factors, process performance indicators (to link to goals and strategy, satisfy process maturity requirements and allow Process Performance Management)
- In the Task:
  - Responsibility according to the RACI concept, i.e. assigning the roles which are responsible, accountable, consulted or informed for a concrete task in a process.
  - Applications/IT-Services required for performing the task
  - References to use cases providing input for system design based on the business processes and allowing to trace back requirements to the business
  - Referenced products

- Assigned risks and controls (for details see the following sub-section on building an Internal Control System)
- Activity times, fixed activity costs and performer assignment (for simulation purposes, see one of the following sub-sections on process costing and simulation for further details)

It is also suggested to provide the user with possibilities to show such added information directly in the diagram, e.g. as can be seen in the following figure to show the responsible role below the task or the used application above it.

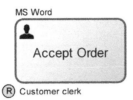

Figure 6 – Task with visualized "Role" and "IT-Application"

Based on the proposed extensions the typical business roles involved can gain different views and run different kinds of analysis, such as:

- Who is responsible for which processes? For which processes is a particular person responsible?
- What are the responsibilities of a particular role?
- For which tasks is a concrete role responsible, accountable, being consulted and/or informed? (➔ essentially delivering job descriptions for the business)
- What are key success factors and the KPIs needed to measure business performance?
- Where are the key operational risks (also in terms of impact on the business) and are sufficient controls in place?
- Where are particular applications and IT-services used?
- Which parts of the business and which processes are concerned or affected when switching to a new IT system/application or planning maintenance windows?
- Who is concerned or affected when changing document templates/forms?
- etc.

Building an Internal Control System (ICS), Enterprise Risk Management

Many companies are obliged by legislation to create and prove an Internal Control System (ICS) [COSO, 1992; COSO, 2004] and adhere to well-drafted standards (SOX in USA, 8th EU Directive, Combined Code in UK, AktG in Germany, URÄG in Austria etc.) as well as sector-specific rules such as Basel II and Solvency II.

ICS projects usually involve several internal and external roles (revision, accountancy, external auditor, risk manager, control owner etc.) and characterize themselves by having a high level of interaction between different participating actors, departments and external partners. The steps within the project are performed in a parallel manner demanding efficient and effective collaboration between the parties involved.

In terms of methodology, the "magic" triangle of Process-Risk-Control as shown in the figure below, provides the framework necessary to implement an ICS.

In the context of BPMN that means:
- having a means to create risk and control objects

- extending the BPMN task with new attributes, where risks can be identified and assigned to them, as well as controls (as counter-measures) that can be documented

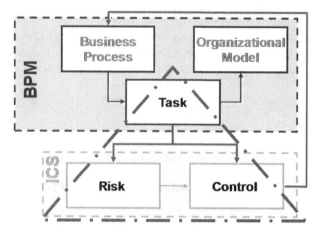

Figure 7 - The "magic" triangle of Process-Risk-Control

In ICS projects risk catalogues are usually (centrally) defined or even directly derived from rule sets like Basel II. Then during the project an assignment of the relevant identified risks to the processes takes place and risk analysts will assign both the risk probability and impact. Subsequently controls are assigned to risks and both have to be properly documented.

Information on assigned risks and controls can also be directly seen in the BPMN diagrams, as you can see in the upper right hand corner of the Task in our example below:

Figure 8 – Task with visualized Risks and Controls

Based on the information captured, business users can generate different forms of reports for their stakeholders: a typical artifact is a so called ICS matrix, which will list processes and activities on the vertical and provide information on risks, their impact, probability and control (execution) on the horizontal side of the matrix.

Process costing, Simulation

The quantitative and dynamic evaluation of business processes and the associated elements such as roles, organizational units, products, services and technical resources is important to provide a sound basis for management decisions based on business process analysis. This is of special interest before business process implementation activities and organizational restructuring initiatives are executed. Typical mechanisms used in this context are process costing and simulation algorithms [BKJ, 2003].

We call the quantitative and dynamic evaluation of business processes without considering the underlying working environment as "path analysis". If the working environment is included as well we call it "capacity analysis" and "workload analysis". Typical questions to be answered in such evaluations are:

- "What is the average cycle time of a process?"
- "What is the critical path of a business process concerning criteria such as consumed execution time, unnecessary waiting time, the percentage of transport time to the overall cycle time of a process etc.?"
- "What is the probability of the process path with the highest process costs?"
- "How many actors (human resources, technical resources) will be needed to execute a new 'to-be' process 10,000 times a month?"
- "Which actors will be affected by the bottleneck if the frequency of a business process is increased by 20%?"

The specification of BPMN 2.0 does not contain sufficient information to be able to answers such questions. The following list provides a proposal for quantitative parameters to extend BPMN 2.0 to apply it for process costing and business process simulation:

- Time-related parameters: the cycle time describes the average time from process start until process end. The execution time covers the time necessary to execute all of the involved tasks of a process. The waiting time describes the time spent before tasks are executed or which is consumed while tasks are interrupted. The resting time represents the time after a task was executed until it will be transported to the next actor. The transport time describes the time needed for transportation of material between two tasks.
- Cost-related parameters: activity costs are directly assigned to tasks and are independent from the assigned actor executing the task. Actor costs occur independently of the tasks an actor executes, while actor-related costs are the costs which occur executing certain tasks. Resource costs occur when actors need certain kinds of resources to execute their tasks. The sum of all kinds of costs which can be directly assigned to and/or computed for a specific business process is referred to as the 'process costs'.
- Capacity-related parameters: the process quantity describes how often a process will be executed in a certain period of time. The resource need describes how many resources of a given resource type, e.g. human resources or technical resources, are needed for the execution of a certain amount of processes. The workload shows how much certain resources are involved or needed to execute a certain volume of business processes or to be able to handle a certain process frequency.
- Other parameters: typical other parameters necessary to allow process costing and process simulation are probabilities when the control or information flow is split into several alternatives. For advanced situations it might even be necessary to describe statistical distributions such as discrete, normal, uniform or exponential distributions.

The following figure shows how business process simulation might look applying BPMN for the underlying process mapping.

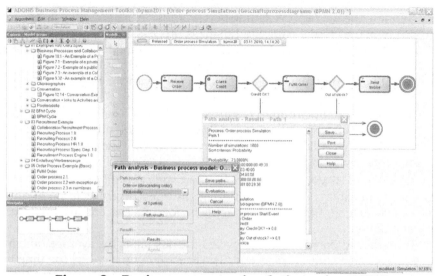

Figure 9 – Business process simulation using BPMN

Test-case management

A methodical approach for creating business test-cases is to derive these test-cases from the existing business process models, e.g. BPMN business process diagrams in a company [KMSZ, 2010]. This is important to not only cover functional tests, but real life test-cases based on business cases. The deduction of business test-cases from business process models provides a maximum coverage of business cases and leads to early detection of possible errors in the software and services used for executing these business process models.

Automated deduction of test-cases based on business process models can be structured into five phases:

    a)   requirement definition and business concept,
    b)   architecture and component concept,
    c)   implementation,
    d)   component, integration- and system tests and
    e)   acceptance tests.

In phase a), b) and e) the knowledge of the process owner and the process performers in the particular operating department and the process advisor from the internal business organization department is needed. For phase b), c) and d) the IT Analyst is the contact person, who knows about the IT support of the business processes and manages the execution of the tests.

The first step to structure the test-cases is to use the process map, already mentioned in section "Organizational analysis and work instructions". In the next step, the referenced business process diagrams are used. For each path in a BPMN business process diagram a test-case chain is derived. In addition to every task the pre- and post conditions concerning the test-case rules are considered. By using an animation of all process paths, see [Figure 10], the standard business cases are defined and recorded.

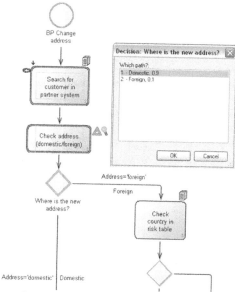

Figure 10 - Animation of process path in a BPMN business process diagram

Finally the data of each path is saved as an XML file, which is used as the source for various test templates. This data contains information about the task, name, description, the responsible role, input and output documents and data structures.

PROPOSED BPMN 2.0 EXTENSIONS FOR BUSINESS USE

The previous section provided a detailed analysis of four important business scenarios and extensions of BPMN to make it fit for use by key business stake holders and help them achieve their related business goals.

Within this section we show how these proposed extensions relate to the defined classes in the BPMN specification and how other, non-flow-related concepts can be mapped to business modeling concepts.

The BPMN specification also foresees, next to the elements needed to define process flows, data (input, output and data flow), messages (and flow) as well as participants and various resources. These elements form the core part of the BPD diagram.

Figure 11 shows how the BPD can been embedded in a business modeling environment covering the four core elements of BPM, creating links between them and thereby integrating BPMN into a full BPM modeling and analysis environment. For this embedding, the method integration approach introduced in [ZKK, 2007] has been used. The numbers 1-4 in Figure 11 reference the extended classes used in each of the business scenarios introduced in the last section.

There are two different kinds of extensions:

- On one hand we have the given BPMN classes that are without a defined notation, like BPMNInputOutputSpecification, BPMNResource-Role and BPMNServices.
- On the other hand we have classes which are not (yet) covered by the BPMN specification, Product, Component, Risk, Control etc.
- The class "Process*" which exists in the BPMN specification and has the notation of a pool has been reused as part of a process map with another notation.

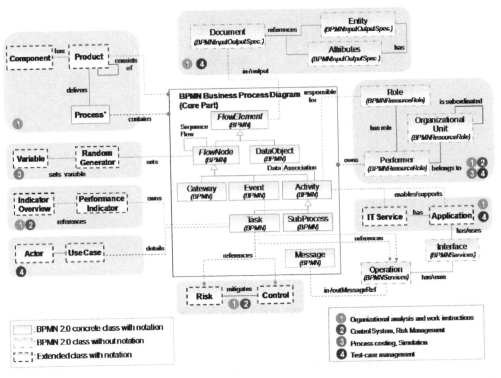

Figure 11 - BPMN 2.0 with extensions for business use

As you can further see in Figure 11 the core element "Information Technology" has been further split up into different modeling concepts (classes). The IT system model provides means to build up an IT service catalogue and application landscape, e.g. to develop and create Service-Oriented Architectures (SOA). Additionally it allows to document interfaces between Applications and Services and identifying infrastructure resources (providing the basis for Enterprise Architecture Management (EAM)).

Furthermore a document repository/catalogue can be built up: documents are used as inputs and outputs to activities (e.g. a task in a process), they can be forms and templates and they can also represent guidelines and procedures which have to be obeyed during the execution of processes and tasks.

The IT systems and documents themselves are further linked with the data model, e.g. to define which entities are processed by applications and which attributes are used to fill in data into a form or template.

Last, but not least, a UML Use Case Diagram is provided to be able to capture business requirements by detailing tasks in business process diagrams for a subsequent system design. The Use Case Diagram hereby serves as an example of possible integration with another OMG standard and it goes without saying that also other UML stereotypes, such as the Class Diagram, Sequence Diagram, State Diagram etc. could be added and foreseen to aid detailed system design.

CONCLUSION AND OUTLOOK

Business Process Management has been a key discipline in managing organizations over the last ten years. With the inclusion of BPMN to OMG's standardization body a big step forward towards a standard business process notation has been taken. The new BPMN version 2.0 can only advance further forward by providing a Business Process Model and Notation, possibly allowing BPMN to become for Process Design and Interchange what UML already is for System Design and Analysis.

As the need for a standardized notation, interchange of models and portability across platforms continues to grow, BPMN is also enjoying steady growth and a greater level of importance. The new version providing a defined meta-model, extended concepts and a new interchange format will certainly help to support this.

However there has been and is much discussion about BPMN's first letter and how well the specification supports business professionals and their needs.

This paper has selected four typical and important real-life business use cases (scenarios) of business professionals and shown where and how the current BPMN specification can be extended to accommodate their needs and requirements. This has been done while ensuring full compatibility and conformance with the BPMN specification.

Thereby BPMN has been made fit for business purposes and professionals and we strongly expect that this will be crucial to the real-life application of BPMN 2.0 through addressing users across the business, going beyond pure process modeling. By doing so, one of the main concerns towards BPMN could be addressed if this was achieved, by offering both a standard for describing process models and the support of key business application scenarios.

Future work in this area can and should look at what business related extensions are generic enough to be standardized and included in a next version of BPMN, as well as to evaluate the concepts currently available in BPMN and see how they have been received and used by end users.

REFERENCES

[BKJ, 2003] Boucher, X.; Kühn, H.; Janke, J.: Integrated Modelling and Simulation of Inter-Organisational Business Processes. In: Proceedings of the Fourth Conference Francophone de Modélisation et Simulation (MoSim'03), "Organisation et Conduite d'Activités dans l'Industrie et les Services", Toulouse, France, April 23-25, 2003.

[BOC, 2010] Homepage of BOC group, http://www.boc-group.com.

[COSO, 1992] Internal Control - Integrated Framework, AICPA, 1992.

[COSO, 2004] Enterprise Risk Management - Integrated Framework , AICPA, 2004.

[JKBK, 2004] Junginger, S.; Kühn, H.; Bayer, F.; Karagiannis, D.: Workflow-based Business Monitoring. In: Fischer, L. (Ed.): Workflow Handbook 2004. Future Strategies Inc., 2004, pp. 65-80.

[KMSZ, 2010] Kühn, H.; Murzek, M.; Specht, G.; Zivkovic, S.: Model-Driven Development of Interoperable, Inter-Organisational Business Processes. In: Yannis Charalabidis (Ed.), Interoperability in the Digital Public Services and Administration: Bridging E-Government and E-Business, ISBN 978-1-61520-887-6, IGI Global, 2010, pp. 119-143.

[OMG, 2010] Business Process Model and Notation (BPMN) Version 2.0, June 2010, OMG Document Number: dtc/2010-06-06, OMG Adopted Beta Specification.

[SILV, 2009] Silver, B.: BPMN Method and Style: A levels-based methodology for BPM process modeling and improvement using BPMN 2.0. Cody-Cassidy Press, 2009.

[SINU, 2010] Sinur, J.: BPMN for Business Professionals: Burn Baby Burn. http://blogs.gartner.com/jim_sinur/2010/08/30/bpmn-for-business-professionals-burn-baby-burn/ (last viewed 03.11.2010)

[SWEN, 2010] Swenson, K. D.: BPMN 2.0: no longer for Business Professionals. http://kswenson.wordpress.com/2010/09/01/bpmn-2-0-no-longer-for-business-professionals/ (last viewed 03.11.2010)

[ZKK, 2007] Zifkovic, S.; Kühn, H.; Karagiannis, D.: Facilitate Modelling using Method Integration - An Approach using Mappings and Integration Rules. In: Österle, H.; Schelp, J.; Winter, R. (Eds.): Proceedings of the 15th European Conference on Information Systems (ECIS2007) - "Relevant rigour - Rigorous relevance", St. Gallen, Switzerland. June 2007, pp. 2038 – 2050.

BPMN and Business Strategy: One Size Does Not Fit All

Lionel Loiseau, BNP Paribas BPM Competency Centre and Michael Ferrari, Analyst, France

ABSTRACT

A five-layer operational translation of business process approach

In BPM, we would like to conciliate the management-oriented abstraction necessary to fully grasp the essence of a process with the exhaustiveness and realism that are essential to an automated solution.

But one size does not fit all!

This led us to develop a classification of the various business process modeling plans and a gradual approach aimed at defining how to move smoothly from one plan to another.

Our classification takes into account the required levels of abstraction, the legacy notations, and the important number of existing process models as well as the contribution of the BPMN notation.

While traditional BPMN approaches present three levels of process modeling, respectively descriptive, analytic and exhaustive, our classification connects BPMN to strategy, indicators, business rules and risks, and breaks down further the separation between general process models and organized process models.

In this chapter, we intend to detail and justify our approach and our classification, as well as explain how they are used in our company. We also intend to shed a new light on the role of the BPM analyst, an emerging position blending several skills, notations, and collaborative tools.

INTRODUCTION

As the adage says, "a picture is worth a thousand words". The human brain is made in such a manner that it is easier and quicker to fully grasp the context and the essence of a process when it is visual rather than text-based.

However, it is not possible to design at the same level the necessary abstraction to grasp the internal running of a process for top managers and the exhaustiveness and realism required by an automation solution.

There is a wide conceptual gap between, for example, a strategic description and business requirements. The required level of parameters for specifying the execution of an IT application is also very different.

These thoughts led us to define a several layer-classification of business process modeling. This classification depends on various levels of abstraction and matters of concern, as well as a gradual approach that aims at smoothing away the cascade from one layer to another. We named this approach: operational translation of business process.

In this context, the BPMN notation stands out in a well-established existing environment with proprietary notations such as Aris, Casewise or Mega, not to mention others with significant investments. We also have a valuable heritage of models that it is completely out of question to either migrate or automate. At BNP

Paribas, among others, no less than 8,000 existing process models need to be maintained.

Does BPMN require the replacement of the existing notations? Do we need to adapt existing process models? What is exactly BPMN contribution? After all, isn't it another additional IT craze? How does it differentiate itself from the other notations? Could it peacefully live together with the others? And, in that case, how?

We, at BNP Paribas, carefully thought about what we could do. These questions do not seem to be well covered by the available literature and materials. At the most, we found some comparisons between several types of notation: some tools to transform from a notation to another with, sometimes, displayed intentions to make proprietary notations evolve toward BPMN.

From our point of view, the most remarkable contribution of BPMN lies in its large expressiveness in exception handling; in its most welcome processes collaboration, compulsory for their automation and in its new ability to be serialized in a comprehensible format for an automation solution.

However, BPMN shows some weaknesses when it comes to linking the process model to functional or application architecture blueprints, strategy, objectives, risks, business rules or to define performance criteria. This is understandable: the notation has not been specifically designed for that purpose. In other words, BPMN is weak when it comes to putting the process back in its working context and performing analysis or communicating to non-technical users.

Our classification of the various layers of business modeling and our translation approach should consequently integrate the existing proprietary notations, the stock of existing business process models as well as the contribution of BPMN.

Our classification and approach, initially based on proprietary notations, took significant advantage of the contribution of BPMN. It is a key point to "stretching down" our layers toward the IT and automation activities.

CLASSIFICATION

While common BPMN classifications present process modeling in three levels, respectively "descriptive", "analytic" and "complete", our classification distinguishes itself by "stretching them up" with two additional upper levels:
- The process heritage blueprint of the company;
- A distinctive separation between general process models and their organized process model view.

We strove towards the following goals:
- Modeling can aim at various objectives : consequently various representations and abstractions are needed;
- In a complementary way, we need to consider the upper levels that are not well covered by BPMN and take into account the lower levels that are not well covered by the proprietary notations;
- Using the most complete and adapted notation according to the objective;
- Introducing a translation approach in order to cascade seamlessly, and with full knowledge of the facts, from one modeling plan to another.
- Identifying the whole potential of a key JUNCTION POINT that spans both the business and IT teams and that requires new skills and the control of the BPMN notation. At this point, BPMN, along with business process modeling environments, brings all its relevance and improves a working mode where the detailed specifications are just "thrown over the wall" for technologists to implement them. They combine the expressiveness and

the thoroughness of the notation with all the power of a collaborative environment.

The five modeling plans that we suggest are the following and illustrated below:

- Business plan – Overall & General View;
- Business plan – Static Process View;
- Business plan – Dynamic Resources View;
- Workflow plan – Translation View;
- Workflow plan – Orchestrated Physical View.

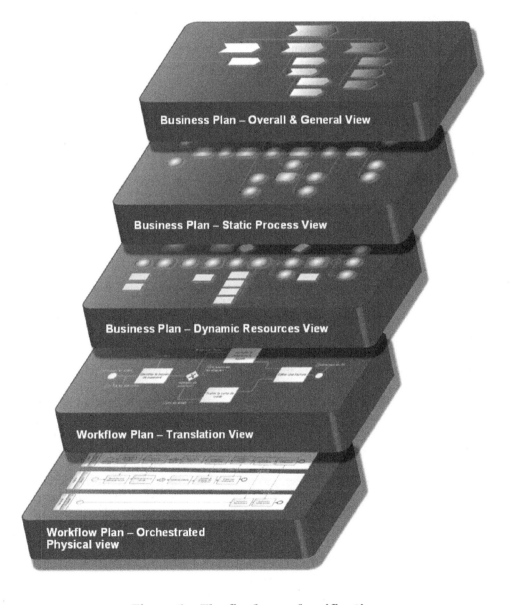

Figure 1 – The five-layer classification

BUSINESS PLAN – OVERALL & GENERAL VIEW

This level aims at identifying, classifying and analysing in a very general manner the main processes of the company. It will provide an answer to the "what?" question, the decision level, rather than the "how?". The latter will be subject of further discussions. It also includes different views containing organization, indicators, risks or any high-level element.

The business process modeling processes which characterize this level provides:
- An overall representation of processes dedicated to the top management in order to ease their understanding and the decisions that are likely to be taken. In other words, it depicts "the big picture"; the corresponding processes are comprehended in a very macroscopic manner;
- The identification of the main mission statements and strategic objectives;
- The classification of processes into families such as the traditional distinction between core business, support and management families;
- The recognition of the heritage value of process assets.

This level is perfect to communicate and establish a common understanding of the organization. It also connects with global performance indicators, general strategic objectives with the prioritization of the corresponding budgets, resources, and projects. It is a powerful tool to assess the core missions of the organization.

Invariance assumption: at this level, the cataloguing of processes into families is invariant from a banking domain to another and from a business line to another. It is the reason why we are able to find general classifications materials such as the American Quality & Productivity Centre cross-industry Process Classification Framework, or IBM' Information Framework for instance. In case of companies' mergers, these general classification frameworks could be used to sort out the most reusable models.

BUSINESS PLAN – STATIC PROCESS VIEW

This level will provide the general analysis of a given process regardless of the organization. In other terms, the process description would still be resilient against massive organizational changes. It globally answers the "how?" question from a business point of view. It provides a high-level representation of the business process and a static description of main business activities.

The business process modeling activities which characterize this level provide:
- The identification of the end-to-end process, that is from the client's request to the corresponding reply of the organization, expressing by this way a value-added chain, crossing all the organization (although they will not be described at this level). It replaces the clients at the very center of matters of concern.
- The identification of high-level business events; corresponding macro-activities within the process, kinds of "moments of truth" in the client relationship, punctuating the process life cycle; decision points; and corresponding transitions between these business events decision points and macro-activities;
- The representation of an abstract, "ideal" running mode, where all the paths are flowing happily in order to extricate the process bulk.

As described, the Business Plan – Static Process View is the natural home for describing processes in their general acceptance: collection of structured business events, activities, and transitions; identified client; client-to-client range; and increasing value chain.

This level is typically used in the banking business to express interactions between a front and a back office without presuming, at this stage, of the possible concentration of activities in one side or the other. The latter will be described in the next lower level.

In addition, it is valuable in case of mergers because it helps to quickly identify the strengths and weaknesses of main activities. It eases, in the case of complex organization such as BNP Paribas, for instance, decision statements should they concern organization, IT or business policy.

Invariance assumption: as mentioned previously, this level is supposed to be invariant of the underlying organisation and applications.

BUSINESS PLAN – DYNAMIC RESOURCES VIEW

This level is the general ground for a thorough examination of the process for analysis purposes, simulation or for detailed documentation (procedure). It aims at detailing the business analysis of a given process in the precise context of its organization and application heritage. It keeps answering the "how?" question from a business perspective based on organization constraints and the application environment and starts answering the "who?", "where?", "when?" questions, and possibly the "how many?" and the consequently "how much?" questions.

The business process modeling activities which characterize this level provide:

- A representation of positions, persons and IT systems, and their interactions within the process; as well as the available document for the process. The latter regards either the available documentation that describes an event, an activity or a decision, or the documents that are consumed or updated by activities in an administrative process for instance;
- A description of business rules applied to make decisions;
- The identification of the main exception paths with the depiction of decisions and gateways;
- If simulation is needed, the emphasis on durations and sensors that we would like to be captured and monitored, such as touch and idle times, average and standard deviations;
- If costs analysis must be performed, the description of costs related to each activity and resources used to produce the activity;
- For enterprise architecture purposes, functional services can also be represented;
- Progressively, we will break up general activities into tasks following the three units of the ancient Greek tragedy: unit of action, unit of time, and unit of place. These three units, even if they are not yet fully respected at this level, help to find the right level of atomicity for the tasks which should not be interrupted. The global notions of process and activity start to be broken into smaller pieces, i.e. procedures, useful to decide whether this process part should be automated or not;
- The progressive identification of sub-processes. According to the BPMN notation, sub-processes should be identified by fragmentation (i.e. breaking down the overall general process into smaller parts), globalization (i.e. gathering several activities into a consistent whole) and, why not at this stage, by factorization (i.e. identifying some process pieces that can be reused). These considerations will govern the creation of either embedded or reusable sub-processes;
- A certain legibility if not aestheticism. For that purpose, we will avoid accumulating activities on the diagram (a good, even attractive, modeling rule-of-thumb is to restrict to seven the number of activities in the dia-

gram) by creating through fragmentation as many sub-processes as required. It will allow the model to be printed on one page or projected on one slide.

At this level, the decision to launch process simulation campaigns can be made because we are not so far from having the required details level.

Invariance assumption: the process description, at this level, is supposed to stay invariant of a decision to implement it in a BPMS (Business Process Management Suite) or not.

WORKFLOW PLAN – TRANSLATION VIEW

As the previous levels were for business analysis purposes, it now becomes clearer that the process is going to be brought to the gates of automation. This level extends the answers to the "who?", "where?", "when?", "how many?" and "how much?" questions with the "how?" from an IT point of view.

The business process activities which characterize this level provide:

- The actual translation of process model toward BPMN notation;
- A real breaking down of the activities into atomic tasks. For automation purposes, we would need to consider alternately the point of view of each performer, which would result into further breaking down the tasks.
- The introduction of a "loose" flow, breaking off in that way the design of the previous levels which tend to consider process in a tightened flow. For instance, in a purchase process, they would consider that a purchaser is waiting for a request and immediately deals with it. In real life, the purchaser would probably be eager to gather all his pending requests in order to optimize his daily work even to the detriment of the process duration. This globalization concern would probably give birth to natural process collaboration;
- The representation of process collaboration. As mentioned above, previous processes are likely to be further broken down into several processes that will collaborate through catch and throw message events;
- The detailed representation of all possible alternative exception paths;
- The identification of interrupting and escalation intermediate events; of activity factorization into reusable sub-processes; of transactions with their corresponding cancel events and compensation activities;
- The optimization of people's daily work through the definition of roles, skills, capabilities and authorizations, as well as the optimization of task distribution, allocation, and strategy offering.

As mentioned before, even if we sink into the IT sphere at this level, the effective collaboration between business and IT teams here is essential to ensure the success of the process automation.

Invariance assumption: the process description, at this level, is supposed to stay invariant from one BPMS solution to another.

WORKFLOW PLAN – ORCHESTRATED PHYSICAL VIEW

This level deals with IT concerns that are likely to be invisible in a diagram. It extends the "how?" question in a significant technical way and brings the process to the gates of automation.

The activities which characterize this level are:

- The management of data, parameters, attributes, correlations, of their value, persistence, of process mapping;

- The synchronisation and navigation within company organization model;
- The integration of external systems, web services calls, WSDL;
- The design and implementation of user forms; workspaces;
- The corresponding coding and scripting;
- The integration of the specific constraints related to a target BPMS solution.

Invariance assumption: the process automation, at this level, is supposed to stay invariant from an execution environment to another (development, tests, user acceptance, production and so on).

APPROACH

Like one says, "the concept of dog does not bark". Obviously, a process model is not executed day-to-day. It is still an abstract concept not tested and confronted to real life.

In this context, the daily application of our approach, superficially introduced so far, strives for providing a gradual and consistent body to process models. At each level, we would try to be watchful and respectful to align each level accordingly to their previous one's objectives.

Of course, all process modeling projects do not have the calling or the ambition to be automated. At any stage, it should be possible to end, considering that the modeling objectives are reached should they concern process identification, analysis, automation, management, control, communication, documentation, mutual understanding, sharing or capitalization.

At any stage, it seems essential to be able to clearly justify the cascade from one level to another considering the modeling project main objectives and the corresponding exponential investment.

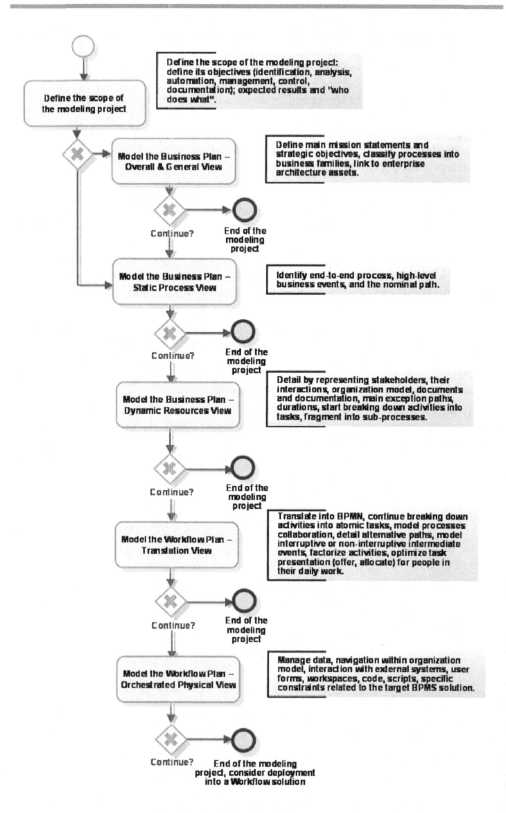

Figure 2 – The operational translation step by step

This approach is rather intended for teams leading large scale modeling projects. Nevertheless, it provides a theoretical or a "self-service" frame useful for smaller scale projects.

Obviously, the "round tripping", from lower to higher levels, is missing in our approach. It is matter of discipline and meticulousness that is out of our scope.

As understood, the upper plans, rather descriptive, aim more at business people. The bottommost, more demanding in term of details, more technical, is more for IT people's concern.

APPLIED CASE: BNP PARIBAS

BNP Paribas (www.bnpparibas.com) is one of the six strongest banks in the world (rated AA by Standard & Poor's i.e. 3rd rating level on a scale of 22) and the largest bank in the Eurozone by deposits. With a presence in more than 80 countries and more than 200,000 employees, including 160,000 in Europe, BNP Paribas is a leading European provider of financial services on a worldwide scale.

It ranks highly in its three core activities: Retail Banking, Investment Solutions and Corporate & Investment Banking. In Retail Banking, the Group has four domestic markets: Belgium, France, Italy and Luxembourg. BNP Paribas is rolling out its integrated model across the Europe-Mediterranean zone and boasts a large network in the United States. BNP Paribas Personal Finance is the leader in consumer lending in Europe.

In its Corporate & Investment Banking and Investment Solutions activities, BNP Paribas also enjoys top positions in Europe and solid and fast-growing businesses in Asia.

In this wide, very challenging and international context, we had the opportunity to work with various teams specialized in every level of our classification.

The most typical cases we met accordingly to BNP Paribas' Norms & Standards Catalog are represented in the following table.

PLAN	POPULATION	NOTATION	TOOL
Business Plan – Overall & General View	Strategic Business Analysts	EPC (Event Process Chain)	Software AG – IDS Scheer ARIS Business Designer
Business Plan – Static Process View	Business Process Analyst, User Representatives	EPC (Event Process Chain)	Software AG – IDS Scheer ARIS Business Designer
Business Plan – Dynamic Resources View	Business Process Analyst, User Representatives	EPC (Event Process Chain)	Software AG – IDS Scheer ARIS Business Designer
Workflow Plan – Translation View	User Representatives, IT Analysts	BPMN 1.2	TIBCO Business Studio
Workflow Plan – Translation View	IT Analysts, IT Developers	BPMN 1.2	TIBCO Business Studio

In order to put our approach into practice and to communicate on it, we launched three initiatives:

- ***PATI (Project Aris Tibco Integration):***

We set up a partnership with IDS Scheer, the ARIS platform vendor, for building a solution able to transform proprietary EPC models into BPMN models, compatible with TIBCO Business Studio.

This solution is intended to make the cascade easier from the Business Plan – Dynamic Resources View to the Workflow Plan – Translation View in the context of a very large scale BPM project addressing several hundreds of business models to be automated in the field of BNP Paribas' French Retail Banking Back Offices.

Currently, due to its experimental features, the corresponding project has been ranked eligible for a European Research Tax Credit.

Figure 3 – PATI two-step transformation

- **Internal training:**

We built an internal BPM training course composed of seven modules ranging from general business process modeling to advanced hands-on exercises in order to experiment in a very concrete manner the operational translation of business processes concepts.

Since 2000, we have had the opportunity to train several hundreds of people.

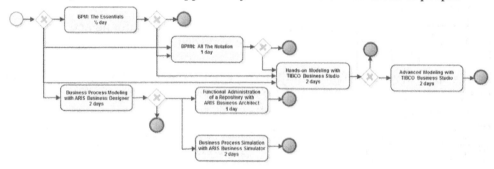

Figure 4 – BNP Paribas internal BPM training course

- **Internal White Paper:**

Lastly, we wrote an internal white paper of which you find the substance here.

DISCUSSION AND CONCLUSION

Our central position as BPM Competency Centre for the whole BNP Paribas Group enabled us to participate, being observers or actors, to more than twenty different automation projects by their ambition, business, budget, duration, internal running mode or constraints.

This led us to confirm that indeed the management of BPM projects is far more difficult than traditional projects' one. First, BPM concepts are quite not yet wide spread across the company and do not beneficiate from the industrialization and maturity of traditional technologies. In addition, BPM addresses very sensitive topics at the very centre of the organization, core business policy and execution. As a consequence, BPM projects reveal early enough an internal politics dimension.

Therefore, we saw a significant amount of projects fail or taking ages in the design, the development or even in user acceptance's phases.

For these reasons, it is essential that business and IT stakeholders come early into a collaborative approach, join and find their way into normative frames.

There is clearly a communication, not to say reconciliation, and change management challenge to take up.

As a matter of fact, the BPMN notation addresses this challenge. Along with the appropriate tools, it encourages a more collaborative and co-responsible way of designing and implementing process automation. It is within the reach of both populations to share BPMN knowledge and interact over the same models.

Through our classification and approach, we strove to make a modest contribution to the discussion. We think that they could contribute to the reinforcement of the BNP Paribas normative frame and to the repeatability of BPM projects successes.

This reinforcement is especially located where it is most needed, that is to say at a pivotal junction point between business and IT. This junction point that we situated at the Workflow Plan – Translation View, leverages the entire contribution of BPMN as unifier and enabler between business process analysis and automation. It enables the business to hand over process modeling, i.e. more than detailed specifications, to IT people in the best conditions by making the effort to assimilate some of the technical constraints that they will take into account afterwards.

Marking a break with the traditional separation between Business and IT, it sheds a light on an emerging and position open to the dialogue, communicative, thorough, skilful with BPMN, and with both business and IT competencies.

In our opinion, it is a key point to secure BPM project successes. It is also the very core mission of the BNP Paribas' BPM Competency Centre.

Human-Readable BPMN Diagrams

Thomas Allweyer, Kaiserslautern University of Applied Sciences, Germany

INTRODUCTION

The Object Management Group (OMG) has published a useful non-normative document for BPMN modelers: "BPMN 2.0 by Example" [BPMNExamples].

While the specification of the BPMN standard describes the BPMN diagrams, elements, and their meanings, the examples document provides suggestions of how to use BPMN for modeling real processes. The reader can get valuable insights and hints for his own modeling practice.

This paper discusses one of the models, the E-Mail Voting Example [BPMNExamples, p. 35]. The E-Mail Voting Example describes how a distributed working group discusses issues and votes on them by e-mail. This process was used during the development of BPMN. The authors claim that "This process is small, but fairly complex [...], and it will help illustrate that BPMN can handle simple and unusual business processes and still be easily understandable for readers of the Diagram" [BPMNExamples, p. 35].

The original BPMN diagram of the process is shown in Figure 1. The process as such may indeed be small, but the diagram is not small. It looks rather complex. So, if this is a small process, it is easy to guess the dimensions of a large process's diagram.

Is this diagram easily understandable? Judge for yourself. If you take the effort to follow the sequence flow step by step you will be able to sort out how the process actually works. So yes, it is understandable for experts – but it is certainly not easy to understand. I would not dare to give this diagram to any business expert. This picture is not worth a thousand words, but it requires a thousand words of explanation in order to understand it. Actually, the explanation in the document contains a bit more than 1.500 words.

It may be unfair to criticize this model, because its main purpose is to illustrate the application of many different BPMN concepts. However, it is still an interesting exercise to re-design this model in order to make it more comprehensible. How should the model look like if its main purpose was to explain the process to one of the participants, maybe to a newly elected workgroup coordinator who needs to carry out that process in the future?

It is recommended to print out the original model from the OMG paper and refer to it when reading this paper.

PARTITIONING THE PROCESS

In order to cope with a large model, it can be divided into sub-processes. When the e-mail voting process is analyzed, four basic phases can be identified:

1. A discussion of the issues by e-mail and by a conference call
2. The submission of the votes by the voting members
3. The dissemination of the voting results
4. An evaluation of the voting results and a decision about how to proceed. For example, if not enough members have voted, there will be a second chance for submitting the missing votes.

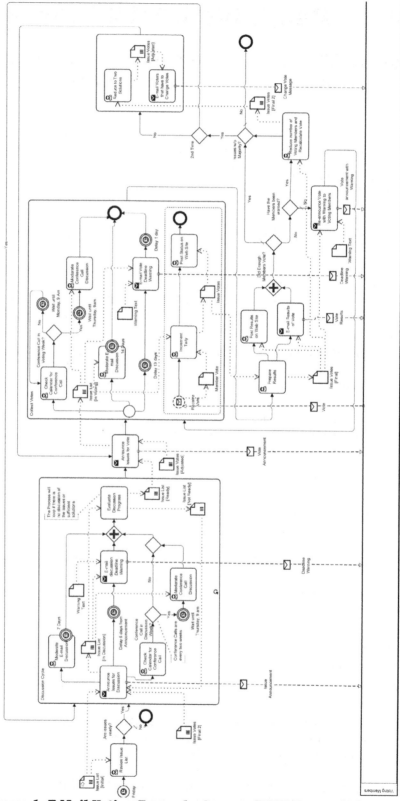

Figure 1: E-Mail Voting Example. Source: [BPMNExamples], p. 36

So the process could be split into four sub-processes. However, the dissemination of voting results would be a rather small process, and the decisions in the fourth phase can also be modeled in a more compact way. There are also strong connections between phase 2 and phase 4, since there are two back-loops from phase 4 to phase 2.

For these reasons it may be a good idea to define only two sub-processes: "Discussion" and "Voting".

Usually, BPMN sub-processes are part of a higher-level process. A first draft of such a higher-level process is shown in Figure 2. This is a simple diagram of the basic structure of the process: First, there is a discussion, then the voting.

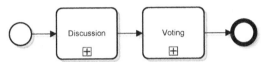

Figure 2: High-level diagram with inaccurate sequence flow

However, the diagram in Figure 2 is a little bit oversimplified. A look at the original diagram reveals that the process is not triggered by a "none" start event, but by a timer event. And there is also a back-loop to the discussion, because it is possible that the voting cannot be completed, but the discussion needs to be re-opened. In order to reflect this, the top-level diagram needs to be modified, as in Figure 3.

Now the diagram is correct, but it is cluttered with details which are not really appropriate for a high-level diagram. Is it important that the process is started every Friday? No, this is a detail. If the process would be started every Thursday instead, it would not be important for the big picture. Is the back-loop important? Probably not, since a detailed analysis of the original diagram's sequence flow shows that the discussion is re-opened only in exceptional cases.

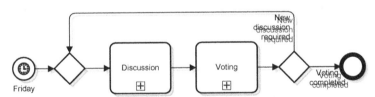

Figure 3: High-level diagram with accurate sequence flow, but with too many details

So, how can you model the simple fact that the process consists of a discussion process followed by a voting process? If you strictly follow the BPMN specification, you cannot.

One possibility is to relax the BPMN rules a little bit for high-level diagrams and simply use the diagram from Figure 2. If you decide to do so, you should define in your modeling conventions at which points you relax the BPMN rules.

The other possibility is not to use BPMN for this purpose, but another notation or free-form diagram, as in Figure 4. Here, arrow symbols have been used which often can be found in value-chain diagrams or process landscapes.

Figure 4: Non-BPMN high-level diagram

SIMPLIFYING THE PROCESS DIAGRAMS

A first attempt to make the two sub-process's diagrams more readable is shown in Figure 5 and Figure 7. First of all, the data objects and the message flows have been removed. In order to understand what is going on in the process, these details are not required. They are only confusing. Since there are only two roles – the workgroup coordinator who carries out the process, and the voting members – it is rather clear from the activities' descriptions which e-mails will be exchanged. Therefore, the message flows do not add valuable information for understanding the process. Nevertheless, a simplified diagram with message flow will be shown later on as an alternative representation.

The data objects, on the other hand, are more interesting. They represent the various documents and lists which are used and created in this process. The workgroup coordinator can see from the original model which documents he requires for each activity, and where the resulting information is used. In the first step, however, it is easier to understand the sequence flow without the data flows. In a second step such additional information may be added to the model. A variant of the model with data flow will also be shown later on.

In the original diagram, the tasks have been marked with icons as "user tasks" or "send tasks". These icons have been removed for two reasons. The first reason is that the definitions of these task types in the BPMN specification are rather restricted: A user task is defined as "a typical 'workflow' task where a human performer performs the task with the assistance of a software application and is scheduled through a task list manager of some sort" [BPMNSpec, p. 167]. Since this process is apparently not supported by a workflow management system, the tasks are not strictly user tasks. A send tasks, on the other hand, only has the purpose of assigning data to a message and sending that message – but nothing else [BPMNSpec, p. 163 and 444]. In this process, however, the tasks with envelope icons apparently require the workgroup coordinator to combine information from various lists with predefined text, before an e-mail is sent. Due to these additional steps, the tasks are not pure send tasks.

Of course, it would be possible to relax the strict task type definitions and simply use the icons for identifying tasks which consist mainly of user actions or which have the main objective of sending out a message.

The second and main reason for omitting the icons is that they do not provide much help for understanding the process. All of the activities involve the user, and the activities' names or descriptions clearly indicate whether messages are sent.

FIRST PART: THE DISCUSSION PROCESS

Just as in the original diagram, the process starts with a timer event. The first original activity, "Review issue list", has been removed, since it is rather trivial. It is not necessary to emphasize that the following decision "Issues ready?" requires a look into the issue list. This decision is followed by an exclusive gateway. It merges the sequence flow with two backwards looping sequence flows.

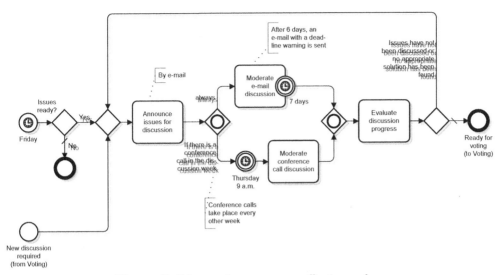

Figure 5: Discussion process, first version

In the original diagram, the discussion cycle is shown as a sub-process with a loop indicator. Since the loop is more clearly visible when modeled with a gateway and a backwards looping sequence flow, this alternative structure has been chosen. This is also more consistent with the representation of the other loops in the voting process.

The e-mail discussion and the conference call discussion have been reduced to one task each. The details concerning the e-mail deadline warning and how to determine whether there is a conference call in the discussion week, have been removed from the model. They are explained in annotations. In this way, the model structure becomes clearer. It is very easy to see what is going on: An e-mail discussion and – in some cases – a conference call discussion. It would be possible to model the omitted details in sub-processes. However, in this case the annotations should be sufficient, so there is no need for the reader to figure out this information from additional models.

Originally, the fact that there is always an e-mail discussion and only sometimes a conference call, has been modeled with parallel sequence flows. One of these parallel flows is split into two alternative flows: One with the conference call, the other without any activity. This rather complex solution for a simple problem has been remodeled with an inclusive gateway. The upper sequence flow is labeled "always", indicating that the condition of this sequence flow is always true and the e-mail discussion takes place in any case.

After evaluating the discussion progress, either the loop is repeated, or the voting process can start. When the discussion process reaches the end event, the start event of the voting process is triggered. There is no obvious way of modeling this connection between processes. If the two processes are regarded as two independent processes, it would be possible to use signal or message events. Both types of events are not entirely satisfying. Signals represent broadcasting behavior: Any process could react to that signal. This is not intended here, since only one specific process should be addressed. Such a behavior can be expressed by sending a message, instead. However, the sending of messages between internal processes rather than between different partners is not very intuitive.

Note that link events cannot be used in this case, since we have two separate processes. Link events are intermediate events which can only be used within one process. If the undivided original process just had been printed onto two different pages, then link events could have been used for providing the connection between the two pages.

If the two processes are not independent processes, but sub-processes of a high-level process (as the one in Figure 3), then the connection is provided by the parent process. When the first sub-process is finished, the parent process moves the control to the second sub-process and thus triggers the start event in this sub-process. Within the sub-processes, the connection to the next sub-process is usually not visible. It is therefore indicated in the label of the end event ("to Voting").

Note that the discussion process also has a second start event: "New discussion required (from Voting)". This label indicates that this start event is triggered from the backwards looping sequence flow originating from the voting process. This loop is also shown in Figure 3.

Unfortunately, the connection between the parent process of Figure 3 and the discussion sub-process is still not modeled correctly. When a sub-process is activated by its parent process, the sub-process's 'none' start event is triggered. So every Friday, the parent process would activate the discussion sub-process, but the process would not start with the timer event, but with the 'none' start event, so that the decision "Issues ready?" would be omitted. The sub-process's timer event "Friday" is independent from the parent process's timer event. Therefore, the sub-process would be started a second time. This second process instance would not be in the context of the parent process, so that it would finish without triggering the voting process.

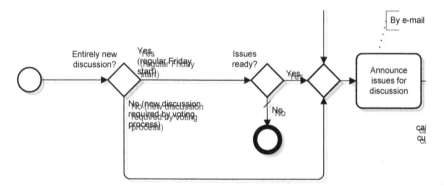

Figure 6: Alternative beginning of the discussion process with only one start event. This makes the model consistent with the parent process from Figure 3.

The correct behavior would be expressed by one single 'none' start event in the sub-process (Figure 6). This would be followed by an exclusive gateway. This gateway would split the flow based on whether the sub-process was triggered via the sequence flow from the start ("regular Friday start"), or via the sequence flow from the backwards loop ("new discussion required by voting process").

Since Figure 6 is less self-explanatory, and since the business reader may not be shown Figure 3 (but rather Figure 4), Figure 5 still seems the better solution.

SECOND PART: THE VOTING PROCESS

The beginning of the voting process is similar to the beginning of the discussion process. Parallel to the voting there is another e-mail discussion and another conference call. Since the voting period is 14 days, there is always one conference call during that period. Therefore a parallel gateway has been used.

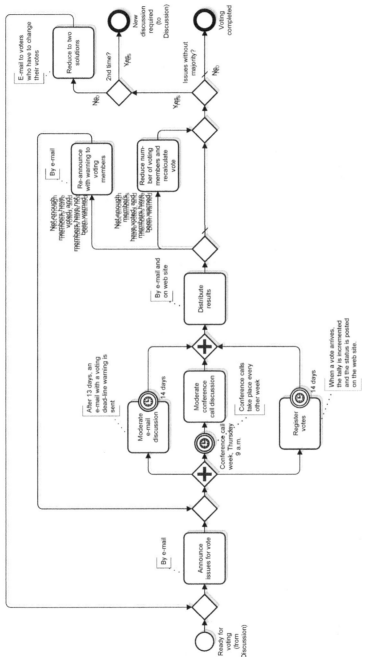

Figure 7: Voting process, first version

In the original diagram, registering the votes has been modeled with a rather unintuitive event sub-process. This has also been simplified and reduced to one task which is carried out in parallel to the e-mail and conference call discussions. Both the e-mail discussion and registering the votes take 14 days. Like in the original diagram, this is modeled with attached intermediate timer events. Again, the details are explained in annotations. The new task "Distribute results" also replaces several smaller tasks.

The following sequence of several gateways has been simplified, too. The number of gateways and different paths has been reduced by creating combined conditions (e.g. "Not enough members have voted, *and* members have not been warned"). The graphical layout and the consequent separation of merging and splitting also improve the readability.

FURTHER RE-DESIGN OF THE MODELS

The re-designed models are certainly easier to comprehend than the original model. However, there are still some details which may not be required for getting a good understanding of how the process works. First of all, the timer intermediate events can be omitted. The details concerning durations and times can be given in annotations without losing significant information. In the discussion process, the decision at the beginning can be combined with the timer start event, so that the process is triggered on Fridays with ready issues. The combined event is not a pure timer event any more. BPMN contains an event-type "multiple" which could be used here. However, the "multiple" information is not important for understanding the process; so a simple "none" event is sufficient.

Since the connections between the processes are still a bit difficult to see, this information can be emphasized by placing it into annotations to the respective events. The resulting diagram is shown in Figure 8.

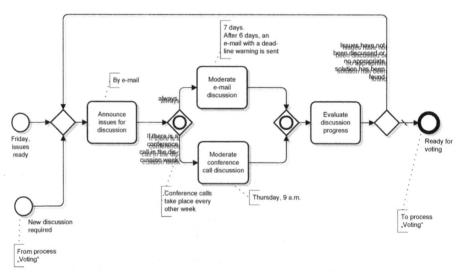

Figure 8: Discussion process, second version

The basic structure is even better visible when the tasks' annotations are hidden (Figure 9). Although this diagram now provides an overview that can be grasped very quickly, the information of the annotations has been lost. Therefore, this information must be provided in a different way.

If the model is printed out in a document, it can be supplemented with a table that contains a short description of each task. If a modeling tool or an interactive web-interface is used for displaying the model, the description of each task can be displayed when it is selected. Such functionality is provided by many modeling tools. Figure 10 shows a screenshot from itp commerce's Process Modeler, as an example.

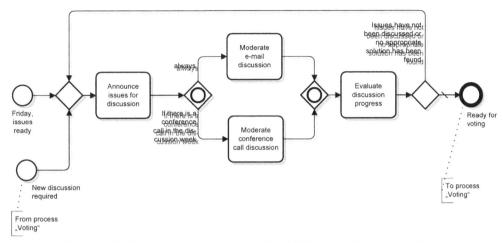

Figure 9: Discussion process with hidden task annotations

The model of the second process, the voting process, can be changed in a similar way to the first one. Although the number of gateways already has been reduced in Figure 7, the decision logic is still fairly complex. Since a process should only focus on the flow but not on complex decision rules, the entire chain of decisions can be hidden in one task "Evaluate voting results". This task produces one out of four possible results which is used for selecting a path at the following exclusive gateway (Figure 11).

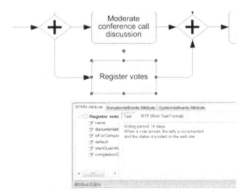

Figure 10: Displaying attributes for a selected element in a BPMN modeling tool (itp Process Modeler)

The decision logic can be described in a separate text or model, such as a decision tree or a decision table. Figure 12 shows a decision table describing what needs to happen within "Evaluate voting results". For each combination of conditions, the necessary actions within the task and the resulting decision are shown. This table could be connected to the task by a hyperlink.

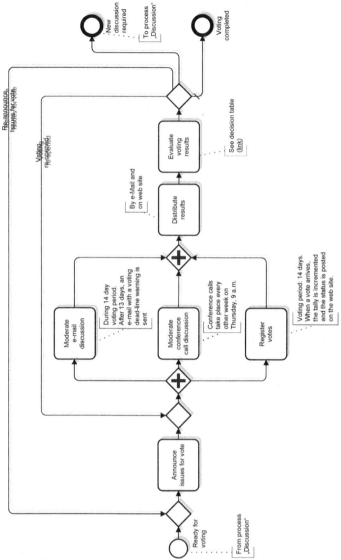

Figure 11: Voting process, second version

This table is a little bit simplified, since for the case "Not enough members have voted" and "members have been warned", a re-calculation of the vote for the re-duced number of members is required, in order to determine whether there are issues without majority. If this needs to be reflected more thoroughly, a sub-process for "Evaluate voting results" can be used to show how the decision is made. In any way, the detailed decision logic is separated from the overall se-quence flow.

Enough members have voted	Members have been warned	Issues without majority	2nd time	Action	Decision
Yes	-	No	-		Voting completed
Yes	-	Yes	Yes		New discussion required
Yes	-	Yes	No	Reduce to 2 solutions and e-mail voters who have to change their votes	Re-announce issues for vote
No	Yes	Yes	Yes		New discussion required
No	Yes	Yes	No	Reduce to 2 solutions and e-mail voters who have to change their votes	Re-announce issues for vote
No	Yes	No	-		Voting completed
No	No	-	-	Re-announce with warning	Voting re-opened

Figure 12: Decision table for activity "Evaluate voting results"

Again, the process structure is easier to see when the task annotations are hidden and only displayed when required (Figure 13).

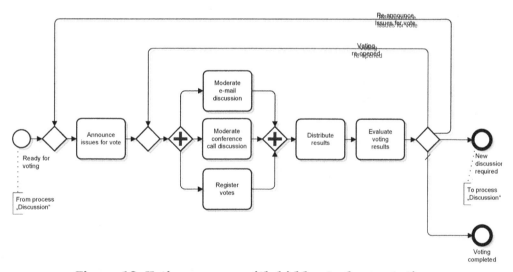

Figure 13: Voting process with hidden task annotations

DATA OBJECTS

In the previous diagrams, no data objects have been show in order to make the sequence flow more clearly visible. However, if the information about input and output data objects is required, data objects need to be included. The discussion process with data objects is shown in Figure 14.

In the original model, there are many long data association arrows crossing other lines. In order to avoid such a confusing structure, the data object symbols have been duplicated. They are always drawn above or below the connected tasks. This layout makes it easy to distinguish between sequence flow and data flow. Note that the data flows with arrows at both ends actually are two separate data flows which have been drawn on top of each other, since there are no bi-directional data flows in BPMN.

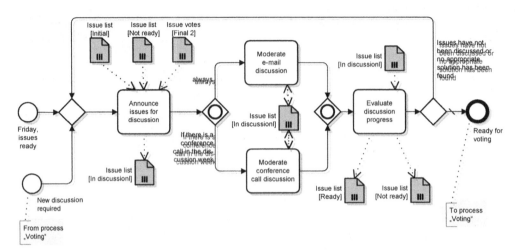

Figure 14: Discussion process with data-objects

Duplicating data object symbols is correct according to the BPMN specification. All data objects with the same name are references to the same data object. They may refer to different states of that object. This state is shown in square brackets.

Copying data objects to another process, however, is different. By definition, a data object only exists within the process in which it is defined. So if the two processes contain data object symbols with the same names, the two symbols represent two different data objects. Data objects are not automatically passed on between processes. If the processes were independent, a message flow would be required in order to exchange data. Another possibility would be to use a data store symbol. However, this is more for permanent data stores which are independent from the processes.

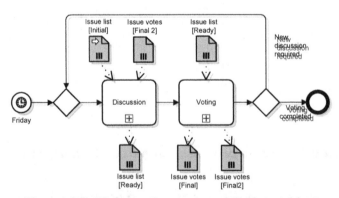

Figure 15: High-level process with data objects

If the two processes are regarded as sub-processes of a common parent process, the data objects can be defined in the parent process. The sub-processes can then refer to these common objects.

Strictly following these rules, the parent process model from Figure 3 would need to be complemented with the common data objects. The resulting high-level diagram is shown in Figure 15. As in the original diagram, the object "Issue list [initial]" is marked as an input object to the entire process. In the sub-process, the input marker is not required any more, since the sub-process only refers to this object that already exists in the parent process.

Again, it is not recommended to present the model from Figure 15 to normal business users. However, this high-level model provides the context for the two sub-processes, so that the overall collection of models conforms to the BPMN specification (with the exception of the start events in the first sub-process). So even if the high-level model is not drawn, the existence of a "virtual" parent model could still be assumed, in order to conform to the specification.

The diagrams contain a few alterations compared to the original model. Some data objects have been omitted, because they are not important in the overall context of the process (such as "warning text" as input object for sending an e-mail with a deadline warning). The "Issue list [in discussion]" is probably changed by the discussions, so that there are data associations between the discussion tasks and the issue list in both directions. All occurrences of the "Issue votes" object now have the multiple marker. This was missing in the original diagram at some places.

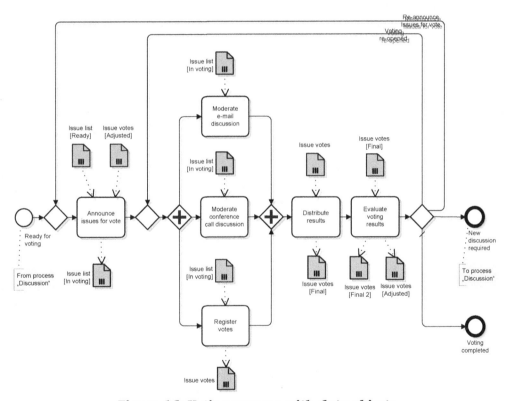

Figure 16: Voting process with data-objects

The diagrams here also show how colors or shadings can be used for increasing the readability. All sequence flow objects are white. The data objects have dark shadings, and the annotations concerning connections to other processes have light shadings. Although there are many elements in these diagrams, the process structure can still be grasped very quickly.

With some modeling tools the user can define which types of information should be displayed. There can be different views on one comprehensive model. In our example, the data objects could be hidden in order to provide the simple views of

Figure 9 and Figure 13. When the user wants to inspect the data flow, he can have the data objects and associations displayed within the same model.

Another means to hide additional information is to attach detailed diagrams to each task. These detailed diagrams can include information like input and output, system transactions, resources etc. However, this requires the user to open a lot of diagrams if he is interested in several tasks.

MESSAGE FLOW

It has been argued that for understanding the e-mail voting process, the modeling of message flows is not really necessary. Nevertheless, the message flows can also be integrated into the re-designed models.

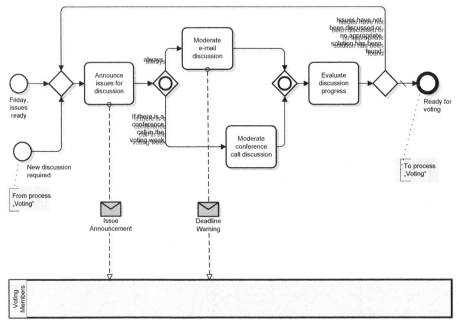

Figure 17: Discussion process with message-flows

In Figure 17 and Figure 18, the same principles as in the previous chapters have been applied:

- The simplified process structure allows for a clearer depiction of the message flows.
- The layout helps visualizing the flow structures. Some of the tasks have been moved horizontally so that it was possible to draw all message flows as straight vertical lines. There are only few crossings of lines. This number could have been further reduced by exchanging the vertical positions of "Moderate e-mail discussion" and "Moderate conference call discussion". However, it was decided not to change the basic structure of the previous diagrams, so that orientation is easier for the reader.
- Shadings have been used for highlighting different aspects of the diagram.
- Other elements, such as task annotations and data objects have been hidden.

Again, a modeling tool can be helpful in order to hide details when they are not required. It could also provide a combined view with data objects and message flows. Without such a tool it is too tedious to draw and update several different diagrams of the same process.

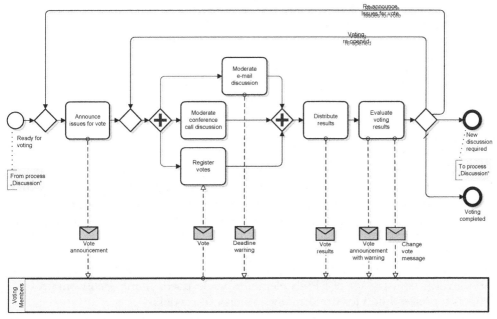

Figure 18: Voting process with message-flows

CONCLUSIONS

It has been demonstrated how a complex BPMN model can be re-designed in order to make it easier to read and comprehend. The re-designed models only serve the purpose of explaining the process to business users. They are neither a basis for workflow automation, nor detailed work instructions.

The re-design included the following changes to the original model:

- Dividing the model into two smaller processes, each fitting on one page
- Defining a simplified high-level model as a freeform diagram
- Creating fewer, but more comprehensive tasks
- Documenting details in annotations, when text is easier to understand than the graphical representation
- Replacing complex structures of parallel and exclusive gateways with inclusive gateways
- Replacing looping sub-processes by backwards-looping sequence flows
- Replacing event sub-processes by parallel sequence flow paths
- Applying uniform rules for modeling splits and merges (always using gateways, each gateway either representing a split *or* a merge).
- Using annotations for defining connections between the two processes
- Moving complex decision logic from the BPMN model to a separate documentation, e.g. a decision table
- Using a consistent layout with horizontal sequence flows and vertical data and message flows
- Highlighting different aspects of the model with colors or shadings
- Hiding annotations, data objects and message flow, and displaying them only when required. Thus, different views onto the process are provided.

During the re-design it turned out as a problem that the BPMN 2.0 concepts still have a strong background in process automation. This creates many challenges for creating process models for business users. Especially creating hierarchical models is rather difficult, since correct BPMN models require high-level models to include many details (e.g. exception flows and data objects). Defining correct connections between different sub-processes also requires rather complex model structures which make it difficult to understand the models (e.g. when a sub-process can be triggered by different incoming sequence flows, each requiring a different start in the sub-process). Another example concerns the markers for different task types. Icons for different task types could also be useful for business modeling; but they are only defined in respect to process automation.

The author hopes that future BPMN versions will reflect the business modeler's needs in a better way.

In order to create easily readable models for business users, modelers are recommended to relax the strict BPMN rules where they make the models difficult to understand. However, this should only be done when there is a good reason, since otherwise the resulting models may be too far away from the standard. Modeling conventions should be defined in which deviations to the standard are documented.

Such modeling conventions should also include rules concerning modeling size and layout, the sub-set of BPMN elements to be used, naming conventions, etc. This is a precondition for uniform and consistent models.

Whether a model is easy to understand is always subject to personal judgment and individual preferences. The models in this paper are therefore only suggestions, and the readers are invited to discuss these models or provide alternative solutions. Although no systematic evaluations of the readability of these models have been made, the author is convinced that they are much easier to understand than the original model.

REFERENCES

[BPMNSpec]   Object Management Group, OMG (ed.): Business Model and Notation (BPMN) Version 2.0. Beta 2. June 2010. OMG document number: dtc/2010-06-05
URL: http://www.omg.org/spec/BPMN/2.0/Beta2/PDF/

[BPMNExamples] Object Management Group, OMG (ed.): BPMN 2.0 by Example. Version 1.0 (non-normative). June 2010. OMG document number: dtc/2010-06-02
URL: http://www.omg.org/spec/BPMN/2.0/examples/PDF/10-06-02.pdf

Business Process Integration in a Defense Product-Focused Company

Kerry M. Finn and J. Bryan Lail
Raytheon Company, U.S.A

INTRODUCTION

Aspects of business process integration (BPI) have been around for many years, with a known value statement in terms of business efficiency and cross-functional life-cycle improvements. The essential concept is that when a business can agree on and build a common model for key business processes that span functional organizations, followed by supporting organizational, user process and technology changes, then very significant life-cycle improvements in cost, cycle time and manpower can be achieved beyond the scope of one business function or organization. The evolution of a globally-recognized Business Process Modeling Notation[1] standard over the last four years, with a leap in business impact from Version 2 in 2010, is providing powerful methods and vendor tools to achieve that integration.

A common language for integrating processes across silos is a significant enabler in ways both obvious and subtle. Once the business organizations that touch a product or execution life cycle can agree on the first priorities where tighter integration is very clearly going to yield measurable benefits, then the common process language immediately leads to communicating one shared model across leadership and stakeholders. From there, modern methods and tools lead to validated processes, key performance indicators that can be tracked during execution, behavior and cultural changes, and executable processes that automate and parallelize legacy practices.

This paper describes how BPMN 2.0 can promote a balance of business agility and enterprise efficiency. The approach takes two tiers to execute for a product-focused company, which the authors call horizontal and vertical integration. The methods and common language around BPMN apply to internal business operations for any sizeable company; however, the approach for applying the methods to the actual products of a defense company is different. The dual benefits come from focusing on the information management for those products in either the battle-space or the business space; this paper will study both areas and deliver a common theme for BPI.

BUSINESS IMPERATIVE

During the 1990s, the Western military-industrial complex went through a dramatic era of consolidation[2] as evidenced in Figure 1. This resulted in multiple legacy business units with distinct product offerings and internal business systems with a large potential for improved business efficiency through enterprise wide

---

[1] http://www.omg.org/spec/BPMN 2.0/Beta2

[2] The Health of the U.S. Defense Industry, P. Chao, 2004

integration. Evolution of these organizations to respond to business needs with agility based on efficient and affordable enterprise solutions is still occurring a decade later. In the meantime, the global economic downturn has led to similar consolidation in some commercial sectors, with many indications that the military industrial complex is going into another era of consolidation. The difference this time is that the imperative for integration and efficiency is happening in an even more complex, ever-accelerating era of technology and globalization. This means the defense sector must learn from successful commercial practices.

There are significant initiatives in the U.S. Department of Defense to apply BPMN methods for enterprise-level integration as evidenced by End-to-End Business Flow[3] models released by the Business Transformation Agency, but recent cost-cutting trends are actually countering the agency's influence on business operations. It is left up to the individual, larger companies to tailor and apply successful commercial practices to the product-focused defense industry.

BPI is a subset of the overall discipline of Business Process Management[4] (BPM), the management approach focused on aligning and integrating all aspects of an organization with the wants and needs of the customer. It is a holistic management approach that promotes business effectiveness and efficiency while striving for innovation, flexibility and integration with technology. BPM attempts to measure and improve processes continually. Vendor support for powerful BPM Suites has grown dramatically in the last several years, tied to both technology advances and the economic and globalization drivers for enhanced enterprise efficiency. Today's companies need increased process efficiencies through linking silos of information with modern Web-based services. The maturation of Internet-based collaborative processes also provides a competitive edge through new sales tools, more efficient finance processes, tighter supply chains, and better workflow management.

Meeting this imperative in today's environment can be accomplished through two levels of integration, both based on BPMN methods and common language. The first is the horizontal integration achieved through instituting a common process language, using it as an anthropological tool to draw together disparate business functions and sharing validated models to drive technology solutions. The second is vertical integration, achieved through building BPMN into the compliance requirements for the company's enterprise architecture, working from the business user level through process logic and service execution to automate and enforce the new integrated processes. Aspects of this approach that differ for a product-focused company in the defense sector, as compared to commercial service-based companies, will be addressed in the next two sections.

---

[3] http://www.bta.mil/products/BEA_7_0/BEA/html_files/end2end.html

[4] http://www.bpm-consortium.org/120407_BPM_SOA_Agile_Enterprise.pdf

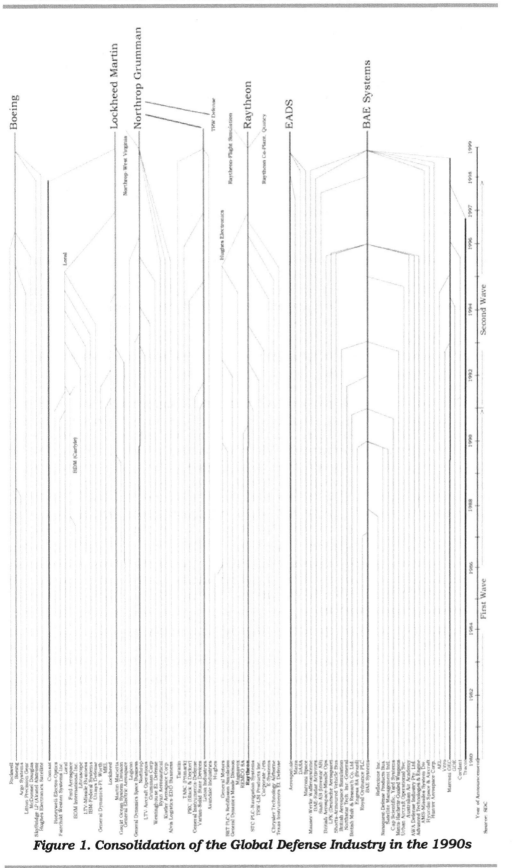

Figure 1. Consolidation of the Global Defense Industry in the 1990s

HORIZONTAL INTEGRATION

Horizontal integration is focused on the business benefits of BPI before applying technologies. Having this tier separate from implementation and execution levels (vertical integration) is critical in a product-focused company. Starting with a focus on integrating high-payoff internal business operations and processes, BPMN certainly enables communications and organizational change that leads to life-cycle improvements and enhanced sales.

To achieve this strategic business goal, the multiple organizations or domains involved must agree on the highest priority processes to integrate across their individual areas. Many studies have found that a mature company will realize the most benefits from integrating across the white spaces, or process linkages across elements of the organization, since the experts within their own domain are likely performing internal processes fairly well. Our company uses a business blitz method to bring a small number of representatives from each domain, work together on the most likely high-payoff life-cycle processes currently limited by shortfalls between domains, and then set that agreed priority for focusing BPI efforts. That common priority should include key stakeholders, key performance indicators (KPI), and a first textual definition of the process. Long product development and investment make this step even more critical.

The actual modeling can now begin, starting with a Level 1 model to enhance that common agreement and understanding of a desired, more integrated and measured process that can achieve the indentified KPIs. Beyond the normal reasons a Level 1 model is necessary in applying the hierarchal methods in BPMN, it is critical here to support two related but distinct paths moving forward. One is the technological path that will be discussed in the next section, applying Level 2 and perhaps even Level 3 modeling to provide services that execute and enforce the new integrated process. The other is just as critical for success; the business must address the anthropological aspects of assigning one owner to an integrated process that cuts across domains and evolving work behavior of the employees to follow the new process and use the power of the new technologies. In this context, a Level 1 model with clear end-to-end description of the desired integrated process and associated KPIs is the key to that change management.

The essence of the BPMN 2.0 contribution is the critical advance in providing both a common language across domains and the power to measure the benefit of process integration before investing significant funds in organizational change or technologies that automate and execute the new process. An example is provided next to explore these benefits.

A company that develops products with some complexity, such as having many components that are integrated in the final product—each potentially coming from a supplier as another assembled part—must have an efficient data management system that tracks product configuration, changes, internal approval, customer approval, relationship to cost and other functions. This example is not intended to cover the topic of product data management, which is reported elsewhere in literature, but rather use that context to explore the benefits of BPI. Figure 2 describes a technical data package (TDP) process that initiates with a specific state of product design and ends with several possible end states noting level of acceptance for design changes. The standardization on BPMN enables many key integration points across roles and organizations.

The lanes within the pool show one orchestrated process across a data manager, an approval agent and a customer-facing contracts role but with clear task responsibility throughout. The choreography with external pools represents both the process trigger due to a change from engineering and the handling of interaction with the customer. The latter provides critical risk mitigation through managing all possible outcomes of customer response, since the process cannot control the customer's actions but can model and measure the company's response regardless of that action (i.e., accept, reject, or no response). The unambiguous events allow assignment of key performance indicators in terms of expected cost, manpower, cycle time or other metrics. The gateways allow assignment of expected occurrence for each logical outcome, and therefore measurement later during execution (along with the metrics) for process control.

Finally, a common process focused on configuration data about the products, rather than on the varied products themselves, enables horizontal integration and resulting efficiency and life-cycle performance across business units in a product-focused company. This starts with the anthropological benefit of clear communications about a desired, common parent process in one process language and with detail that is unimportant to leadership left to tightly linked sub-processes (shown in five portions of the figure), which can be expanded whenever necessary. With this kind of horizontal integration, the company is then ready to proceed to vertical integration focused on automating and executing the workflow for that common process.

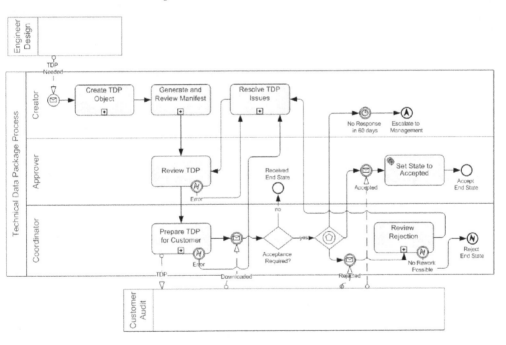

Figure 2. Technical Data Package Process

VERTICAL INTEGRATION

Vertical integration shifts from the business focus to an information technology and organizational change management focus, while still heavily applying the methods and common language benefits of BPMN. After the business stakeholders agree on and model a common desired process with associated key performance indicators, BPMN Level 2 and 3 methods lead directly to automation and enforcement of the integrated process resting on service oriented architecture (SOA) suites and other workflow technologies. For a business that sells defense system sensors, weapons, radios and control systems, however, the significant features of BPMN for vertical integration don't apply directly to many of the company's market offerings. As such, this section will explore first how BPMN can be leveraged for vertical integration for internal business operations. Then an example will be given for where BPMN does apply to defense products, which is the planning and interoperability to optimize usage of these devices.

For internal business efficiency, there are multiple BPM vendors that at least partially support the BPMN standard in their tools and product suites, with intent to achieve full Version 2.0 compliance in the future. BPM Suites provide the capability to generate human-to-service orchestration scripts and generally support integration to a SOA suite, promoting interoperability and modularity across business systems for a growing (or consolidating) company along with disparate business users. BPMN provides the common language to describe cross-domain business processes, with events and tasks implemented as services within the enterprise. As the company promotes this practice through enterprise architecture, more and more foundational services (beyond the basic package provided with a SOA suite) are available to compose new business services and replace point-to-point integrations that are hard to sustain in later years.

The advent of BPMN Version 2.0 and the strategic roadmap for some of the vendors in this space (some of whom helped create and build consensus on the standard) are leading to a more seamless integration straight from business-driven Level 1 models to measurement of events and attributes in Level 2 and execution right on the SOA suite through Level 3. The company that can agree on the highest payoff business processes to integrate, build a model that includes significant automation of manual tasks and parallelization of serial queues, execute vertically to new services based on a standard foundation, and change user behavior to align, will outpace less agile competitors.

In the defense industry, these same methods can be applied to enterprise wide systems supporting the military and to the associated battle-space planning for and interoperability between defense products. In fact, various academia and commercial successes around the Internet and associated Web services led to the Net-Centric Operations[5] or net-enabled operations concepts for Western defense agencies. For defense products such as planes, weapons, sensors, ships, radios, or other tactical systems that are not part of the enterprise services, the equivalent of process integration comes from a net-ready requirement that expects an architectural definition for achieving integration with the enterprise services (core business processes following a framework standard), and then certain technical standards addressing how to expose services and data from those devices.

To further draw the distinction from internal business operations or the enterprise service layer, military products are generally deployed into challenging envi-

---

[5] http://disa.mil/news/pressreleases/2010/nces_foc_102010.html

ronments with interrupted communications. In this stressing environment, security must be at the level associated with the need to save lives. This leads to unique needs for policy-based management, in which the integration of battle-space processes from the enterprise level out to the device level can still leverage agile services but with very well–understood, pre-defined policy enforcement and clear ownership at every point in the process (although that ownership can change dynamically, within policy limits). Finally, the flexibility and loosely-coupled architecture that are driven by net-centric services and BPI will enable next generation acquisition strategies for refresh and upgrade over replacement.

A fictional coalition operations use case will be referred to as the business management planning-tactical (BMP-T) process. The BMP-T process focuses on seamless integration of a number of planning applications (e.g., satellite planning, sensor planning) built by numerous global defense companies into a single automated workflow for operations. The current process might consist of multiple silos with some point-to-point integrations among planning systems with different methods for sharing information and no combined linkage out to the desired end effect of an integrated process, such as better allocation of the available assets across a coalition operation. Using outdated data integration methods is primarily driven by development as siloed systems that don't allow the quick addition of new interoperable services and an end-to-end model of the whole business process.

The future BMP-T process in Figure 3 depicts the common business process flow that orchestrates a number of tactical theater planning services, focusing on just the internal process (excluding the external process triggers and subsequent messaging). With agreement among the multiple stakeholders in a coalition force on common processes applying one BPMN language, then BPM tools or experienced developers can compose one set of workflow services and data system accesses that execute the same for all users. Notice that critical security and policy management issues are called out right in the first level business process, in tasks such as Define Limits & Risks for Engagement, as explicit tasks and clear process ownership. For the full process model in a realistic scenario, this task would be expanded into a subprocess with specific steps to set policy on authorized roles and access to services, all within the responsibility of the Theater Planning role. Then other roles such as the Operational Planning would work within a service-oriented environment that enabled maximum flexibility and service availability (including to military products), but controlled within policy limits.

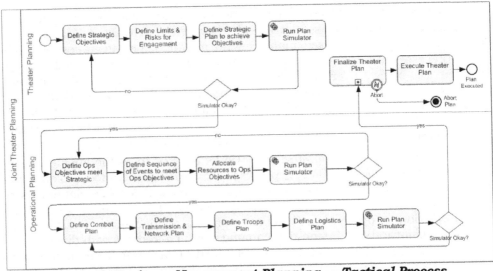

Figure 3. Business Management Planning — Tactical Process

With a common process among the coalition stakeholders and across multiple legacy planning systems, the Level 2 process model can relay detailed events, automated workflow, service-based publish and subscribe tasks, and attributes that flow down the key performance parameters to execution. A BPM suite or skilled SOA developer can then leverage SOA standards and the enterprise services to integrate a very cost-effective and powerful integrated solution. With the loose coupling and common business processes from the partnership of SOA and BPMN, there is enhanced support for new services and technology refresh across multiple domains.

CONCLUSIONS

Finally, stepping back from the Defense example, the relationship between the two tiers of integration, enterprise architecture, and BPMN can now be drawn. If a company has an enterprise architecture that drives common methods and standards across units and organizational domains, then the power of BPMN can be threaded throughout. Horizontal integration promotes development of more tightly integrated processes across domains using the same language for the common process itself, while maintaining the distinct practices and product focus within each domain. Vertical integration takes those high-priority process models and applies powerful methods to execute and enforce them with modern technologies. Enterprise architecture provides the standard methods and independent review to ensure the tiers are addressed beyond the scope of an individual project to achieve the greatest benefits.

The differences between a product-focused company and a services- or information-technology company, such as long product development cycles, lead to an even greater importance for getting the horizontal integration aspects correct before investing in execution methods. Aspects of the defense sector, such as a greater demand for security and policy management than the commercial sector, along with an acquisition strategy not driven by free market efficiency, lead to tailoring of the vertical integration approach. Taken together, these aspects can help a company achieve significant benefits from BPI.

Section 3

Reference and Appendices

Reference Guide—XPDL 2.2: Incorporating BPMN 2.0 Process Modeling Extensions[1]

Robert M. Shapiro, WfMC Chair XPDL Technical Committee, USA

Introduction

In June 2009 the OMG[2] voted to adopt the BPMN 2.0 specification which then entered the Finalization Task Force (FTF) phase. At that time the WfMC[3] initiated work revising XPDL2.1. The new version, XPDL2.2, is described in this paper.

As of March 1, 2010 the FTF was still hard at work. Many issues in BPMN2.0 remain unresolved. If the FTF completes its task in June, the original objective, it will do so only by deferring a large number of issues. The principle reason for this is that many new ideas were introduced that extend or change what was in the previous version, BPMN1.2.

XPDL2.2 is intended as a preliminary release which supports the graphical extensions to process modeling contained in BPMN2.0. In fact, the BPMN specification addresses four different areas of modeling, referred to as:

- Process Modeling
- Process Execution
- BPEL Process Execution
- Choreography Modeling

We focus only on Process Modeling. Within that we define several sub-classes to support process interchange between tools. This is discussed in a later section of this paper.

For a review of XPDL we refer the reader to a prior paper which describes the historical development of XPDL and a review of the major elements in XPDL2.1[4] . Here we discuss significant additions in XPDL2.2.

Another part of the process interchange story is the serialization of a process diagram, which is used to persist a process model and to transport it to other tools. XPDL has been used for this purpose and XPDL2.1 is the only standardized way of serializing earlier versions of BPMN[5]. The OMG is committed to providing a serialization of BPMN2.0, but the draft specification contains a serialization only for the semantic portion of the specification; the graphical aspects of diagram inter-

---

[1] This paper was originally published in the *2010 BPM and Workflow Handbook*, (Future Strategies Inc. Lighthouse Point, FL)

[2] Object Management Group

[3] Workflow Management Coalition

[4] XPDL 2.1 - Integrating Process Interchange & BPMN
    http://www.wfmc.org/Specifications-Working-Documents/XPDL/

[5] 1.0,1.1,1.2

change are being worked on by the Diagram Interchange subgroup of the FTF. We return to this topic in a later section of this paper.

OVERVIEW OF ADDITIONS AND CHANGES

In the next sections we discuss changes in the following areas:

- Pools and Lanes
- Call Activity/Re-usable Sub-Process
- Event Sub-Process
- Event Types
- Data Objects, Data Flow and Input/Output Specifications

For a complete description of BPMN2.0 refer to the OMG specification[6]. For a complete description of XPDL2.2 refer to the WfMC specification[7].

POOLS AND LANES

In prior versions of BPMN all the process modeling elements pertaining to flow, i.e. Activities, Gateways, Events and SequenceFlow, were always contained in a Pool. All the flow elements in a Pool were part of the same process. Multiple processes were depicted using multiple pools. Message communication between processes was depicted by message flow between Pools. The Pool boundary was optional for a single Pool in the diagram. Lanes were a way of subdividing Pools.

In BPMN2.0 a distinction is made between Collaboration diagrams and Process diagrams. A Collaboration diagram involves two or more Pools with Message flow between them. A Process diagram has no Pool. To support the Lane construct, a new element, LaneSet, was introduced. The Lane structure is contained in Lane-Set. Both Pool and Process may have LaneSets.

Eliminating Pool from a process diagram creates an inconsistency between prior versions of BPMN and BPMN2.0 with little apparent benefit. Consequently in XPDL2.2 we retain the idea of a background Pool for a single process with no pool border displayed. Lanes remain a way of subdividing Pools.

CALL ACTIVITY/RE-USABLE SUB-PROCESS

BPMN2.0 introduces a graphical distinction between embedded Sub-Process and Re-Usable Sub-Process which is incorporated in XPDL2.2. However, the manner in which input and output parameters are passed between the caller process and the called process remains complicated and confusing. XPDL retains the mechanisms provided for accomplishing this: providing conventional parameter lists (actual and formal parameters) as well as straightforward data mapping between data fields in the two processes upon entry and exit.

EVENT SUB-PROCESS

An Event Sub-Process is similar to an Embedded Sub-Process. It shares the data environment of the Process or Sub-Process in which it is defined. The instantiation is different. Instead of being instantiated by a SequenceFlow, it is triggered by an Event. In XPDL both Event and Embedded Sub-Process are defined by Activity Sets within a Process. An Embedded Sub-Process is instantiated by execution of a Block Activity in the Sequence flow of the containing Process, whereas the Event

---

[6] OMG, BPMN (version 2.0 – June, 2009)

[7] WfMC, XPDL 2.2 WFMC-TC-1025 (Version 1.0 April 2009)

Sub-Process is triggered by an Event. An attribute of Activity Set 'TriggeredByEvent' distinguishes between Event and Embedded.

EVENT TYPES

Event Types in BPMN2.0 are more complex for three reasons:

- Support for both interrupting and non-interrupting Events.
- Introduction of the Event Sub-Process.
- Introduction of a new Event type: EscalateEvent.

Changes in XPDL to support this are minimal:

- A new attribute 'Interrupting' with a default value 'true' for the appropriate Start and Intermediate Events.
- Addition of Escalation Event for:
  - Interrupting or non-interrupting Start Event in Event Sub-Process.
  - Interrupting or non-interrupting Boundary Intermediate Event.
  - Intermediate or End Throw Event

The following chart (from the specification) portrays all the Event types and the contexts in which they may occur.

Types	Start			Intermediate				End
	Top-Level	Event Sub-Process Interrupting	Event Sub-Process Non-Interrupting	Catching	Boundary Interrupting	Boundary Non-Interrupting	Throwing	
None	◯			◎				◯
Message	📨	📨	📨	📨	📨	📨	📨	📨
Timer	⏰	⏰	⏰	⏰	⏰	⏰		
Error		ⓐ		ⓐ				ⓐ
Escalation		Ⓐ	Ⓐ	Ⓐ	Ⓐ	Ⓐ	Ⓐ	Ⓐ
Cancel				⊗				⊗
Compensation		ⓚ		ⓚ			◀◀	◀◀
Conditional	🗒	🗒	🗒	🗒	🗒	🗒		
Link				⬡			⬡	
Signal	△	△	△	△	△	△	▲	▲
Terminate								◉
Multiple	⬠	⬠	⬠	⬠	⬠	⬠	⬠	⬠
Parallel Multiple	✚	✚	✚	✚	✚	✚		

DATA OBJECTS, DATA FLOW AND INPUT/OUTPUT SPECIFICATIONS[8]

Data and data flow, as represented in the diagram by the *data object* shape and *association*, were classified in BPMN 1.x as *artifacts*, meaning essentially annotations of the diagram with no defined semantics.

That has all changed in BPMN 2.0. Data has been elevated to a first-class semantic element. A data object, together with a handful of other types of *data-aware elements*, now signifies a *process variable*, defined with a specific schema. It is no longer connected to flow elements by a regular association, which still just applies to artifacts, but with a new type of connector, a *data association*. The details of the data association actually define the mapping of data from one flow element to the next.

The *data object* is the primary construct for modeling data within a process. Each data object is contained within a specific process or subprocess element, and its lifetime and visibility are constrained within that element. In other words, a data object could represent a *global variable* for the process or a *local variable* for a particular activity. The lifetime of a data object is limited to the lifetime of the process or activity instance.

Data Object   Collection Data Object   Data Store

A data object representing a *collection* of variables is depicted in the diagram with the multi-instance marker. A *data store* represents a data structure that the process can read or write but which persists beyond the lifetime of the process.

Processes, tasks, and global tasks specify their input and output parameters, or data requirements, as *data inputs* and *data outputs*. A data input represents information needed to start an activity, and each data input can be defined as required or optional; it cannot have incoming data associations. If a required data input is unavailable when a process or task is invoked, start is delayed until that data input becomes available. A data output represents information that may be output from an activity; it cannot have outgoing data associations.

Data input (left) and data output (right)

The collection of data inputs and data outputs required by a particular activity is called an *inputSet* and *outputSet*, respectively, and together these comprise the *ioSpecification* for the activity or process. It is possible to define multiple inputSets and outputSets, in which case the implementation determines which ones apply.

A *data association*, depicted in the diagram using the dotted line connector, represents a mapping between a data object, property, or data store (i.e., persisted data) on one end and a data input or data output (i.e., parameter) on the other end. A data association connected to an activity or event in the process diagram

---

[8] This section is taken from BPMN Method and Style, Bruce Silver 2009

represents a visual shorthand for connection to the data input or output of that activity or event. Activities have two types of data association, *dataInputAssociation* and *dataOutputAssociation*, respectively. A catching or throwing event has only one, as appropriate.

A data association defines a *source* and a *target*, and optionally a *transformation*. When a data association is executed, data is copied from the source to the target, and possibly transformed in the process.

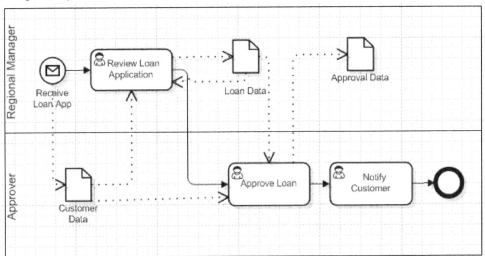

The example shown above illustrates the use of data objects and data associations in executable BPMN.

For non-executable modeling,

- Data Input and Data Output are typically omitted from the model.
- Data Object is used in the same way as the Data Object artifact of XPDL2.1.
- DataStore is used to graphically emphasize **persistent data**.

PROCESS METAMODEL

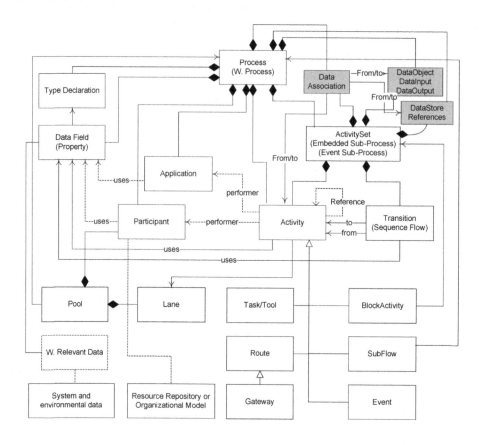

The meta-model depicts the relationships between all the elements in a Process. The shaded elements represent new graphical elements added to XPDL.

PACKAGE METAMODEL

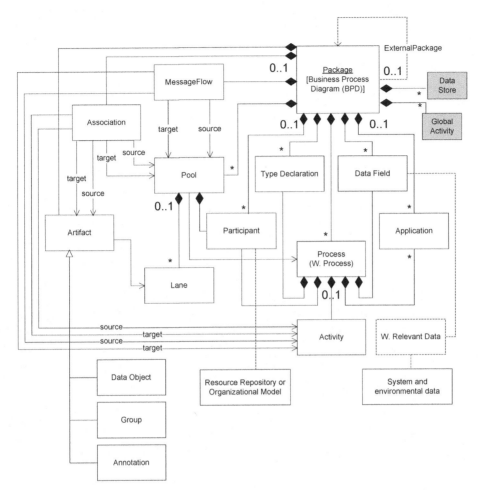

This meta-model describes the relationship between elements on the Package or Business Process Diagram level. The shaded elements represent new graphical elements added to XPDL.

PROCESS INTERCHANGE

Common meta-model allows tools to exchange models

Type of tools:

- Simulation tools
- Monitoring tools
- Execution tools
- Modeling tools
- Repository tools

The following diagram illustrates the use of process interchange in a BPM suite.

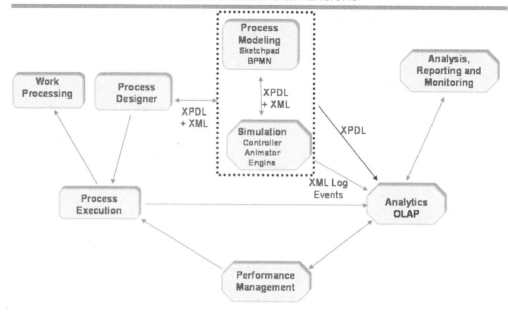

BPMN MODEL PORTABILITY CONFORMANCE

BPMN can be used for both "abstract" activity flow modeling and for complete executable design. Many tools, however, make use of BPMN for the abstract modeling but add executable detail in tool-specific activity properties. One goal of XPDL 2.2 is to promote portability of abstract activity flow models between tools. This requires separating the elements and attributes of BPMN related to activity flow modeling from those related to executable design. The BPMN2.0 spec does not define this separation, but a proposal being considered by the OMG BPMN2.0 Finalization Task Force would add Conformance sub-classes for this. XPDL2.1 did this, in the form of BPMN Model Portability conformance classes. XPDL2.2 modifies and extends the conformance classes.

In broad terms, the "abstract model" elements are those that represent BPMN constructs that are printable in the business process diagram, such as those defining the flow object type or subtype (e.g., looping User task, collapsed subprocess, exclusive gateway, timer event), including only attributes specifying the subtype, label (Name attribute), and unique identifiers for the object itself and pointers to other identifiers in the diagram. Elements and attributes representing data, messages, or other implementation detail are omitted from the abstract process model. In other words, the model describes the "what" and the "when" of process activity flow, but not the "how" of flow object implementation.

There are three conformance sub-classes defined:

- SIMPLE
- DESCRIPTIVE
- ANALYTIC

SIMPLE is contained in DESCRIPTIVE, which is, in turn, contained in ANALYTIC.

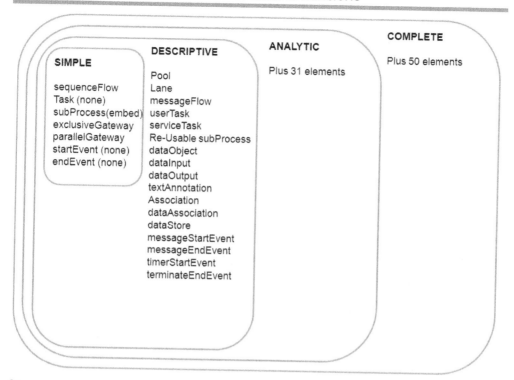

SIMPLE

ELEMENT	ATTRIBUTES
sequenceFlow (unconditional)	id, name, sourceRef, targetRef
task (None)	id, name
subProcess (expanded)	id, name, flowElement
subProcess (collapsed)	id, name, flowElement
exclusiveGateway	id, name
parallelGateway	id, name
startEvent (None)	id, name
endEvent (None)	id, name

DESCRIPTIVE

All the elements in SIMPLE plus:

ELEMENT	ATTRIBUTES
participant (pool)	id, name, processRef
laneSet	id, name, partitionElement, childLaneSet, flowElementRef
messageFlow	id, name, sourceRef, targetRef
userTask	id, name
serviceTask	id, name
callActivity	id, name, calledElement

dataObject	id, name
textAnnotation	id, text
association/dataAssociation	id, name, sourceRef, targetRef, associationDirection*
dataStoreReference	id, name, dataStoreRef
messageStartEvent	id, name, messageEventDefinition
messageEndEvent	id, name, messageEventDefinition
timerStartEvent	id, name, timerEventDefinition
terminateEndEvent	id, name terminate EventDefinition

* associationDirection not specified for dataAssociation

ANALYTIC

All the elements in DESCRIPTIVE plus:

ELEMENT	ATTRIBUTES
sequenceFlow (conditional)	id, name, sourceRef, targetRef, conditionExpression*
sequenceFlow (default)	id, name, sourceRef, targetRef, default**
sendTask	id, name
receiveTask	id, name
Looping Activity	standardLoopCharacteristics
MultiInstance Activity	multiInstanceLoopCharacteristics
exclusiveGateway	Add default attribute
inclusiveGateway	id, name, eventGatewayType
eventBasedGateway	id, name, eventGatewayType
signalStartEvent	id, name, signalEventDefinition
signalEndEvent	id, name, signalEventDefinition
Catching message IE***	id, name, messageEventDefinition
Throwing message IE	id, name, messageEventDefinition
Boundary message IE	id, name, attachedToRef, timerEventDefinition
Non-int Boundary message IE	id, name, attachedToRef, cancelActivity=false, messageEventDefinition
Catching time rIE	id, name, timerEventDefinition
Boundary timer IE	id, name, attachedToRef, timerEventDefinition
Non-int**** Boundary timer IE	id, name, attachedToRef, cancelActivity=false, timerEventDefinition
Boundary error IE	id, name, attachedToRef, errorEventDefinition
errorEndEvent	id, name, errorEventDefinition
Non-int Boundary escalation IE	id, name, attachedToRef, cancelActivity=false, escalationEventDefinition
Throwing escalation IE	id, name, escalationEventDefinition
escalationEndEvent	id, name, escalationEventDefinition

Catching signal IE	id, name, signalEventDefinition
Throwing signal IE	id, name, signalEventDefinition
Boundary signal IE	id, name, attachedToRef, signalEventDefinition
Non-int Boundary signal IE	id, name, attachedToRef, cancelActivity=false, signalEventDefinition
conditionalStartEvent	id, name, condtionalEventDefinition
Catching conditional IE	id, name, condtionalEventDefinition
Boundary conditional IE	id, name, condtionalEventDefinition
Non-int Boundary conditional IE	id, name, cancelActivity=false, condtionalEventDefinition
message	id, name

* conditionExpression allowed only for sequenceFlow out of gateways, may be null.

**default is an attribute of a sourceRef (exclusive or inclusive) DecisionGateway.

***IE= intermediateEvent

****Non-int=nonInterrupting

For a tool to claim support for a sub-class the following criteria must be satisfied:

- All the elements in the sub-class must be supported.
- For each element, all the listed attributes must be supported.

The tool must be able to read and write syntactically correct serializations that include any other elements and attributes. In particular, if a tool reads in such a serialization and edits it, when writing it out all elements and attributes not in the supported sub-class must also be written out.

SIMPLE PERSONA

A common situation for use of the SIMPLE class is *process capture.*

- A business analyst is sitting in a room with a group of process owners.
- The session is attempting to map out a currently deployed set of processes that have never been suitably documented.
- Technology for such a session may range from a low-tech whiteboard to a laptop and projector.
- A process map is drawn by the business analyst as the process owners describe their operations step by step.

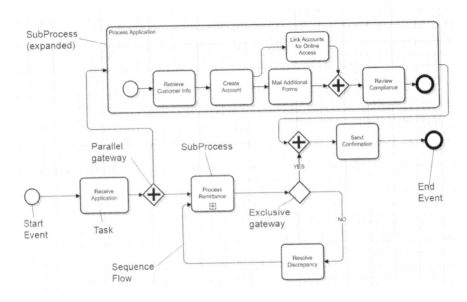

SIMPLE Example

Descriptive Persona

A common situation for use of the descriptive class is fleshing out the details omitted in a process capture session

Using elements familiar from traditional flowcharting, the business modeler

- extends the routing logic to include the more critical exceptions (such as time-outs) and special cases,
- adds information about resource or role requirements for performing activities,
- adds some basic information about data flow
- and provides an overview of communications between participants/processes pertaining to the start and end of processes.

DESCRIPTIVE Example

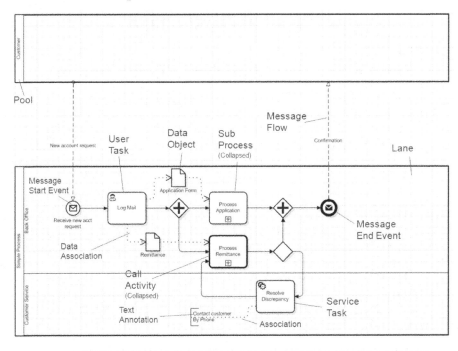

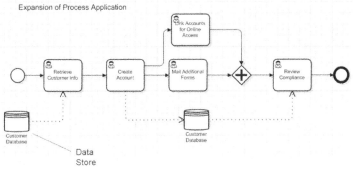

CONCLUSION

XPDL 2.2 provides a standard graphical approach to Business Process Definition based on BPMN graphics. XPDL 2.2 provides a standard file format for persisting BPMN diagrams and interchanging Process definitions. The file format is based on the WfMC meta-model which establishes a framework for defining, importing and exporting process definitions for numerous products including execution engines, simulators, BPA modeling tools, Business Activity Monitoring and reporting tools. The schema defining the format is extensible and provides vendor and user extension capabilities as well as a natural path for future versions of the standard. Mappings to specific execution languages (e.g. BPEL) and other XML-based specifications (e.g. ebXML) are possible. Finally, BPMN Model Portability conformance classes greatly increase the likelihood of true portability at the design level among a significant number of different vendor tools.

Author Appendix

Thomas Allweyer
Professor, University of Applied Sciences Kaiserslautern, Germany
Thomas Allweyer is a professor for enterprise modeling and business process management at the University of Applied Sciences Kaiserslautern, Germany. He is a regular speaker at national and international conferences and has published many papers and several books, among them an introduction into BPMN 2.0. He holds seminars and consults international companies on process management and modeling. He is the author of the process management blog www.kurze-prozesse.de (in German).

Conrad Bock
National Institute of Standards and Technology, USA
Conrad Bock specializes in formal product and process modeling at the U.S. National Institute of Standards and Technology. He is a primary contributor to BPMN 2 interaction modeling, and founding editor for Activities and Actions in the Unified Modeling Language, and Systems Modeling Language at the Object Management Group. His experience includes research and development of model-based tools in commerical and government initiatives, with SAP, Microsoft, and the U.S. Defense Advanced Research Projects Agency.

Marco Brambilla
Researcher, Politecnico di Milano, Italy
Marco Brambilla is researcher and professor at Politecnico di Milano and partner of Web Models Srl, the company that commercializes WebRatio. He got his Ph.D. in Information Engineering in 2005 from Politecnico di Milano. His interests are on conceptual modeling of processes, web applications, and services. He was visitor researcher at Cisco and at UCSD. He is involved in evaluation of EU research projects and he is senior analyst for large-scale industrial projects on web, BP, and SOA solutions. He is co-author of the book "Designing data-intensive web applications", Morgan-Kauffman, USA and of several journal and conference papers. Details available at: http://home.dei.polimi.it/mbrambil.

Thomas Brennan
Consultant, BOC Ltd, Ireland
Thomas Brennan has worked as a consultant for the BOC Group in the English speaking markets for the last 3 years. He is responsible for key customer account management and business development in these regions. He has been involved in process harmonization and improvement projects and delivers training on the core products of the BOC Management Office. He is also responsible for the maintenance of the ADONIS NGOSS reference library. Thomas studied Business Information Systems at the Dublin Institute of Technology and was awarded a BSc degree in 2001.

Stefano Butti
CEO, Web Models S.r.l. - WebRatio, Italy
Stefano Butti graduated at the École Nationale Supérieure de Techniques Avancées (ENSTA) in Paris and at Politecnico di Milano. He has been one of the founders of Web Models, the spin-off of Politecnico di Milano that produces the toolsuite WebRatio, a model-driven development tool for business process based

web applications. Over the years he played different roles within the company: analyst of Web applications developed with WebRatio, sales engineer, application development manager, software factory manager, sales manager. Since June 2006 he is the CEO of Web Models.

MICHELE CHINOSI
Grantholder, European Commission, Joint Research Centre (JRC), Italy
Michele Chinosi has a PhD in Computer Science with a thesis titled: "Representing Business Processes: Conceptual Model and Design Methodology". He is doing research on dynamic workflows modelling and composition for distributed geoprocessing at the European Commission Joint Research Centre, where the main duties are: define scenarios for multidisciplinary interoperability; identify connectivity, interoperability and sharing obstacles as well as user requirements; investigate advanced service chaining/orchestration methods for modelling workflow of distributed geoprocessing services. He took part in the BPMN 2.0 FTF. Some publications: BPM and Workflow Handbook (2009), Journal of Research and Practice in Information Technology (2009), Process.gov conference (2009), BPMN 2009 Workshop at CEC09.

LLOYD DUGAN
Senior Project Director/CTO, Information Engineering Services, Inc., USA
Lloyd Dugan manages and leads the delivery of high-value IT services and the sizing, design, development, implementation, and operation of integrated business systems for IES, where he functions as its Senior Project Director/CTO and Chief Architect. He helps clients to achieve business goals and objectives through the creative and disciplined use of leading and emerging IT methodologies, tools, and solutions. In addition to an MBA, he has a successful track record of over 24 years of experience in providing services to a variety of public and private sector clients. He specializes in BPM and SOA technologies, and has spoken over the years on these topics at numerous national conferences (sponsored by AIIM, WfMC, ARMA, etc.) and published an article in AIIM's e-Doc magazine about the realization of ECM via web services.

MICHAEL FERRARI
Independent BPM Consultant and Business Analyst, France
Michael Ferrari is a BPM consultant with a 5-year experience in BPM. Thanks to his knowledge that ranges from enterprise architecture to business strategy he has been able to work on both business process management and the critical link between information systems and business users. He focuses on using modeling to make companies more efficient. He is specialized in the Aris platform and regularly teaches training courses on business process modeling.

KERRY FINN
Enterprise SOA Lead, Raytheon, USA
Kerry M Finn is an Enterprise Architect at Raytheon who is a seasoned, results-driven Senior Director of Technology, Enterprise Architect / Chief Architect with 20+ years experience aligning Commercial Product Development, Global IT and Department of Defense organizations with key business objectives to achieve dramatic bottom-line results. He has extensive expertise in leading large-scale on-time/on-budget projects, enterprise architecture federation, deliver customer facing SOA & Web 2.0 initiatives that scale to support massive number of users, agile product development initiatives through the software architecture & development life cycle. He has been fortunate to work with some of the best technolo-

gists and product development companies (e.g. Sun Microsystems, EMC Corporation, Progress Software and Kronos Corporation), defense companies (e.g. Raytheon Corporation, General Dynamics) and global IT firms (e.g. Pearson Education, Arbella Insurance). Kerry has received Innovation Recognition Awards at Sun Microsystems as a key architect to the Java micro-edition platform as well as Excellence Awards at Pearson Education and EMC Corporation. He has been an active member of numerous industry, technology and business standard consortiums like SNIA, ISM-GLC, JCP (Java) and ACORD. Kerry holds an MS in Computer Science.

LAYNA FISCHER
Publisher, Future Strategies Inc,

As the Editor and Official Publisher to WfMC and Director of the annual Global Awards for Excellence in BPM and Workflow, Layna Fischer was previously the Executive Director of WfMC and continues to work closely with the organization to promote industry awareness of BPM and Workflow. Ms Fischer was also the Executive Director of the Business Process Management Initiative (now merged with OMG) and is on the board of BPM Focus (previously WARIA, Workflow And Reengineering International Association), where she was CEO since 1994.

Future Strategies Inc., (www.FutStrat.com) publishes unique books and papers on business process management and workflow specializes in dissemination of information about BPM and workflow technology, business process redesign and electronic commerce. As such, the company contracts and works closely with individual authors and corporations throughout the USA and the world.

Future Strategies Inc., is the also publisher of the business book series *New Tools for New Times*, as well as the annual *Excellence in Practice* volumes of award-winning case studies and the annual Workflow Handbook, published in collaboration with the WfMC. Ms. Fischer was also a senior editor of a leading international computer publication for four years and has been involved in international computer journalism and publishing for over 20 years. She was a founding director of the United States Computer Press Association in 1985.

JAKOB FREUND
CEO, camunda services GmbH, Germany

Jakob Freund is Co-Founder and CEO of the camunda services GmbH. He worked with Ivana Trockovich and Denis Gagné in OMG FTF for BPMN 2.0. Jakob is co-author of the OMG document "BPMN 2.0 by Example" and author of "Praxishandbuch BPMN", a German book about BPMN. He is also founder of "BPM-Netzwerk.de", a German online-community about BPM with more than 7,000 members.

DENIS GAGNE
CEO & CTO, Trisotech, Canada

M. Gagné is responsible for the solutions and technology vision at Trisotech. He has led Trisotech through the process of developing unique services and product offerings and provided leadership in plotting out Trisotech's market strategy. M. Gagné's current research interest focus on technological and know-how innovation in the fields of business process management and business transformation.

HARTMANN GENRICH
Consultant, Germany
Hartmann Genrich worked for Gesellschaft für Mathematik und Datenverarbeitung (GMD), the German National Research Institute for Information Technlogy. He holds a Dr. rer. nat. (PhD) in Mathematics from University of Bonn, and published various papers on the mathematics of Petri Nets. Later he got involved in the modelling, simulation and analysis of workflow systems. He retired from GMD in 2001 and works as a consultant to US-American and German companies.

JOHN JANUSZCZAK
Vice President, Meta Software Corporation, USA
John Januszczak is a software architect with Meta Software, a leading provider of capacity planning and workforce management solutions for the financial services industry. His extensive expertise in software development, process modeling and simulation has been applied in a broad spectrum of enterprises, including telecommunications, insurance and banking. Most recently, John Januszczak has been focused on the integration of process modeling and simulation technology with workforce management applications and web services.

HARALD KUEHN
Managing Director, BOC AG, Austria
Dr. Harald Kühn is member of the board of the BOC Group. He is responsible for the product management, development and support of BOC's ADONIS and ADOxx product platforms, where he is also one of the chief architects. In addition to his industry activities, Harald Kühn works actively in the research of IT-supported management approaches, meta modeling, interoperability and integrating software technology and semantic technology.

BRYAN LAIL
Chief Architect, Raytheon, USA
J. Bryan Lail is an IT Fellow at the Raytheon Company, leading business architecture methodology for the enterprise and chairing regular BPMN in Practice sessions. He represents the Missile Systems business unit on the enterprise architecture review board and in driving business process integration across organizational functions. Previous to the last two years as Chief IT Architect, he worked for Engineering in Raytheon for nine years leading the application of netcentric technologies to tactical systems, including the formation of the Tactical Services Community of Interest for the U.S. Department of Defense. Earlier professional experience included ten years working for the U.S. Navy as a scientist at the Naval Air Warfare Center at China Lake. Bryan is a Raytheon Certified Architect, a program accredited by The Open Group to include Master Certified IT Architect status. He holds two pending patents in information management for tactical systems and multiple Excellence Awards from Raytheon. He holds an M.S. in Physics.

LIONEL LOISEAU
Head of BPM Competency Center, BNP Paribas, France
Lionel Loiseau has 24 years of experience in the financial industry. As new technology project leader, he has been involved at an early stage in subjects at the crossroad between IT technologies and organization. Then, starting 2000, he became deeply involved in core business matters as manager of a department dealing with document management, workflow, knowledge management and

collaborative solutions. Three years ago, he took over the BPM competency centre for the entire BNP Paribas Group dealing with a broad BPM community of 130 people, ensuring norms and standards for the BPM family, supporting several dozens of BPM projects and managing an internal consultancy and service provider company.

EDITA MILEVICIENE

Cameo Business Modeler Product Manager, No Magic Europe, Lithuania

Edita Mileviciene is a Product Manager for Cameo Business Modeler, a plug-in to MagicDraw modeling platform enabling BPMN 2.0 modeling capabilities. Edita has been working in MagicDraw R&D team since 2002 in various roles: QA engineer, analyst, and product manager. Edita is also an experienced UML and BPMN consultant and regularly runs online and onsite trainings to MagicDraw customers worldwide. She holds Master degree in Computer Science from Kaunas University of Technology and OMG Certified UML Professional Advanced certificate. Currently, Edita is working on UML Profile for BPMN Processes submission to OMG.

MARION MURZEK

Software Architect, BOC GmbH, Austria

Dr. Marion Murzek is a software architect at the BOC Group. Her research and development activities are focused on the design and development of business process modeling languages and model transformation mechanisms for the software products of the BOC group. Her work in industry is complemented with active research involvement in the field of model-driven development approaches and environments and the application of model transformation approaches, which has resulted in several publications. Dr. Marion Murzek studied computer science and business administration at the University of Vienna, Austria, where she received the M.Sc. (Mag.) degree in 2004. She received her Ph.D. (Dr.) degree in business informatics at the Vienna University of Technology, Austria, in 2008.

NATHANIEL PALMER

Chief BPM Strategist of SRA International and Executive Director, Workflow Management Coalition, USA.

Nathaniel Palmer is Chief BPM Strategist of SRA International and Executive Director of the Workflow Management Coalition (WfMC). In addition he was recently appointed Editor-in-Chief of BPM.com – the BPM market's most-trafficked destination site. He is also the founder and chairman of the successful Transformation and Innovation event series, widely regarded as the leading conference on business transformation. Previously he was Director, Business Consulting for Perot Systems Corp, where he worked for business process guru Jim Champy. He spent over a decade with Delphi Group as Vice President and Chief Analyst. The author of over several dozen research studies as well as co-author of the critically-acclaimed management text "The X-Economy" (Texere, 2001) and the "BPM and Workflow Handbook" (FSI, 2007), Nathaniel has been featured in numerous media ranging from Fortune to The New York Times. He is on the advisory boards of many relevant industry publications, as well as the Board of Directors of Association of Information Management (AIIM) NE, and was nominated to represent the Governor of Massachusetts on the Commonwealth's IT Advisory Board.

TOBIAS RAUSCH
Management Consultant, BOC AG, Austria

Tobias Rausch works as a Management Consultant within the BOC Group and is actively involved in BPM projects in different industries. His main research area lies in business process improvement and automation, modeling and management of the organization and systems and workflow technology. A specific focus in all these areas lies in the standardization of the underlying technology. He graduated at the University of Vienna in 1999 and since 2001 published several articles in these fields. Over the last decade Tobias also acted as a member of EU teams in ICT projects and as an independent expert for reviews and the monitoring of the implementation of indirect actions under the IST Program.

VISHAL SAXENA
Founder and CEO, Roubroo, USA

Vishal Saxena is one of the authors of the BPMN 2.0 specification. He brings extensive experience in the enterprise software development, integration and BPM industry over the past 15 years. He worked extensively on the BPMN 2.0 submission at OMG. Besides leading development teams in multiple time zones, he is out evangelizing BPM solutions with customers, partners and analysts. Recently, he was the VP of Engineering at Intalio, the leading open source vendor of BPMS. Earlier he led the development of Oracle Business Process Analysis (BPA) Suite. His blog can be found at http://vishals.blogspot.com

MATTHIAS SCHREPFER
Management Consultant, camunda services GmbH, Germany

Matthias Schrepfer works as Management Consultant at the camunda services GmbH. His focus is on process modeling with BPMN. Matthias is actively involved in BPM projects in different industry sectors. He focuses on the development and application of BPMN modeling guidelines in customer projects. Matthias holds a Master degree in Computer Science from Växjö University, Sweden, and a Master Degree in Information Systems from Humboldt-Universität zu Berlin, Germany.

ROBERT SHAPIRO
SVP Research, Global 360, USA

Robert Shapiro created the first open-architecture object-oriented graphical modeling toolkit for process modeling. It was the platform for Design IDEF in support of SADT (Structured Analysis and Design Technique) and used to build the first version of CPN (Colored Petri Net) modeling and simulation technology.

Robert Shapiro is founder and manager of Process Analytica. He is Senior Vice President: Research, for Global 360. He founded Cape Visions (acquired in 2005) where he directed the development of Analytics and Simulation software used by FileNet/IBM, Fujitsu, PegaSystems and Global 360 Business Process Management products. Prior to founding Cape Visions, as founder and CEO of Meta Software Corporation, he directed the implementation of a unique suite of graphical modeling and optimization tools for enterprise-wide business process improvement Products based on these tools are used by Bank America, Wells Fargo, JPMChase and other major banks to optimize their check processing and Lock Box operations As a participant in the Workflow Management Coalition and chair of the working groups on conformance and process definition interchange, he plays a critical role in the development of international standards for workflow and business process management. He has been instrumental in the creation and evolution of XPDL and BPMN. In 2005 he was awarded the Marvin L Manheim Award for outstanding contributions in the field of workflow.

Darius Silingas
Principal Consultant, No Magic Europe, Lithuania
Dr. Darius Silingas is a Principal Consultant at No Magic, the vendor of award-winning modeling tool MagicDraw, which supports BPMN 2.0. Since 1998, he participated in numerous international software development projects in various roles. In 2005, Darius has been assigned as the leader of a newly established Training Department. Since then he has run over 100 consultancy and training sessions on business and software modeling using BPMN and UML in 18 countries including USA, UK, Germany, France, Finland, Russia, South Africa and others. He has published a number of papers on modeling and spoke at premier conferences like Architecture and Design World, JAX, OOP, Code Generation, and EuroSTAR.

Bruce Silver
Independent Industry Analyst and Consultant, Bruce Silver Associates,
Bruce Silver is principal of Bruce Silver Associates, provider of BPM consulting and training services, and founder and principal of BPMessentials.com, the leading provider of BPMN training. He served on the BPMN 2.0 technical committee in OMG, and is the author of *BPMN Method and Style*, still the number one BPMN book on Amazon.com. He also writes the popular BPMS Watch blog (www.brsilver.com), offering reports and commentary on both BPMN and leading BPM Suites.

Gerardo Navarro Suarez
Consultant, camunda services GmbH, Germany
Gerardo Navarro Suarez is Consultant at the camunda services GmbH. His focus is on process modeling with BPMN. Gerardo applies BPMN in a number of customer projects. He is co-author of the OMG document "BPMN 2.0 by Example". Gerardo consults to customers on modeling approaches and prepares processes for technical implementations in process engines.

Stephen White
BPM Architect, International Business Machines, USA
Stephen A. White is currently a BPM Architect at IBM. He has 25 years experience with process modeling—ranging from developing models, consulting, training, process modeling tool design, product management, and standards development. In the mid-1990s he was product manager at Holosofx (which was later acquired by IBM), where he gained a lot of experience with the business analyst's perspective through training and consulting. After Holosofx, he was at SeeBeyond (later acquired by Sun Microsystems) where he began working in standards, including the start of BPMN. From SeeBeyond he moved to IBM where he continued work in standards and with BPMN.

While at SeeBeyond and IBM, he served on the BPMI.org Board of Direc-tors (which later merged with the OMG). Within the OMG, he is currently a member of the BPM Steering Committee and is co-chair of an Architecture Board sponsored Special Interest Group on Process Metamodels. As Working Group chair and Specification Editor since its inception, Stephen A. White was instrumental in creating the BPMN standard and is now guiding its continuing refinement at the OMG.

DENNIS WISNOSKY
CTO and Chief Architect, DCMO, US Department of Defense, USA
Dennis Wisnosky is the CTO and Chief Architect of the Deputy Chief Management Officer for the US DoD with over 25 years of leadership experience in Information Technology. He created the Integrated Definition language and contributed to the SOA Design Patterns book. He has received numerous honors for his work, including Fortune magazine "one of the five heroes of manufacturing" in 1997, and the Federal 100 Award in 2007. He is the author of several books and over 100 papers including DoDAF Wizdom, considered the decisive source within DoD and other government organizations for managing EA projects.

JACK XUE
Manager of IT Architecture, Conseco Service LLC & Butler University, USA
Xinjian Jack Xue has a MBA in Finance from Ball State University, Muncie, IN, 2005, a Ph.D. in Mathematics from Swiss Federal Institute of Technology, Lausanne, Switzerland, 1996, and a MS in Electrical Engineering from Shanghai University of Technology, Shanghai, China, 1987. He did his postdoctoral study at Pennsylvania State University, University Park, PA. He has been working with Conseco Service LLC, Carmel, IN., for last five years as a Manager of IT Architecture after worked with Regenstrief Institute for Healthcare, Indianapolis, IN and IBM/Tivoli, Indianapolis, IN. Since 2007, he has been an adjunct faculty of Butler University, Indianapolis, IN. His main interests are operations research, online optimization, reliability and Service Oriented Architecture.

MICHAEL ZUR MUEHLEN
Director, Center for Business Process Innovation, Stevens Institute of Technology, USA
Dr. Michael zur Muehlen is Assistant Professor of Information Systems at Stevens Institute of Technology in Hoboken, NJ. He directs Stevens' BPM research center (Center of Excellence in Business Process Innovation) and is responsible for the University's graduate program in Business Process Management and Service Innovation. Prior to his appointment at Stevens, Michael was a senior lecturer at the Department of Information Systems , University of Muenster , Germany, and a visiting lecturer at the University of Tartu , Estonia. He has over 14 years of experience in the field of process automation and workflow management, and has led numerous process improvement and design projects in Germany and the US and serves as Enterprise Chief Process Architect of the U.S. Department of Defense Business Transformation Agency. An active contributor to standards in the BPM area, Michael was named a fellow of the Workflow Management Coalition in 2004 and chairs the WfMC working group "Management and Audit." He studies the practical use of process modeling standards, techniques to manage operational risks in business processes, and the integration of business processes and business rules. SAP Research, the US Army, the Australian Research Council, and private sponsors have funded his research. Michael has presented his research in more than 20 countries. He is the author of a book on workflow-based process controlling, numerous journal articles, conference papers, book chapters and working papers on process management and workflow automation. He has also published widely on BPM standards and standard making in general. He is a founding director of the AIS special interest group on process automation and management (SIGPAM) . Michael holds a PhD (Dr. rer. pol.) and an MS in Information Systems from the University of Muenster, Germany .

Acknowledgements

BPMN 2.0 Specification

SUBMITTING ORGANIZATIONS (RFP PROCESS)

The following companies are formal submitting members of OMG:

Axway
International Business Machines
MEGA International
Oracle
SAP AG
Unisys

SUPPORTING ORGANIZATIONS (RFP PROCESS)

The following organizations support this specification but are not formal submitters:

Accenture	Intalio
Adaptive	Metastorm
BizAgi	Model Driven Solutions
Bruce Silver Associates	Nortel
Capgemini	Red Hat Software
Enterprise Agility	Software AG
France Telecom	TIBCO Software
IDS Scheer	Vangent

Finalization Task Force Voting Members

The following organizations have been Voting Members of the BPMN 2.0 Finalization Task Force:

Adaptive	KnowGravity Inc.
Axway Software	Lombardi Software
BAE SYSTEMS	MITRE
BizAgi Ltd.	U.S. National Institute of Standards and Technology
CA Inc.	
Camunda Services GmbH	No Magic Inc.
Cordys	oose Innovative Informatik GmbH
DICOM	Oracle
France Telecom R&D	PNA Group
Fujitsu	Red Hat
Global 360 Inc.	SAP AG
Hewlett-Packard	Softeam
iGrafx	Software AG Inc.
Inferware	TIBCO
Intalio	Trisotech
International Business Machines	Visumpoint

The following persons were members of the core teams that contributed to the content of this specification:

Anurag Aggarwal	Antoine Lonjon
Mike Amend	Sumeet Malhotra
Sylvain Astier	Falko Menge
Alistair Barros	Jeff Mischkinsky
Rob Bartel	Dale Moberg
Mariano Benitez	Alex Moffat
Conrad Bock	Ralf Mueller
Gary Brown	Sjir Nijssen
Justin Brunt	Karsten Ploesser
John Bulles	Pete Rivett
Martin Chapman	Michael Rowley
Fred Cummins	Bernd Ruecker
Rouven Day	Tom Rutt
Maged Elaasar	Suzette Samoojh
David Frankel	Robert Shapiro
Denis Gagné	Vishal Saxena
John Hall	Scott Schanel
Reiner Hille-Doering	Axel Scheithauer
Dave Ings	Bruce Silver
Pablo Irassar	Meera Srinivasan
Oliver Kieselbach	Antoine Toulme
Matthias Kloppmann	Ivana Trickovic
Jana Koehler	Hagen Voelzer
Frank Michael Kraft	Franz Weber
Tammo van Lessen	Andrea Westerinen
Frank Leymann	Stephen A. White

In addition the following persons contributed valuable ideas and feedback that improved the content and the quality of this specification:

Im Amsden	David Marston
Mariano Belaunde	Neal McWhorter
Peter Carlson	Edita Mileviciene
Cory Casanave	Vadim Pevzner
Michele Chinosi	Pete Rivett
Manoj Das	Jesus Sanchez
Robert Lario	Markus Schacher
Sumeet Malhotra	Sebastian Stein
Henk de Man	Prasad Yendluri

Acknowledgements

XPDL Implementations

A

- Active Endpoint's ActiveVOS visual orchestration system supports XPDL 2.1
- ActiveModeler, see "KAISHA-Tec"
- Adobe has successfully implemented XPDL within Adobe LiveCycle Workflow
- ADVANTYS WorkflowGen supports XPDL
- Amazonas Workflow is a Java based workflow engine which supports XPDL
- Arachnea EverSuite supports XPDL
- Appian Enterprise and Zynium's Byzio use XPDL for interchange of Visio process models
- Ascentn AgilePoint Server is a .NET-based BPMS that supports XPDL
- Aspose's Aspose.Workflow is a .Net workflow engine using XPDL
- Assetlink Corporation uses XPDL to define and store processes in Marketing Workbench

B

- BOC ADONIS 3.7(and higher) supports XPDL export
- BEA Systems supports XPDL in the AquaLogic Enterprise Repository and BPM Suite
- Brein VB's InProces uses XPDL 2.0
- Bonita is an open source workflow solution using XPDL
- ProEd Workflow Editor is a XPDL compliant design tool on top of Bonita

C

- Canto CanFlow uses XPDL within this Digital Asset Management solution
- CapeVisions supports XPDL including a free plugin to Visio that edits XPDL
- CHALEX BPM Framework supports XPDL
- ComActivity supports XPDL in its process design tool and runtime engine
- Cordys BPMS supports XPDL for process definition important and export
- COSA Designer and the COSA BPM engine support XPDL
- Cubetto Toolset is a generic modelling tool which can export XPDL

D

- Documentum, see "EMC"

E

- Eclaire Group Lynx Flow Designer supports XPDL
- EMC Documentum ApplicationXtender Workflow supports import and export of XPDL
- EMC Documentum Process Suite supports XPDL
- Enhydra Shark is an open source XPDL workflow engine in Java
- Enhydra JaWE an openSource graphical XPDL workflow editor

F

- First Trace's Kinnosa Workflow supports XPDL for process model exchange
- Finantix Studio FXS supports BPMN and XPDL for Business Process Modelling
- Fujitsu Interstage BPM (i-Flow) supports XPDL and BPMN
- FileNet Business Process Manager 4.0 supports XPDL 1.0 and 2.0 as well as BPMN

G

- Global 360 Business Optimzation Server (BOS) supports XPDL 2.0 and BPMN
- GlobalSight, see "Transware"

H

- HOGA.PL'S intraDok supports import and export of process definitions in XPDL

- IBM FileNet Business Process Manager 4.0 supports XPDL 1.0 and 2.0 as well as BPMN
- IDS Scheer Business Architect supports export of process models to XPDL through an optional add-on
- iGrafx supports XPDL 2.1 within iGrafx 2009 (import and export)
- Interwoven WorkRoute MP supports XPDL for both import and export.
- Infinity Process Engine supports XPDL for import/export and Wf-XML 2.0 deployment
- Infor (formerly SSA Global) supports XPDL in a BPM engine within its ERP suite
- ITP-Commerce Design provides a XPDL 1.0 validation module

J

- jawFlow is an open source workflow engine supports XPDL
- Jenz & Partner's BPEdit is an ontology-based business process editor that supports XPDL

K

- KAISHA-Tec's ActiveModeler Avantage supports XPDL 2.0

L

- Lombardi's Blueprint supports XPDL 2.1 and BPMN

M

- Metoda S.p.A OpenMet BPMF supports XPDL
- Mono-sys's Tigris BPM solution supports XPDL 2.0 as well as BPMN

N

- Nautica uses XPDL process definition data with GUI based definition editor

O

- Open Business Engine is an open source Java workflow engine based on XPDL

- OpenPages Governance Platform solution for enterprise-wide business governance using XPDL
- Openwork is validating support for XPDL and Wf-XML
- Oracle 9i Warehouse Builder 9.2 saves process definitions in XPDL

P

- Pentaho's B1 Platform uses an XPDL-based workflow engine to execute activities within the system
- Projekty Bankowe Polsoft's BPB Workflow supports import/export in XPDL 2.0

Q

- QualiWare supports XPDL 2.1 for both import and export of process models

R

- R-Data's E-SOD business process export using XPDL 2.0 and import using version 1.0 and above
- Rodan Systems OfficeObjects Workflow is an embedded, commercial workflow engine using XPDL

S

- Savvion supports XPDL for import and export of process models through its Process Modeler
- Simprocess from CACI supports XPDL for simulation models
- Software AG's Crossvision BPM supports XPDL 1.0 and XPDL 2.0
- SpeechCycle's LevelOne virtual CSR platform uses XPDL
- SSA Global, see "Infor"

T

- Tell-Eureka, see "SpeechCycle"
- TIBCO iProcess Suite supports XPDL
- Together Workflow Editor is a graphical XPDL-based workflow editor
- Transware Ambassador embeds an XPDL-compliant workflow engine

U

- Unisys has done significant BPM development using XPDL

V

- Vignette Process Workflow Modeler supports XPDL

W

- W4's W4 BPM Suite supports XPDL
- WfMOpen is an open source workflow engine that uses XPDL
- Workflow::WfMC is an OpenSource lightweight Workflow Engine in PERL based on XPDL 2.0

Z

- Zynium's Byzio is a Visio plugin enabling two-way transformation of Visio diagrams and XPDL

XPDL is the Serialization Format for BPMN

BPMN is a visual process notation standard from the OMG, endorsed by WfMC, and broadly adopted across the industry. But the BPMN standard defines only the look of how the process definition is displayed on the screen. How you store and interchange those process definitions is outside the scope of the standard, and this is where XPDL comes in.

XPDL provides a file format that supports every aspect of the BPMN process definition notation including graphical descriptions of the diagram, as well as executable properties used at run time. With XPDL, a product can write out a process definition with full fidelity, and another product can read it in and reproduce the same diagram that was sent.

XPDL Enables a Process Definition Ecosystem

XPDL is used today by more than 80 different products today to exchange process definitions. As a greater percentage part of the organization starts to use process tools for everyday work, it will become less and less reasonable to take a single-vendor strategy to process definition work.

Users need to go beyond the vendor lock-in, and take a "best of breed" approach that allows the use of their favorite process technology to accomplish specific process oriented tasks, such as simulation and optimization, and future tasks that we can only dream of today.

XPDL is extensible so that it allows each different tool to store implementation specific information within the XPDL, and have those values preserved even when manipulated by tools that do not understand those extensions. This is the only way to provide for a "round trip" through multiple tool and still be able to return to the original tool with complete fidelity.

How Does XPDL Compare to BPEL?

BPEL and XPDL are entirely different yet complimentary standards. BPEL is an "execution language" designed to provide a definition of web services orchestration.

It defines only the executable aspects of a process, when that process is dealing exclusively with web services and XML data. BPEL does not define the graphical diagram, human oriented processes, subprocess, and many other aspects of a modern business process: it simply was never defined to carry the business process diagram from design tool to design tool.

XPDL 2.1 Approved by WfMC Membership

Following a 60-day review and comment period, as well as voting by member, the WfMC Steering Committee voted on 23 April 2008 to approve version 2.1 of XPDL. This release includes all new functionality that was submitted to the working group and accepted by the working group.

Also included is new functionality to update the BPMN to version 1.1 as well as specific descriptive material on BPMN as well as the BPMN E-Mail Voting process[1], plus an extended section on conformance to support portability of BPMN design-level models.

For additional information: http://wfmc.org/xpdl.html

---

[1] [BPMNExamples, p. 35 See BPMN 2.0 Companion CD available from the publisher, Future Strategies Inc. www. FutStrat.com

BPMN 2.0 Glossary

A

Activity Work that a company or organization performs using business processes. An activity can be atomic or non-atomic (compound). The types of activities that are a part of a Process Model are: Process, Sub-Process, and Task.

Abstract Process A Process that represents the interactions between a private business process and another process or participant.

Artifact A graphical object that provides supporting information about the Process or elements within the Process. However, it does not directly affect the flow of the Process.

Association A connecting object that is used to link information and Artifacts with Flow Objects. An association is represented as a dotted graphical line with an arrowhead to represent the direction of flow.

Atomic Activity An activity not broken down to a finer level of Process Model detail. It is a leaf in the tree-structure hierarchy of Process activities. Graphically it will appear as a Task in BPMN.

B

Business Analyst A specialist who analyzes business needs and problems, consults with users and stakeholders to identify opportunities for improving business return through information technology, and defines, manages, and monitors the requirements into business processes. **Business Process** A defined set of business activities that represent the steps required to achieve a business objective. It includes the flow and use of information and resources.

Business Process Management The services and tools that support process management (for example, process analysis, definition, processing, monitoring and administration), including support for human and application-level interaction. BPM tools can eliminate manual processes and automate the routing of requests between departments and applications.

BPM System The technology that enables BPM.

C

Choreography An ordered sequence of B2B message exchanges between two or more Participants. In a Choreography there is no central controller, responsible entity, or observer of the Process.

Collaboration Collaboration is the act of sending messages between any two Participants in a BPMN model. The two Participants represent two separate BPML processes.

Collapsed Sub-Process A Sub-Process that hides its flow details. The Collapsed Sub-Process object uses a marker to distinguish it as a Sub-Process, rather than a Task. The marker is a small square with a plus sign (+) inside.

Compensation Flow Flow that defines the set of activities that are performed while the transaction is being rolled back to compensate for activities that were performed during the Normal Flow of the Process. A Compensation Flow can also be called from a Compensate End or Intermediate Event.

Compound Activity An activity that has detail that is defined as a flow of other activities. It is a branch (or trunk) in the tree-structure hierarchy of Process activities. Graphically, it will appear as a Process or Sub-Process in BPMN.

Controlled Flow Flow that proceeds from one Flow Object to another, via a Sequence Flow link, but is subject to either conditions or dependencies from other flow as defined by a Gateway. Typically, this is seen as a Sequence flow between two activities, with a conditional indicator (mini-diamond) or a Sequence Flow connected to a Gateway.

)

Decision A gateway within a business process where the Sequence Flow can take one of several alternative paths. Also known as "Or-Split."

E

End Event An Event that indicates where a path in the process will end. In terms of Sequence Flows, the End Event ends the flow of the Process, and thus, will not have any outgoing Sequence Flows. An End Event can have a specific Result that will appear as a marker within the center of the End Event shape. End Event Results are Message, Error, Compensation, Signal, Link, and Multiple. The End Event shares the same basic shape of the Start Event and Intermediate Event, a circle, but is drawn with a thick single line.

Event Context An Event Context is the set of activities that can be interrupted by an exception (Intermediate Event). This can be one activity or a group of activities in an expanded Sub-Process.

Exception An event that occurs during the performance of the Process that causes a diversion from the Normal Flow of the Process. Exceptions can be generated by Intermediate Events, such as time, error, or message.

Exception Flow A Sequence Flow path that originates from an Intermediate Event attached to the boundary of an activity. The Process does not traverse this path unless the Activity is interrupted by the triggering of a boundary Intermediate Event (an Exception - see above).

Expanded Sub-Process A Sub-Process that exposes its flow detail within the context of its Parent Process. An Expanded Sub-Process is displayed as a rounded rectangle that is enlarged to display the Flow Objects within.

F

Flow A directional connector between elements in a Process, Collaboration, or Choreography. A Sequence Flows represents the sequence of Flow Objects in a Process or Choreography. A Message Flow represents the transmission of a Message between Collaboration Participants. The term Flow is often used to represent the overall progression of how a Process or Process segment would be performed.

Flow Object A graphical object that can be connected to or from a Sequence Flow. In a Process, Flow Objects are Events, Activities, and Gateways. In a Choreography, Flow Objects are Events, Choreography Activities, and Gateways.

Fork A point in the Process where one Sequence Flow path is split into two or more paths that are run in parallel within the Process, allowing multiple activities to run simultaneously rather than sequentially. BPMN uses multiple outgoing Sequence Flows from Activities or Events or a Parallel Gateway to perform a Fork. Also known as "AND-Split."

Intermediate Event An event that occurs after a Process has been started. An Intermediate Event affects the flow of the process by showing where messages and delays are expected, distributing the Normal Flow through exception handling, or showing the extra flow required for compensation. However, an Interme diate Event does not start or directly terminate a process. An Intermediate Even is displayed as a circle, drawn with a thin double line.

J

Join A point in the Process where two or more parallel Sequence Flow paths are combined into one Sequence Flow path. BPMN uses a Parallel Gateway to per form a Join. Also known as "AND-Join."

L

Lane A partition that is used to organize and categorize activities within a Pool. A Lane extends the entire length of the Pool either vertically or horizontally. Lanes are often used for such things as internal roles (e.g., Manager, Associate), systems (e.g., an enterprise application), or an internal department (e.g., shipping finance).

M

Merge A point in the Process where two or more alternative Sequence Flow paths are combined into one Sequence Flow path. No synchronization is required be cause no parallel activity runs at the join point. BPMN uses multiple incoming Sequence Flows for an Activity or an Exclusive Gateway to perform a Merge. Also know as "OR-Join."

Message An Object that depicts the contents of a communication between two Participants. A message is transmitted through a Message Flow and has an iden tity that can be used for alternative branching of a Process through the Event-Based Exclusive Gateway.

Message Flow A Connecting Object that shows the flow of messages between two Participants. A Message Flow is represented by a dashed lined.

N

Normal Flow A flow that originates from a Start Event and continues through activities on alternative and parallel paths until reaching an End Event.

P

Parent Process A Process that holds a Sub-Process within its boundaries.

Participant A business entity (e.g., a company, company division, or a customer) or a business role (e.g., a buyer or a seller) that controls or is responsible for a business process. If Pools are used, then a Participant would be associated with one Pool. In a Collaboration, Participants are informally known as "Pools."

Pool A Pool represents a Participant in a Collaboration. Graphically, a Pool is a container for partitioning a Process from other Pools/Participants. A Pool is not required to contain a Process, i.e., it can be a "black box."

Private Business Process A process that is internal to a specific organization and is the type of process that has been generally called a workflow or BPM process.

Process A sequence or flow of Activities in an organization with the objective of carrying out work. In BPMN, a Process is depicted as a graph of Flow Elements, which are a set of Activities, Events, Gateways, and Sequence Flow that adhere to a finite execution semantics.

R

Result The consequence of reaching an End Event. Types of Results include Mes sage, Error, Compensation, Signal, Link, and Multiple.

S

Sequence Flow A connecting object that shows the order in which activities are performed in a Process and is represented with a solid graphical line. Each Flow has only one source and only one target. A Sequence Flow can cross the boundaries between Lanes of a Pool but cannot cross the boundaries of a Pool.

Start Event An Event that indicates where a particular Process starts. The Start Event starts the flow of the Process and does not have any incoming Sequence Flow, but can have a Trigger. The Start Event is displayed as a circle, drawn with a single thin line.

Sub-Process A Process that is included within another Process. The Sub-Process can be in a collapsed view that hides its details. A Sub-Process can be in an expanded view that shows its details within the view of the Process that it is contained in. A Sub-Process shares the same shape as the Task, which is a rectangle that has rounded corners.

Swimlane A Swimlane is a graphical container for partitioning a set of activities from other activities. BPMN has two different types of Swimlanes. See "Pool" and "Lane."

T

Task An atomic activity that is included within a Process. A Task is used when the work in the Process is not broken down to a finer level of Process Model detail. Generally, an end-user, an application, or both will perform the Task. A Task object shares the same shape as the Sub-Process, which is a rectangle that has rounded corners.

Token A theoretical concept that is used as an aid to define the behavior of a Process that is being performed. The behavior of Process elements can be defined by describing how they interact with a token as it "traverses" the structure of the Process. For example, a token will pass through an Exclusive Gateway, but continue down only one of the Gateway's outgoing Sequence Flow.

Transaction A Sub-Process that represents a set of coordinated activities carried out by independent, loosely-coupled systems in accordance with a contractually defined business relationship. This coordination leads to an agreed, consistent, and verifiable outcome across all participants.

Trigger A mechanism that detects an occurrence and can cause additional processing in response, such as the start of a business Process. Triggers are associated with Start Events and Intermediate Events and can be of the type: Message, Timer, Conditional, Signal, Link, and Multiple.

U

Uncontrolled Flow Flow that proceeds without dependencies or conditional expressions. Typically, an Uncontrolled Flow is a Sequence Flow between two Activities that do not have a conditional indicator (mini-diamond) or an intervening Gateway.

NOTE

Excerpted from the BPMN 2.0 Specification from OMG™
http://www.omg.org/spec/BPMN/2.0/Beta2/PDF/

2010 BPM & WORKFLOW HANDBOOK

Spotlight on Business Intelligence

Linking BI and BPM creates stronger operational business intelligence. Users seek more intelligent business process capabilities in order to remain competitive within their fields and industries. BPM vendors realize they need to improve their business processes, rules and event management offerings with greater intelligence or analytics capabilities.
Retail $75.00

BPM EXCELLENCE IN PRACTICE 2010

Award-winning Case Studies in BPM & Workflow

The companies whose case studies are featured in this book have proven excellence in their creative and successful deployment of advanced workflow process and business process management concepts. The positive impact to their corporations includes increased revenues, more productive and satisfied employees, product enhancements, better customer service and quality improvements. **Retail $39.95**

BPMN GUÍA DE REFERENCIA Y MODELADO

Comprendiendo y Utilizando BPMN

Desarrolle representaciones gráficas de procesos de negocios, que sean rigurosas pero al mismo tiempo de fácil comprensión.

En BPMN, los "Procesos de Negocio" involucran la captura de una secuencia ordenada de las actividades e información de apoyo. Modelar un Proceso de Negocio implica representar cómo una empresa realiza sus objetivos centrales; los objetivos por si mismos son importantes, pero por el momento no son capturados por la notación. Con BPMN, sólo los procesos son modelados. **Precio $49.95**

BPMN MODELING AND REFERENCE GUIDE

Stephen A. White, PhD, Derek Miers
Understanding and Using BPMN
Develop rigorous yet understandable graphical representations of business processes
BEST SELLER for the Beginner!
Business Process Modeling Notation (BPMN™) is a standard, graphical modeling representation for business processes. It provides an easy-to-use, flow-charting notation that is independent of the implementation environment. **Retail $39.95**

BPMN 2.0 Handbook Companion CD

Additional Material

A Companion CD is planned for release in early 2011 which will contain, in addition to the complete *BPMN 2.0 Handbook Digital Edition,* substantial material on BPMN 2.0 helpful to readers. This includes free BPMN and XPDL Verification/Validation files, webinars, videos, product specs, tools, free/trial modelers etc.

BPMN 2.0 HANDBOOK COMPANION CD

BPMN and XPDL verification/validation files, modeling tools, simulation tools, videos, webinars and more

Published in collaboration with the Workflow Management Coalition (WfMC)

Contents

- Specifications and Examples
  BPMN
  XPDL

- Free Trials/Tools
- Free Validation Files
- Papers/Slideshows
- Webinars/Videos
- Complete **Digital Edition BPMN 2.0 Handbook** with additional author material.

Several BPMN 2.0 Handbook authors have contributed additional files and explanatory diagrams to the CD. This important material gives readers exposure to a larger resource on BPMN 2.0 and XPDL than a book alone can offer.

An early mock-up of the CD has been posted to http://bpmnhandbook.com/ together with information on sponsorship of tools, trials and other BPMN-related products, including product demo videos.

More Unique Books on BPM can be found at
www.FutStrat.com

Made in the USA
Monee, IL
12 December 2021

85029965R00142